I0753244

Decolonising Animals

ANIMAL PUBLICS

Melissa Boyde & Fiona Probyn-Rapsey, Series Editors

The Animal Publics series publishes new interdisciplinary research in animal studies. Taking inspiration from the varied and changing ways that humans and non-human animals interact, it investigates how animal life becomes public: attended to, listened to, made visible, included, and transformed.

Animal Death
Ed. Jay Johnston and Fiona Probyn-Rapsey

Animal Dreams
David Brooks

Animal Welfare in Australia: Politics and Policy
Peter Chen

Animal Welfare in China: Culture, Politics and Crisis
Peter J. Li

Animals in the Anthropocene: Critical Perspectives on Non-human Futures
Ed. The Human Animal Research Network Editorial Collective

Australian Animal Law: Context and Critique
Elizabeth Ellis

Cane Toads: A Tale of Sugar, Politics and Flawed Science
Nigel Turvey

Dingo Bold: The Life and Death of K'gari Dingoes
Rowena Lennox

Decolonising Animals
Ed. Rick De Vos

Engaging with Animals: Interpretations of a Shared Existence
Ed. Georgette Leah Burns and Mandy Patersonn

Enter the Animal: Cross-Species Perspectives on Grief and Spirituality
Teya Brooks Pribac

Fighting Nature: Travelling Menageries, Animal Acts and War Shows
Peta Tait

The Flight of Birds: A Novel in Twelve Stories
Joshua Lobb

A Life for Animals
Christine Townend

Meatsplaining: The Animal Agriculture Industry and the Rhetoric of Denial
Ed. Jason Hannan

Obaysch: A Hippopotamus in Victorian London
John Simons

Decolonising Animals

Edited by Rick De Vos

SYDNEY UNIVERSITY PRESS

First published by Sydney University Press

Sydney University Press
Gadigal Country
Fisher Library F03
University of Sydney NSW 2006
AUSTRALIA
sup.info@sydney.edu.au
sydneyuniversitypress.com.au

A catalogue record for this book is available from the National Library of Australia.

ISBN 9781761540295 hardback
ISBN 9781743328606 epub
ISBN 9781743328927 pdf

Cover image: *Dingo in the bush*, by Peter Waples-Crowe
Cover design: Naomi van Groll

We acknowledge the traditional owners of the lands on which Sydney University Press is located, the Gadigal people of the Eora Nation, and we pay our respects to the knowledge embedded forever within the Aboriginal Custodianship of Country.

Cultural safety

Aboriginal and Torres Strait Islander readers are advised this publication contains names and images of people who have died.

In addition, some quotations from scholarly sources may contain terms or views that were considered acceptable within mainstream Australian society when they were written but may no longer be considered appropriate. The wording in these quotes does not necessarily reflect the views of Sydney University Press or the authors.

Contents

Acknowledgements

I am very grateful for the advice and support of Agata Mrva-Montoya, Susan Murray, Jo Lyons, Naomi van Groll and the staff of Sydney University Press in the preparation of this book. Fiona Probyn-Rapsey provided me with valuable guidance in completing the volume. I also wish to thank Fiona and Annie Potts for their encouragement and advice in the early stages of the project.

I am indebted to the wonderful group of anonymous reviewers who read draft chapters and provided such valuable advice and guidance. I am thankful for your expertise and generosity.

The idea for this volume emerged from the 2019 Australasian Animal Studies Association Conference, Decolonizing Animals, convened by Annie Potts and hosted by the New Zealand Centre for Human-Animal Studies, University of Canterbury, which took place in Ōtautahi/Christchurch. The conference was guided by Māori tikanga (values, practices and forms of etiquette), and conducted in a warm, collegial and encouraging manner. I am grateful to the principal organisers, Philip Armstrong, Nik Taylor, Pieta Gray, Cressida Wilson, Emily Major, Kirsty Dunn and Annie Potts, as well as the team of brilliant volunteers, for this valuable and generative hui. Thank you also to AASA for helping me get there.

Finally, I would like to thank my fellow contributors for their generosity, collegiality, enthusiasm and perseverance, and for making this a very enjoyable experience.

Introduction: Unsettling subjects

Rick De Vos

In the prelude to Kim Scott's novel *That Deadman Dance*, the central character, Bobby Wabalingany, starts to write with chalk on a thin piece of slate.[1]

> Roze a wail …

These three words, defiant of grammar and spelling but anthemic to the novel, simultaneously inscribe the start of a new story, the remembering of a story told but never before written, and the narrative uncertainty of what the whale's rising means to Bobby. The spectacle of a southern right whale suddenly leaping from the ocean can be frightening, affirming, promising or disorienting, with the thunderous slap as the whale falls and hits the ocean surface echoing for great distances. Whales have a reason for rising and falling, but the action is beyond the control or complete understanding of humans. For Bobby, narrating the whale story serves different purposes for different audiences and in different spaces. The words relate to the presence of

1 Scott 2010. Kim Scott is a descendant of the Noongar people of south-western Western Australia. *That Deadman Dance* is inspired by early contact between Noongar people and Europeans in the early nineteenth century near Scott's hometown of Albany.

whales, not merely as spectacle but as ancestors, kin, prey and capital. Fatefully, it is their absence from the space in which they traditionally lived, close to the coast near the King George Town settlement, that shapes Bobby's later reflections as he struggles to reconcile his cultural and familial ties to the whales, with his earnest and well-intentioned interactions and attachments with the colonial settlers and his part in the hunting and killing of the whales:

> Too many people in this camp and this town should not be here. Once he was a whale and men from all points of the ocean horizon lured him close and chased and speared and would not let him rest until (blood clotting his heart) Bobby led them to the ones he loved, and soon he was the only one swimming.[2]

Southern right whales live on the margins of the colonial space but within the colonial imaginary. They provoke spatial arrangements that must be enforced in order to imagine them as possessions. Their bodies describe and endure subjectivity and subjection. While both their presence and their absence influence the natural and cultural world around them, their perspectives, intentions and desires lie beyond the grasp of humans.

In Alexis Wright's *The Swan Book*, the central character Oblivia Ethylene experiences, while still a young girl, a deep and unspoken bond with a group of black swans who arrive at the swampland where she is living, a bond that will endure for the rest of her life.[3] The attachment is a mutual one, the swans also captivated by her:

> This child! The swan could not take its eyes away from the little girl far down on the red earth. The music broke as if the strings had been broken, and the swan fell earthwards through the air for

---

2 Scott 2010, 160.

3 Wright 2013. Alexis Wright is a descendant of the Waanji people from the southern Gulf of Carpentaria. *The Swan Book* is a speculative, dystopian, multi-layered novel, set in the future, that responds to Australia's conservative, racist governance, border insecurities, social inequities and response to climate change.

> several moments. Maybe, it was in those moments of falling, that the big bird placed itself within the stories of this country, before it restored the rhythm of its flapping wings, and continued on its flight.[4]

The Swan Book balances the narrative thread of the swans as guides for Oblivia with that of their distinct journeys and desires. While care and guidance characterise the relationship between the swans and Oblivia, the swans' actions and interactions exceed this relationship, bearing the weight of their own experiences and understandings, and their own connection with the swamp they recognise as their home.

The black swans in Wright's novel and the whales in Scott's novel provide readers with a glimpse of the indeterminate, unspoken (in human language) and yet profound agency of non-human animals. While filtered through the lens of human perceptions and perceived connections, both the whales and the swans are depicted as finding meaning and purpose in relation to their own spaces, to their own journeys, and to those with whom they share these spaces. Whales and swans are cast not merely as constituents of Indigenous Country but also as its active custodians.

Eva Meijer and Bernice Bovenkerk argue that non-human animal agency matters, both to animal studies and to the academy in general, as evidenced by the accumulation of research and the growing awareness of animal languages, animal cultures, animal emotions, animal cognition and animal politics:

> In our view, in order to do justice to animal agency in our moral deliberations, we need a relational model that takes animals' perspectives into account, as well as the socio-historical context, and that does not measure other animals to a human standard.[5]

Animals have an interest in shaping their own lives. Without decentring humans, Meijer and Bovenkerk argue that it is impossible to come to any understanding of non-human animal perspectives. They offer a

4 Wright 2013, 41.
5 Meijer and Bovenkerk 2021, 55.

preliminary working definition of agency as the capability of a subject to influence the world in a way that expresses will or desire. The swans and whales in Wright's and Scott's novels indicate the indeterminate yet profound nature of this ability when considered in specific spaces, times and social relations. In each case, this ability is revealed in response to an oppressive human regime and social order.

Animal perspectives, interests and personhood, and the ways in which they have endured in the face of colonial settlement, are a key focus of this volume, which brings together a set of situated analyses and case studies, by a diverse group of Indigenous and non-Indigenous writers and researchers, that focus on the lives of specific non-human animals and groups of animals, and their agency, experiences, knowledge and relationships with other animals as well as humans. *Decolonising Animals* presents a set of animals that in the course of their lives, their relationships and their responses to the conditions of their specific subjectivity disrupt and trouble colonial settlement narratives, processes and assumptions. The title refers to the agency of non-human animals in unsettling, disturbing and eluding settler colonial logics, as well as to the challenges for animal studies scholars in rethinking animal perspectives, knowledges and power in settler colonial contexts.

Colonialism and settlement shape and mark our shared landscapes and habitats, our ways of seeing the world around us and our relationships with others, both non-human and human. Colonialism privileges Western epistemologies, assuming patriarchal, capitalist, heteronormative, ableist and speciesist values and criteria. It produces persistent exclusions and inclusions, foregrounding some forms of life while obscuring others. Importantly, the memories and desires of colonialism are experienced within the conditions of our subjection, repositioning us in relation to political, social and scientific authorities. As a Sri Lankan–Australian resident currently living and writing in Naarm/Melbourne on Bunurong and Wurundjeri Country, I recognise some of the ways in which the experiences of my parents growing up in colonial Ceylon and my experiences of growing up as the non-white son of migrants in Boorloo/Perth on Whadjuk Nyoongar Country have shaped my sense of identity, my aspirations and my expectations of how others might respond to me.

Animals undoubtedly continue to be the subjects of colonial domination and displacement, the objects of colonial knowledge and at times the agents of colonial conquest and settlement. Non-human animals have been used and exploited in order to take over lands and exclude and eradicate existing animals as part of the process of eliminating Indigenous peoples. They have also been used and exploited in the imposition of imperial animal practices. In their refusal to recognise colonial authority and subjection, and the times and spaces of empire, however, non-human animals have also displayed resilience, resistance and persistence in the face of colonialism. Non-human animals disrupt history, politics, space, society and culture, and in doing so bring into question any seamless or dogmatic notion of resistance, subversion or decolonisation as exclusively human domains. The ethical demands of non-human animals mean responding to the ways they are defined, confined, displaced, translocated, excluded, consumed and eradicated in the continuing process and rationale of colonial settlement.

The chapters in this volume are not intended as qualified acts of decolonisation, nor do they assume that such a process can indeed be initiated in the absence of animals; rather, they constitute efforts to address specific contexts, centred around or marshalled by specific groups of animals, in which settler colonial structures and logics and the conditions of animal and human subjection can be identified and questioned. In particular, the stories encapsulated in these chapters seek to question colonial animal epistemologies. Each of the authors has attempted to position themselves clearly in relation to the non-human animals and other knowledge-holders with whom they have engaged. The discursive space marked out by *Decolonising Animals* is one in which non-human animal, Indigenous and European colonial knowledges and perspectives are brought into contact with one another in order to question previous and ongoing encounters and hierarchies. The perspectives, knowledges, experiences and representations of horses, dingoes, bison, dung beetles, fish, jaguars, birds in extant, extinct or hybrid forms, and other non-human protagonists are juxtaposed, acknowledged and explored, with a focus on the times, spaces and physical conditions of their subjection within settler colonial regimes, and on their diverse responses to the structures and processes imposed on them. While each of the chapters may at first glance appear to address non-human animals in the wild, or at least animals that are free-ranging, each story as it unfolds reveals ties to colonial demands, animal agriculture and industry, or the process of settlement. Each is tied to specific political, historical and environmental relations and imaginaries.

This volume responds to and is part of a growing body of research addressing the positioning of non-human animals in settler colonial contexts. Animal studies scholars have in recent years attempted to reflect on the ways in which their research has benefited from the academy's colonial history and authority, and have sought to question their social and cultural positions in relation to Indigenous studies and decolonial studies. Connected to this is an increased focus on the experiences and consequences of settler colonialism for non-human animals. A provocative catalyst for this research has been Driftpile Cree writer and scholar Billy-Ray Belcourt's essay "Animal bodies, colonial subjects: (re)locating animality in decolonial thought", which challenges animal studies researchers to understand the conditions of subjectivity experienced by non-human animals within settler colonialism and to theorise animals as colonial subjects who need to be centred in decolonial thought.[6] Belcourt contends that most animal activism and academic animal advocacy continues to operate within and to perpetuate spaces of settler coloniality, while avoiding and deferring a reflective critique of the settler subject position in relation to animals.[7]

In the introduction to their recent edited collection entitled *Colonialism and Animality*, Kelly Struthers Montford and Chloë Taylor argue that Western settler colonial projects have assumed and fostered human exceptionalism in enforcing a restrictive conception of culture based on race, gender and species:

> Dualisms such as nature/culture, body/mind, female/male, and animal/human have been used to mark those labelled as closer to nature, such as racialized persons, women, and animals, as less human and therefore a-cultural non-agentic non-subjects.

6 Belcourt 2015.
7 Belcourt 2015.

> The cultural position of animals has also been used as a marker of civility. Reverence, respect, and spiritual communion with animals and nature were used by colonists as evidence of the savagery of Indigenous peoples – a position used to justify the settler project.[8]

In their introduction to a special issue of the *Journal of Intercultural Studies* entitled "Animal Nationalisms", Kathryn Gillespie and Yamini Narayanan emphasise the importance of the relationship between racism and anthropocentrism to colonial projects, in particular in regard to the ideologies disseminated in the building and maintenance of settler colonial nations.[9] They propose a "multispecies cultural politics that attends to racial/ethnic and species othering".[10] Such a proposition identifies a key challenge for addressing settler colonial and decolonial relationships, one that feeds back to the challenge issued in Belcourt's essay: to theorise non-human animals as colonial subjects with specific, multi-layered conditions of subjectivity, and to unravel the anthropocentrism bound within settler colonial logics, where the establishment of settler humanity occurs at the expense of animalities.

Animal agriculture, with its facade of benign pastoralism and bucolic normality, conceals a vast set of insidious, brutal and cruel animal practices deployed in the processing and killing of selected animal bodies while excluding and eradicating others. Such practices also implicate and exploit racialised and marginalised humans. At the same time, however, settler colonial states display an overt but selective objection to Indigenous animal practices, such as hunting and fishing, which are highlighted as barbaric and threatening biodiversity, at the same time ignoring Indigenous community practices promoting land, water and species protection. While it is clear that some animal practices have a more devastating and widespread effect than others, it might be reasonable to assume that non-human animals would prefer to avoid all practices entailing or leading to their killing by humans.

8 Struthers, Montford and Taylor 2020, 8–9.
9 Gillespie and Narayanan 2020.
10 Gillespie and Narayanan 2020, 4.

Focusing on the colonisation of Australia as a human–animal practice, Fiona Probyn-Rapsey and Lynette Russell take up the challenge of addressing the incipient anthropocentrism that persists, and at times appears unavoidable, in conflicting settler colonial and Indigenous cultural perspectives on animals:

> Disputes over animals are never simply between Indigenous and settler Australians, but also within and across these groups, with contestations framed by tensions around traditional/modern, conservation/ extinction, introduced/native, and human/animal, with animal advocacy and animal welfare issues (raised by both settler and Indigenous Australians) also frequently at odds with mainstream pastoralism, Indigenous hunting practices, and conservation efforts that include species eradications.[11]

They propose examining colonisation from distinct animal, Indigenous and settler colonial perspectives – a triadic approach that reasserts the interests of non-human animals while decentring human perspectives. Such an approach resists the tendency to exclude animal perspectives from consideration when examining colonial violence involving them, as well as the tendency to conflate all humans as a homogeneous group in relation to animals. Considering each perspective separately also allows for the interests of each perspective to be examined in more critical detail, without assuming that all non-human animals share similar perspectives, or that all Indigenous people or all colonial settlers do likewise.[12]

The advantages of such an approach for animal studies scholars include the provision of a discursive space for considering specific relationships between animals and groups of animals and their diverse, distinctive and multi-layered non-human experiences of colonisation, hunting and other interactions, while avoiding the tendency to view animals exclusively through their connections to humans or through species hierarchies, behaviourist models or larger environmental assemblages. At the same time, such an approach allows Indigenous

11 Probyn-Rapsey and Russell 2022, 63.
12 Probyn-Rapsey and Russell 2022, 38–39.

animal knowledges and relationships to be examined without mediation by or comparison with Western science: "interrogating western frameworks is not the same as engaging with radically different approaches in Indigenous knowledges".[13] It is in this space of critical thinking that the discounting or erasure of Indigenous animal knowledges can be seen as epistemic violence, as a strategic colonial practice, and that the aims and demands of a decolonial approach become clearer. Identifying the spatial, temporal and cultural limits of settler colonial knowledges and reasserting both Indigenous and non-human perspectives and knowledges is a conceptually unsettling project, one that does not seek simple resolutions but respects difference and incommensurability. One of the challenges for animal studies scholars, following on from this suggested approach, is to reconsider the way in which they position themselves in relation to Indigenous animal knowledges and the way in which they acknowledge the authority of these knowledges.

Kelsey Dayle John's chapter in this volume engages with this process of erasing and silencing Indigenous and non-human knowledge. John presents a narrative of horses in North America that focuses on kinship and relationalities of care, utilising a Diné worldview that not only accommodates horse personhood but emphasises it as central to understanding the place of horses in ceremony and traditional knowledge. John's decolonial history works against the grain of Western narratives of settlement that assume horses were introduced to the continent as agents of conquest and colonisation, challenging this idea by demonstrating how a shared landscape was marked, and a shared history erased, by a settler colonial regime that rendered the already-settled space "empty", Indigenous relationalities non-existent and more-than-human knowledges confined to the category of myth. John's account of Navajo horse relations speaks directly into that space of silencing, giving witness to the world created by horses and Navajo people.

The discounting of Indigenous knowledge of non-human animals and their relationships in settler colonial histories is also a critical concern of Rowena Lennox's chapter. Through an examination of the

---

13 Probyn-Rapsey and Russell 2022, 47.

representation and conceptualisation of dingoes in contemporary public contexts and in historical settler accounts of specific dingoes and their relationships with one another, with other animals and with Indigenous and non-Indigenous people, Lennox presents an account of more specific and contextualised experiences and knowledges of dingoes. The concepts of epistemic injustice and prejudicial exclusion inform a reconsideration of the ways in which Indigenous knowledge of dingoes, and by extension the guiding principles of Country, are devalued and obstructed in settler colonial biological, historical and legal discourses. Lennox examines the differences in the alternative taxonomic names placed upon dingoes as a space of epistemological tension in settler colonial knowledge, with dingoes unsettling the norms of categorisation as wild/tame, native/introduced and keystone predator/feral pest, demonstrating how naming and writing work within Western and scientific knowledge systems to possess and dominate non-human animals and land, and create hierarchies and hierarchical ways of interpreting the world.

The importance of research approaches and methodologies to affirming Indigenous knowledge and resisting colonial structures and processes is an idea that the influential Māori (Ngāti Awa and Ngāti Porou) scholar and educator Linda Tuhiwai Smith has highlighted and detailed in her work. Smith's Kaupapa Māori research principles reflect the fact that research methods require appropriate guiding principles and frameworks, and that Māori research should be undertaken by Māori, for Māori and with Māori.[14] Her critique of Western research demonstrates how the very concept of research is inextricably tied to and historically founded on colonialism and the annexation of Indigenous peoples, spaces and times, and that reclaiming Indigenous ways of knowing and being requires careful planning, consciousness and commitment in conducting research.

The development and deployment of a decolonising methodology addressing animals, mass extinction and responsibility provide the focus for Katarina Gray-Sharp's chapter, which constructs an approach to the study of anthropogenic mass extinction grounded in Māori and Indigenous studies. This approach is distinctly interdisciplinary,

14 Smith 2015.

displaying openness and careful attention to all analytic techniques. Gray-Sharp's research framework utilises polyvocality, allowing for different voices to articulate and interpret the structure and meaning of anthropogenic mass extinction: scientific/mathematical, linguistic/etymological and philosophical/conceptual. While a Western colonial approach might assume or demand a separation of these discursive sites of inquiry, Gray-Sharp's methodology connects them as a set of constructs confirming the continuation of the current mass extinction event, an event whose discursive shaping can be viewed as structural violence, calling all researchers to respond to it in an ethical and responsible way. Gray-Sharp proposes suggestions for such a response based on mātauranga Māori and Levinasian ethics. Through this polyvocal process, insights are also revealed into the lives and deaths of extinct avifauna in Aotearoa.

While framed as critical responses from settler positions, two other chapters in this volume also engage with decolonising methodologies. The chapter by Susan McHugh works towards framing a critical methodology for literary animal studies, while the chapter by Ana Paula Motta and Martin Porr focuses on decolonial approaches in archaeology, considering how such approaches can structure and inform a specific case study of jaguars.

McHugh's chapter acknowledges two compelling and connected concerns: the marginalisation of race and racism in animal studies, and in particular literary animal studies; and the relegation and exclusion of non-human animal perspectives and interests in contemporary fiction and literary criticism. The chapter commences by posing an uncomfortably familiar question regarding the whiteness of animal studies. McHugh uses this discomfort as a springboard to examine recent debates regarding the relationship between speciesism and racism, using literary critical research on the influential African American writer Toni Morrison, in order to suggest a literary critical methodology that foregrounds and values different reading and writing experiences, highlights narrative paths of inequality, questions objectivity and mastery in textual reading and reasserts what is not known and what lies outside a reader's cultural knowledge. These "far reading practices" are employed alongside more recognisable close reading techniques in analysing Morrison's novel *A Mercy* and how depictions of slavery and non-human animals may be read and interpreted. The chapter presents a case for practising more critical ways of accounting for the responsibility of responsiveness to animal-and-human-worlds.

Motta and Porr compare and connect the discursive and analytic practices of archaeology to those of animal studies. In emphasising the need for a stronger commitment to decolonial approaches, they advocate working towards more resistive and inclusive archaeological practices, highlighting recent archaeological work, particularly in the Global South, that questions how different species perceive the world around them and how these perceptions and responses have changed through time and space. Motta and Porr's case study of jaguars in Mexico and Central and South America examines Eurocentric and colonial conceptions, critically comparing and countering these with jaguar representations and meanings in Mayan, Olmec, Aztec and other Indigenous art, myths, legends and cosmologies. They explore how changing perceptions of jaguars influenced the way jaguars were interpreted in archaeology, as well as their conservation status and the contemporary knowledge held by Indigenous populations. The case study points to the notion of "walking with", in which knowledge is produced through experiencing and re-creating connections between people, land and existence, as helping researchers become more intimately aware of how coloniality is enacted in the process of research. Motta and Porr argue that in dismissing and discounting relational entanglements, colonial epistemologies erase both Indigenous animal and human bodies, citing the work of Haudenosaunee and Anishinaabe scholar Vanessa Watts.

Watts' research provides a critical account of the persistence of animal agency in the face of colonial encounters.[15] Grounding her argument within Haudenosaunee and Anishinaabe cosmologies, Watts describes the process in which shared agency (shared between the land, non-humans and humans) is an integral part of Indigenous environments. Natural environments are always also social environments, or societies: "Non-human beings are active members of society. Not only are they active, they also directly influence how

15 Watts 2013.

humans organise themselves into that society."[16] Watts identifies the framework in which land, non-humans and humans are connected, a framework formed by real Creation events, as Place-Thought. Western political and educational structures enforce a restrictive framework, the epistemological- ontological, in which knowledge and being are separated, with agency reconfigured as an exclusively human capacity. Watts argues that such a framework leads to alienation from the land and from non-human animals:

> As Indigenous peoples, it is not only an obligation to communicate with Place-Thought (ceremonies with land, territory, the four directions, etc.), but it ensures our continued ability to act and think according to our cosmologies. To prevent these practices deafens us. It is not that the non-human world no longer speaks but that we begin to understand less and less. This is why, despite five hundred years of colonialism, we are still not fully colonized and we are still continuing to fight; we have within us the ability to communicate with the land but our agency as Indigenous peoples has been corrupted within this colonial frame.[17]

While the work of Métis scholar Zoe Todd has focused on fish and their relations with humans and with their environment, it has had resonances for animal studies researchers in thinking about human–non-human kinship in other human–animal contexts. Todd's notion of fish pluralities – manifested in their various bodily states of existence, including as non-human beings with agency and knowledge, as food for humans and non-humans, as scientific objects of study and as sites of memories and connections – draws on the fact that fish can be known, recognised and made sense of in many different ways.[18] Todd's concept of fishy refraction works towards understanding how spaces and sites of difference mediate the ways fish and humans engage with each other and with water and air.[19] Together these concepts

16 Watts 2013, 23.
17 Watts 2013, 32.
18 Todd 2014.
19 Todd 2018.

help to build an understanding of how fish contribute to shaping their shared environments and demand ethical responses. Todd's interdisciplinary approach to understanding fish as kin who have been here before humans is framed in Métis legal traditions and cosmology, and focuses on specific groups of fish and humans in specific times and spaces in northern Canada.

Todd's notions of pluralities and kin, as well as Cree political theorist Kiera Ladner's conception of pluralities, are taken up in Danielle Taschereau Mamers' critical interrogation of bisons' relational lifeworlds.[20] The chapter commences by considering a 1907 stereographic image taken by N.A. Forsyth. The image carries with it a set of assumptions about its discursive significance: the enactment of settler colonial power and the processes of extraction, the social and cultural hierarchy established by economic and colonial demands, the removal of a keystone species from a grassland ecosystem, settler colonial alienation in action. Taschereau Mamers' focus, however, is on the bison as a transformative presence, a subject with her own history and agency. The chapter draws on Indigenous multispecies philosophies, practices and protocols in positing an approach that shifts the focus away from a conventional critique of settler colonial state practices, alienation and infrastructure, and towards bison perspectives and agency. Taschereau Mamers interrogates the bisons' entangled lifeworlds both in and outside their colonial contexts, exploring bison world-making and how their presence transforms their place of living, and speculating on the lifeworlds, pluralities and agencies operating in bison dung pats. Thinking through this leads to a way of attending to the unravelling and ending of these worlds.

My own chapter is concerned with fish, in particular how Western scientific knowledge of fish is shaped by a history of colonial violence that is often disposed of in its representation. Stories of miraculous discoveries, the overcoming of danger, the enduring of hardships and the commitment of natural historians and fishing communities provide the cornerstone for fish narratives, and for the establishment of Western science as the unquestioned reference for determining the status of fish, and their ultimate fate. Fish, however, can provide a problem for

20 Ladner 2003.

colonial authority and postcolonial demands, in the way they transgress the times, spaces and structures of colonisation. Their oceanic and fluvial movements and relationships can transgress the boundaries of nation or colony, their histories exceed the temporalities of colonisation, and their knowledges and perceptions surpass the determinations of science. Indigenous fish knowledges, by contrast, suggest less formal distinctions between fish and humans, less hierarchical relations of power and a deeper awareness of ongoing relationships of ecological and cultural connection and kinship. They also point more clearly to what fish know about us. My approach to cultural relationships with fish is informed by Zoe Todd's call for us to see the connections between terrestrial and aquatic environments and to be aware of kinship relationships and obligations in "fish-places".

Kirsty Dunn's chapter presents a critical reflection on the significance and potential of pūrākau in understanding human–non-human kinships and connections, in holding together alternative narrative perspectives, and in experiencing storytelling as a developing, ongoing process. While the Māori term pūrākau does not translate in an easy and definitive way into English, it is understood in this chapter to mean narratives that have been passed down through generations and that hold historical, geographical, genealogical and ecological knowledge as well as moral and ethical guidelines. Non-human kin are often addressed in pūrākau by way of shapeshifting, hybridity and more-than-human behaviours. Dunn analyses two short stories by Māori authors and their portrayals of birdwomen, mother birds and narrative perspectives: "Te Karaka o te Tītī" by Karl Wixon, and "Kurungaituku", a provocative retelling of the story of Hatupatu and Kurungaituku the birdwoman by Ngahuia Te Awekotuku. The stories are considered for the ways in which they represent specific, alternative non-human kin perspectives. Within these stories we see animals as observers, as adversaries, as kai (food), as tohu (signs), as guardians and protagonists with agency and their own perspectives. In keeping with the broader themes of this volume, Dunn's chapter calls attention to the way these stories foreground our inclusion and participation in human–non-human kinships and ecological relationships, and our obligations to non-human animals.

In a foreword to *Colonialism and Animality*, Dinesh Wadiwel posits a reminder that our relationships with non-human animals, as well as those activities that come together as animal studies (such as research, art and activism), are always already tied up with the settler colonial project.[21] Given this fraught attachment, Wadiwel questions how we might resist complicity with the project and avoid reflecting settler rationalities in presenting research about animals. A further question raised, one that is particularly relevant to this volume, concerns the efficacy of presenting alternative perspectives and alternative knowledges, and the extent to which they can bring about change. This is a daunting question with which to engage. While *Decolonising Animals* might seek to present case studies of specific animals and groups of animals that might trouble and unsettle the process of colonialism in specifically framed contexts, the question of radical change remains deferred, to other sites, other animals, other human–animal relationships. Perhaps making space for these knowledges, perspectives and relationships can serve as a beginning.

References

Belcourt, Billy-Ray (2015). Animal bodies, colonial subjects: (re)locating animality in decolonial thought. *Societies* 5(1): 1–11.

Gillespie, Kathryn and Yamini Narayanan (2020). Animal nationalisms: multispecies cultural politics, race, and the (un)making of the settler nation-state. *Journal of Intercultural Studies* 41(1): 1–7.

Ladner, Kiera L. (2003). Governing within an ecological context: creating an alternative understanding of Blackfoot governance. *Studies in Political Economy* 70(Spring): 125–52.

Meijer, Eva and Bernice Bovenkerk (2021). Taking animal perspectives into account in animal ethics. In B. Bovenkerk and J. Keulartz, eds. *Animals in Our Midst: The Challenges of Co-existing with Animals in the Anthropocene*, 49–64. Cham, Switzerland: Springer.

Probyn-Rapsey, Fiona and Lynette Russell (2022). Indigenous, settler-coloniser, animal: a triadic approach. *Animal Studies Journal* 11(2): 38–68.

Scott, Kim (2010). *That Deadman Dance*. Sydney: Picador Australia.

21 Wadiwel 2021.

Smith, Linda Tuhiwai (2015). Kaupapa Māori research – some kaupapa Māori principles. In L. Pihama and K. Southey, eds. *Kaupapa Rangahau: A Reader*, 47–54. Hamilton, New Zealand: Te Kotahi Research Unit. http://hdl.handle.net/10289/9531.

Struthers Montford, Kelly and Chloë Taylor (2020). Colonialism and animality: an introduction. In K. Struthers Montford and C. Taylor, eds. *Colonialism and Animality: Anti-colonial Perspectives in Critical Animal Studies*, 1–16. London: Routledge.

Todd, Zoe (2018). Refracting the state through human-fish relations: fishing, Indigenous legal orders and colonialism in north/western Canada. *Decolonization: Indigeneity, Education & Society* 7(1): 60–75.

Todd, Zoe (2014). Fish pluralities: human-animal relations and sites of engagement in Paulatuuq, Arctic Canada. *Études/Inuit/Studies* 38(1–2): 217–38.

Wadiwel, Dinesh (2021). Foreword: thinking "critically" about animals after colonialism. In K. Struthers Montford and C. Taylor, eds. *Colonialism and Animality: Anti-colonial Perspectives in Critical Animal Studies*, xvii–xxiv. London: Routledge.

Watts, Vanessa (2013). Indigenous Place-Thought & agency amongst humans and non-humans (First Woman and Sky Woman go on a European world tour!). *Decolonization: Indigeneity, Education & Society* 2(1): 20–34.

Wright, Alexis (2013). *The Swan Book*. Sydney: Giramondo Publishing.

1

The horse is Indigenous to North America: Why silencing the horse is so important to the settler project

Kelsey Dayle John

Introduction

"The horse was brought over by the Spanish." I have heard this phrase many times since I was young. But another statement echoes: the words of my Diné father, who knew he needed to teach his daughter the *real* story. He would say: "For Navajos, *the horse has always been here.* They've been with us since the beginning of time. They'll try to tell you it came through colonisation, but that's not true." My sister and I grew up knowing that the creatures adorning our pasture had always been our people's companions. I've done a few presentations on horse knowledges for different audiences. In my presentations, I talk about horsemanship as a specific practice in my community that helps to preserve our overall philosophy. One major part of understanding the horse in a Diné worldview is to understand they were introduced in our creation narratives. I am almost always challenged by an audience member who claims that the horse is *not* indigenous to North America or American Indian peoples but that it was introduced to Native Americans through colonisation. Despite two bodies of evidence (oral indigenous histories and archaeological evidence), this story of the horse still persists with an iron grip on history. Strangely, the narrative seems to fly under the radar while other historically inaccurate narratives about Indians, like the first Thanksgiving or Pocahontas, have been largely accepted as myths. I started to examine scholarly sources and I realised it wasn't for a lack of evidence; rather, it seemed to be that settler stories *need the horse not to be indigenous to this continent*. So I ask why. Why is it so important to the settler narrative that the horse was brought to the Americas by Spanish colonisers?

In this chapter, I weave together two knowledge narratives – American Indian studies and settler colonial studies – to tell a story about horses. I illustrate why settler narratives of identity hold on so tightly to the idea that horses are tools and agents of colonialism rather than persons. I will highlight three key sub-narratives to show how it is less about where the horse originated and more about whose histories are told, and what sacrificing the validity of the settler colonial narrative does to the historical identity of settler societies. In other words, narratives that lay claim to the horse are not just about horses; they're about the right to access and to know. I invite you to listen to and respect the horse as a person and knowledge-holder. Instead of the unchallenged historical narratives about "taming the Wild West with horses", I'll relate a narrative that Indigenous people have been telling in our communities all along: the horse is indigenous to North America; the horse is a relative, a teacher, and our partner. The personhood of horses shows they are agents who belong to place, which fundamentally challenges the standard American creation narrative that described the Americas as empty lands. Horse persons reaffirm Native (human and animal) rights and relationships with lands and have their own stories to tell. I close this chapter with a discussion of how this theoretical intervention might inform some of the current conversations regarding free-range horses in North America today.

The horse is a person

> I am an equine; a member of the Equus family, and I've been on this continent for over 5,000 years. – Bambi

My horse Bambi brags about this to me one day in our corral. She likes to remind me about her personhood any time my humanness becomes too central, or if I start to think our relationship is about doing what I want. This helps me, though, because in my limited experience of the moment when things seem … bad … I think, I wonder, how many events she has seen, how many stories have been passed down to her like a thread thousands of years long. What would she say about her ancestors and how they evolved for the best ways of living? How did they teach her to embody her steadfastness? I didn't have to teach her anything. I had to unbind my mind enough to build a relationship with her. That is why she is so good at communicating and why she is so loving, wise and diplomatic. You don't survive thousands of years as a herd animal being selfish. That's why she gathers around with all the friends in the wash – the bob cat, the coyotes, the birds, the ants and the rabbits. All congregate in her corral to have what I assume are dialogues. Any time I think my way is the best way, I remember that her kin have survived on these lands for longer than my kind. Or perhaps we have survived together and that's why she sees me. She doesn't need me, but I need her. I think all the creatures need her too and that's why they arrive every day to hear her stories.

My horse companion Bambi colours the pages of any manuscript I write, helping me to remember that relationships with the more-than-human world are central to Navajo epistemology. Indigenous persons see the horse as a partner, an autonomous being and a collaborator; they see the horse as they see all things: relationally. Indigenous and decolonial scholars have named, through countless mediums, the differences between a colonial worldview and an Indigenous paradigm.[1] One of the major differences is that all things are interrelated, meaning that whatever happens to one person in the Navajo universe affects every connected person (human or non-human). Horses' autonomy to tell their own stories should be recognised by humans. They are so much more than just servants in the human story of empire.

Navajos understand horses to be sacred, and by this I mean a high holder of knowledge. They are the experts and diplomats of the animal community. The fundamental relationality that underscores Indigenous beliefs about relationships with the more-than-human world is that

---

1 Bang, Curley et al. 2014; Cajete 2005; Kimmerer 2013; Smith 2012.

these persons hold all the characteristics necessary to be granted personhood status.[2] The horse deserves to be untangled from colonial histories and to have a history and identity of its own outside of the framework provided by colonisation. The beginning of the horse's story is not the beginning of ranching, the beginning of human mobility/riding or even the beginning of warfare via horseback, but this is often where the horse's story begins. My community has stories that contextualise these beings as place-based knowledge-holders who participate in ceremony and society. The settler framework needs the horse to be "a colonial tool", as it refuses to see that Native societies have consistently described their fundamental difference in worldview. Native societies have argued that animals are not valuable based on their ability to produce labour for us. They are valuable because they are persons.

An Indigenous horse challenges the narrative of the American West and westward expansion. Expansion into Native territory desired the Native wildness while at the same time desiring to control it. The idea of the Wild West facilitates a socio-constructed narrative about how the US nation came to be. Violence is cloaked in masculinised tropes of taming, breaking and civilising the vast Indigenous scapes of wildness. The colonial figure is typically found atop a horse and engaging in genocidal acts, as in familiar cowboy and Indian storylines, where the cowboys must save the settlers from wild Indians. The basis of this conflict or dichotomy is the basic binary that underlies US expansion: Indian savage versus civilised settler. Indigenous relationalities disrupt the idea that the Wild West can be tamed, because our relationships to horses are not about dominance, utilitarianism or progress: they are about kinship and relationalities of care. The best way to erase Native horse knowledge is to espouse the belief that the horse was a gift brought to the Natives by more civilised colonists. This story argues the horse is a tool that helped to civilise the Natives.

What is lost when we ignore Native horse narratives is the personhood of horses. Indigenous and animal studies scholars alike argue that animals are more than just food or labour.[3] Contrary to American progress narratives, Indigenous folks have been innovative,

---

2 John 2022.

3 Bang, Curley et al. 2014; Belcourt 2015; John 2019; Reo and Whyte 2011.

researching and engaging in technology for centuries and doing so in partnership with more-than-human persons.[4] Indigenous scholars have pointed out that animals are also colonised subjects[5] and an ally for Indigenous persons as they protect their land, their families and their hunting/farming practices.

Diné scholar Rudy Shebala tells a story about a horse ally for a Navajo woman. In the story, a young Navajo woman is captured as a slave by Mexican colonists. She is deeply traumatised as they put her on a horse and take her away from her community. She pleads with her horse to take her home. The horse listens and at a moment when nobody is watching, the horse turns and bolts back home, carrying the young woman back to the safety of her family.[6] To counter the narrative of horses and agriculture, Shebala tells how the horse is a co-conspirator helping Navajo people push back against a practice many don't know about: the capture of Indians for slavery. I love this story because it confirmed to me what I thought all along, which is that horses understand what it's like to be oppressed and enslaved. In the story, the horse understands the violence of forced labour and the desire of the girl to return to her community, and chooses to act with agency to help the girl return safely home.

Indigenous horses challenge the American creation narrative

When I drive through miles of corn fields in Nebraska or eastern Colorado, or see the statistics about cattle ranching or public lands leased to ranchers, I begin to understand the scope and magnitude of land used for agriculture in the American West. For Natives, this transformation of land happened quickly; these places were not always cattle ranches and corn fields sectioned off into square mile parcels. According to many tribal stories, they were places where horses, among other creatures, roamed.[7] Looking at the land now, it's hard to believe

4 John 2019; Kimmerer 2013.
5 Belcourt 2015.
6 Shebala 2018.
7 Collin 2017; Hubbard 2009.

entire societies of animal, plant and human life once thrived in these lands in a different set of relations, but Native people have a collective memory of a time when these places blended together in stories and communities. We have stories where animal partners talk with us and participate in decision-making. Stories where the opinion of the animal is respected. Of course, all these stories are considered myths to non-Native audiences now.

Narratives of erasure

American settler narratives permeate the collective knowledge about American history, often going unnoticed by non-Natives. Indigenous educators have highlighted these narratives and disentangled them from curricula using settler colonial studies.[8] Narratives about the beginning of the United States reflect continual refusals, justifications or "moves to innocence"[9] that excuse or conceal the systematic erasure of Indigenous persons, their knowledge systems, their land relationships and, most importantly for this chapter, their relations with animal persons. Narratives order and shape how collective memory and knowledge inform our understandings about who we are, where we are and how we got here. In turn, these narratives drive communal value systems.

Brian Burkhart explains this as "the coloniality of power" or an underlying epistemology which continues to view every aspect of existence through a duality. This is often referred to as the separation between mind and body. In an effort to make sense of this dualism, persons fall into categories of object or body (read: Indians), and other persons are minds with personhood (read: Europeans). Burkhart argues: "Nature, animals, Indians, and sexuality are physical, and civilisation, European humans, and rationality are mental/spiritual by definition."[10] This ubiquitous dualism projects itself onto the meaning-making systems and relationships, effectively perpetuating

8 Brayboy 2014; Tuck and Yang 2012; Wolfe 2006.
9 Tuck and Yang 2012.
10 Burkhart 2019, 15.

racialised narratives about Black persons, Indian persons and animal persons, positioning them at the "less-than-human" end of the continuum. The less-than-human category then serves as a justification for objectifying people as labour producers or excuses the dehumanisation and genocide of those people.[11] The Native experiences of historical moments are silenced by excluding their histories, dismissing their methods of remembering, or physically erasing persons who carry those knowledges and histories.[12] Billy-Ray Belcourt points out that these systems of unjust violence play out on the bodies of both human and animal persons, ultimately connecting the colonisation of human bodies to the colonisation of animal bodies.[13]

Though there are variances in how versions of the same grand narrative unfold, it is similar in several respects: Natives are always less rational, more primitive and less capable of relating to beings appropriately (land, animals, humans). Because of this, colonisers, settlers and the US government justify acts of assimilation or erasure by arguing that they are helping Natives progress.[14] What results is that Natives, their ways of life and their relationships are disconnected and erased in a process that is always massively violent.

There are many counter-narratives about the origin of the horse. Yvette Running Horse Collin, for example, conducted interviews with Indigenous Elders, medicine people, scientists and horse experts, gathering stories from traditional and oral history experts in Indigenous communities and curating evidence about the horse as a significant person in creation who influenced Native cultures prior to settler colonisation.[15] Collin analysed historical, academic and scientific records in order to produce data that speaks back to the commonly accepted mythic horse history. This collection of oral histories and archaeological evidence suggests horses could have survived through the Ice Age on the North American continent. Collin

11 Deckha 2018; Hubbard 2009; John 2019; King 2019.

12 I am reminded of the horrors of erasure by the discoveries of hundreds of unmarked graves at Indian residential schools found in 2021. See McGreevy 2021.

13 Belcourt 2015.

14 Deloria 2003; Dunbar-Ortiz 2014; Smith 2012.

15 Collin 2017.

cites Russell, Rich et al., who argue that it was possible that horses migrated south during the Ice Age.[16] Collin writes:

> If what Russell et al., discovered is accurate, it is possible that the Indigenous Peoples of the Americas and the Indigenous horse of the Americas co-existed and had a continuous relationship before the arrival of the first load of horses that were brought to the Americas (to what are now the Caribbean Islands) by the Spanish in 1493, and the first horses to be brought by the Spanish to the mainland (to the area now known as Mexico) in 1519.[17]

When one follows this train of thought, it opens up possibilities for extensive ways of knowing that could have existed for thousands of years prior to colonial contact.

This begs the question: "If the horse is new to Natives, how does one explain the advanced level of horsemanship that Native communities have obtained in such a short amount of time?"[18] Or why are there stories of different training methods that include songs and stories?[19] What about different relationships between Native and horse persons, relations outside of settler ranching, farming and imperial domestication? When the horse is considered a new tool, then Native relations with this "new tool" are explained in the standard American progress story. For Navajos, the discussion isn't so much about proving whether the horse was or wasn't here; it is about the continuance of our philosophies and ways of being with the horse even through layers of erasure. There is no denying that horses increase mobility for Navajos. One Navajo will say the horse was here all along; another will tell you that the horse *returned* with Spanish folks. The point is that one narrative helps us see the horse as a person and the other frames the horse as a worker.

As Natives enact their own practices of agriculture outside the settler paradigms of private property,[20] animal domination, exploited

16 Russell, Rich et al. 2009.
17 Collin 2017, 34.
18 Shebala 2018.
19 Collin 2017; John 2019.
20 John 2020; Rotz and Kepkiewicz 2018.

and racialised labour and hierarchies of human/animal, these methodologies fundamentally challenge the US agricultural system. They speak back, saying: "We have our own way of relating to the world and these ways belong to these places and have since time immemorial." This way of relating doesn't begin and end with private property, cattle ranching or expansion. The idea that Natives have sophisticated agricultural systems disrupts the narrative used to justify their erasure and assimilation.

Settler agriculture

Central to the ongoing narrative of progress is American agriculture, and the horse appears in every chapter of this history. Sarah Rotz draws connections between racialised hierarchies, settler colonialism and agricultural systems in Canada, identifying a narrative that operates in the US too, the myth of a frontier. She writes: "The idea of the 'frontier' – carried out by (largely male) 'unlicensed mavericks' and 'explorers' (fur traders, bounty hunters, gold-seekers, ranchers and farmers) rather than formal state procedures – was foundational for settler colonialism."[21] The frontier is a place of no rules, the Wild West if you will, and before the policies of assimilation, the West was an unregulated mesh of violence and land grabs. Patrick Wolfe explains the tensions of settler agriculture and how it works as an arm of settler colonialism to eliminate Native peoples.[22] The destruction of food systems is central to systematic erasure of Indigenous relationships for the purpose of settler colonial national expansion. Belcourt writes:

> Anthropocentrism is […] a politics of space whereby land is commodified and privatised for animal agriculture. Although this unsustainable food system uses approximately thirty percent of the Earth's land mass and accounts for "nearly half of all water used in the United States" decolonial thought has yet to deconstruct the settler-colonial, anthropocentric, and capitalist

21 Rotz 2017, 159.
22 Wolfe 2006.

> logics governing animal agriculture that assume the facticity of settler colonialism.[23]

Belcourt helps us to understand that the American narrative assumes that agriculture is harmless and benevolent, without looking at the logics of reorganising space and relations that were largely destructive in Indigenous communities. Indigenous food sovereignty scholars explain that entire tribal food systems have been disrupted by waves of violent destruction, from crop scorching to livestock slaughter.[24] Steve Price describes how horse slaughter was used as a tool for controlling and exterminating Navajo people: "Kit Carson, appointed a colonial of New Mexico Volunteers and ordered to subdue both the Mescalero Apaches and Navajos, killed both their horses and sheep."[25]

Central to the discourse of civilisation are elevated modes of technology produced from Western epistemology. These advancements, whether railroads, private property, patriarchy or Christianity, are seen as for the ultimate good and are enforced through policies and institutions like the Dawes Act, livestock slaughter,[26] world's fairs, land-grab universities[27] and residential boarding schools, all of which continue to enact separations and fissures in proper relationalities among all persons.[28] In the narrative, all is carried out in the name of progress and expansion, including taming the West, ranching and all things that aid in these processes. Apart from being an aid to colonial empire, horses are rarely seen as stand-alone persons with agency, or as cohabitants in Indigenous communities. In the story of ranching, exploring, US cavalry activities and farming, the horse is central, though often unrecognisable from either of two settler colonial narratives: the horse as a tool to the settler society, or the romantic tale of the horse gifted to Indigenous society by colonisers.

---

23 Belcourt 2015, 5.
24 Mihesuah and Hoover 2019; Weisiger 2009.
25 Price 2017, 73.
26 Weisiger 2009.
27 Lee and Ahtone 2020.
28 John 2019.

Horse histories

In an introductory chapter on equine science outlining equine history, Parker writes that "settlers saw the horse as a means of expansion and as power for taming the wilderness and cultivating virgin soil".[29] Here we see the gendered trope of wild, virgin lands ready to be conquered by horses and tools. Horses were used for operating farm machinery, transportation and driving cattle. Americans believe their agriculture reflected superior land practices and used this superiority to justify land theft, forced removals and exploited labour. The horse is introduced alongside proper farming/ranching techniques for Native communities – it is just another tool of the colonial project. These techniques were introduced and enforced through fairs, land-grab institutions and Indian agents. Horse histories are folded neatly into the American creation narrative as simply another marker of rationality, civilisation and reason. As mentioned earlier, Native methods of knowing (oral history, story, song and ceremony) are erased further by being labelled unreasonable, savage or mythic. Furthermore, if Natives accept and build relationships with horses, then they are characterised as "getting on board" with the colonial project. Karuka writes about the horse in the way most historians interpret generic horse/Native relationships where the horse is a tool for Native participation in agriculture:

> The ecological and social relationships emanating from horses and bison for Lakota society bear a relation to Marx's model of the two departments of capital. The first department, geared toward the means of production, mirrors the role of horses in the buffalo economy. The second department, revolving around production for consumption, mirrors the place of bison in the buffalo economy.[30]

In other words, Spanish colonialism brought Indians culture and more specifically, *real* agri*culture*. The horse helps the Native participate in the settler economy. The horse is re-presented as a pillar of settler

29 Parker 2018, 14.
30 Karuka 2019, 62.

technology along with the idea that these technologies and their accompanying ideologies are a gift, a justification or, worse yet, a blessing.

"If the horses weren't here, neither were the Indians"

Nobody ever actually said to me, "If the horses weren't here, neither were the Indians," but that's what they said without saying it. The utter disbelief that horses could be persons on the lands with histories and a right to access land reminded me of the disbelief people have when they learn that history books tell crudely inaccurate Native histories. Considering horses as original inhabitants in the Americas interrupts comfortable narratives because it reminds us that vibrant communities of humans and more-than-humans thrived across the entire continent of North America. Settler narratives need the horse to be a newcomer, because if Native/horse relationships embedded in creation stories are inaccurate, this inconsistency drives a wedge through the credibility of Native knowledges and stories, which is imperative to perpetuating settler narratives of emptiness. In other words, recognising robust nations (horse and human) prior to colonisation does not align with the American creation narrative. As social psychology scholars remind us, humans can easily dismiss narratives that do not fit into the dominant narratives they encounter regularly. Dismissing Native history delegitimises Native American rights to land by arguing that these spaces were empty and so everyone is an immigrant. The Spanish introduction of the horse is tied directly to the delegitimisation of other histories that Natives tell about their origin, their beginning and their relations. If the horse is a newcomer, this means Natives are newcomers too. Vine Deloria Jr explains that when science traces the movements and migrations of animals, like horses and bison, it is also tracking the movements of human persons.[31]

31 Deloria 1997.

Bering Strait and empty lands

Vine Deloria Jr wrote extensively about how the Bering Strait migration theory is offensive to American Indian peoples because it positions their beginning within this land as sometime "a little bit before" Europeans. He explained that

> coupled with this belief is the idea that American Indians were not the original inhabitants of the Western Hemisphere but latecomers who had barely unpacked before Columbus came knocking on the door. If Indians had arrived only a few centuries earlier, they had no real claim to land that could not be swept away by European discovery.[32]

In the end, this makes people think that Native communities don't have any legal right to the land, and that claims of sovereignty erode alongside American exceptionalism. Land theft seems more acceptable if Natives are immigrants too. If settlers can prove the horse wasn't here, it helps to reaffirm the idea that the Americas were empty.

Settler horse histories are suspicious because they erase horses' place-based relations to land and instead make it seem like the horse came into being when they joined the linear thread of domestication. It could be stated like this: horses were once wild, long ago, and then they were tamed through colonisation, so no real wild horses exist anymore; they are fading away just like nature and real Indians. Because they were not here for thousands of years, it creates a picture of emptiness in the settler imaginary. The image of empty frontiers continues to be a remedy because:

> considerable residual guilt remains over the manner in which the Western Hemisphere was invaded and settled by Europeans. Five centuries of brutality lie uneasily on the conscience, and consequently two beliefs have arisen which are used to explain away this dreadful history. People want to believe that the Western Hemisphere, and in particular North America, was vacant,

32 Deloria 1997, 68.

> unexploited, fertile land waiting to be put under cultivation according to God's holy dictates.[33]

The trope of emptiness permeates US history, acting as a central mode of Indigenous erasure. If we presume horse to be new, and Native to be new, then what is left are vast empty lands waiting to be tamed.

Horse migrations

Price writes another brief horse history that might be included in an equine science, archaeology or Mustang history text:

> Many [horses] migrated to Eurasia across the Bering Land Bridge, and as they were crossing, they likely passed the first paleolithic humans migrating from Asia to North America. In a strange twist of fate, this westward migration is literally what saved horses from extinction, for between ten thousand and twelve thousand years ago, the animals disappeared entirely in North America. They weren't alone … many scientists postulate that those same prehistoric humans the horses passed while crossing the Bering Strait hunted them all to extinction in North America.[34]

Putting this excerpt in conversation with Deloria's work, I recognise a familiar story reflected in a short introductory section that is meant to give a simple explanation about horse origins. When I read this I hear: "Horses went extinct, but luckily they climbed a land bridge to Asia and eventually were domesticated (which is what saved them, by the way). And if you're wondering why they didn't survive in North America, it's because current settler narratives claim the Indians killed them all, even though many Native cultures have strict protocols prohibiting taking more than they need, and revere many animal persons as sacred beings."[35]

---

33 Deloria 1997, 68.

34 Price 2017, 4.

35 Collin 2017; John 2019; Kimmerer 2013; Shebala 2018.

The story of wild mustangs in North America is told using a collection of breed identification, DNA tracking and very specific ideas about domestication. Native ways of knowing, like oral histories and songs that include equines, are silenced. If horses were on the continent all along, imagine the stories they would tell: stories of times before settlement, stories of partnership, resistance and survival through all that humans have done to these lands. Furthermore, acceptable methodologies for knowing Natives generally tell the same kinds of stories about Natives, either positioning them as myths, overly romanticised peoples or backward savages. Any new piece of knowledge offered by Native American people for Native American people is nearly always suspected to be mythic in academic circles.

Communities more entrenched in the science will agree that horses evolved on the North American continent but are careful to insert a pause in time when they are believed to have gone extinct.[36] This pause is extremely important because it helps to perpetuate the idea of emptiness, so it can fit neatly into the American creation story. To me, the pause signals a huge gap in knowledge: What happened during this pause? Who was here? Wouldn't we be curious about Native stories that might contain creation narratives with horses? Why is Native knowledge not taken seriously? Collectively, I see a similar underlying judgement: whatever Natives say about themselves, their histories and their knowledges is fundamentally not true. Consequently, whatever Natives say about their more-than-human partners and their joint histories is also not true. This translates to: "If we can disprove what Natives say about horses, then we can disprove what they say about everything." Or: "If we cannot trust Native origin stories, we cannot trust what they say about horse origins either." In contrast, what science, history, anthropology and archaeology say about these histories is true, even when these stories are incomplete, inconsistent or incongruent.[37] I believe this is what keeps scholars from interrogating the pause in horse history and privileging Native knowledge systems.

36 See e.g. Haynes 2009; Solow, Roberts and Robbirt 2006.
37 Deloria 1997.

Free-range horses today

Today, wild horses still roam free on Navajo Nation and other public and tribal lands. Explanations about origins and lineages vary in different regions and by tribal community. Some American Indian tribes understand that their horse populations descend from various horse herds and are the most naturally occurring horse populations.[38] Today, the same narratives and politics of origin inform the stories that are told about these horses and their purposes. In many ways, they remain a threat to settler colonialism, American agriculture and the control of lands. Ranchers are still unhappy about the high population of free-range horses and the lack of access to grazing on public lands. However, the intersections of rancher, Indian and agriculture couldn't be blurrier.[39] Now more than ever, it is important to consider what Native persons say about knowledge systems of place and all the persons in that place.[40]

There is a trend of controversial politics around how to manage free-range horse herds, and various documentaries[41] and news articles[42] have addressed the issue of free-range horses and all the different stakeholders. Rarely do sources consider what horses think. The Navajo Nation has been criticised for its management (or lack thereof) of wild horse populations, but what is left out of those scathing articles is the centuries of land grabs, forced relocations, extractive mining, environmental pollution, settler encroachment and human/animal extermination.

I love wild horses because they don't care about fencing, private property, public lands or grazing permits. They simply exist and connect to the relationships they need; they live by a different set of rules. Wild horses challenge our understanding of private property, from the horses that tiptoe over cattle guards, to the horses that don't care whose grass belongs to whom. They challenge our allegiance to

38 Snowshoe and Starblanket 2016.
39 Carlisle 2021.
40 Whyte 2017.
41 Aig and Baribeau 2016.
42 Baca 2017.

the structure of private property by not caring about it at all. They break through barbed wire fences to graze alongside the road, or kick a person in the face who tries to "break" them, always reminding us this isn't just a human world. The horse is a being that challenges settler colonialism by challenging cattle-centred agriculture and the American creation story that so often erases any beings in these lands.

If we think about who has right to land and right to graze, we never consider that Indigenous more-than-human persons have the right to land, a story to tell about this land, or knowledge about how to relate to the land. Today, wild horse populations are characterised in the same ways that Indian people were characterised – as a problem in the way of progress. But American mustangs have a narrative all their own about these lands and other ways of being. This is why it's so important to make them colonial, to keep them silent.

References

Aig, D. (producer) and P. Baribeau (director) (2016). *Unbranded*. United States: Implement Productions, Cedar Creek Productions.

Baca, Kim (2017). The Navajo Nation has a wild horse problem. *High Country News*, 6 October. https://bit.ly/3AUzyAh.

Bang, Megan, L. Curley, A. Kessel, A.E. Marin, S. Suzukovich III and G. Strack (2014). Muskrat theories, tobacco in the streets, and living Chicago as Indigenous land. *Environmental Education Research* 20(1): 37–55. https://doi.org/10.1080/13504622.2013.865113.

Belcourt, Billy-Ray (2015). Animal bodies, colonial subjects: (re)locating animality in decolonial thought. *Societies* 5(1): 1–11.

Brayboy, Bryan (2014). Culture, place, and power: engaging the histories and possibilities of American Indian education. *History of Education Quarterly* 54(3): 395–402.

Burkhart, Brian (2019). *Indigenizing Philosophy through the Land: A Trickster Methodology for Decolonizing Environmental Ethics and Indigenous Futures*. East Lansing: Michigan State University Press.

Cajete, Gregory (2005). American Indian epistemologies. *New Directions for Student Services* 105: 69–78.

Carlisle, Alexandra (2021). Stakeholder analysis of the sociocultural, economic, and political dynamics of the feral horse overpopulation crisis on the Navajo Nation. Unpublished Capstone Project, Justice Institute of British Columbia.

Collin, Yvette Running Horse (2017). The relationship between Indigenous peoples of the Americas and the horse: deconstructing a Eurocentric myth. PhD dissertation, University of Alaska Fairbanks.

Deckha, M. (2018). Postcolonial. In L. Gruen, ed. *Critical Terms for Animal Studies*, 280–93. Chicago: University of Chicago Press.

Deloria, Phillip (1998). *Playing Indian*. New Haven, CT: Yale University Press.

Deloria, Vine, Jr (2003). *God is Red: A Native View of Religion*. Golden, CO: Fulcrum Publishing.

Deloria, Vine, Jr (1997). *Red Earth, White Lies: Native Americans and the Myth of Scientific Fact*. Golden, CO: Fulcrum Publishing.

Dunbar-Ortiz, R. (2014). *An Indigenous Peoples' History of the United States*. Boston: Beacon Press.

Haynes, Gary (2009). Estimates of Clovis-era megafaunal populations and their extinction risks. In G. Haynes, ed. *American Megafaunal Extinctions at the End of the Pleistocene*, 39–53. New York: Springer.

Hubbard, Tasha (2009). "The buffaloes are gone" or "return: buffalo"? The relationship of the buffalo to Indigenous creative expression. *Canadian Journal of Native Studies* 29(1/2): 65.

John, Kelsey Dayle (2022). What does it mean when Indigenous peoples say animals are sacred? In Molly Bassett and Natalie Avalos, eds. *Indigenous Religious Traditions in Five Minutes*, 146–8. Sheffield, South Yorkshire: Equinox Publishing.

John, Kelsey Dayle (2020). Fences tell a story of land changes on Navajo Nation. *Edge Effects Digital Magazine*. https://bit.ly/3k6jHth.

John, Kelsey Dayle (2019). Animal colonialism – illustrating intersections between animal studies and settler colonial studies through Diné horsemanship. *Humanimalia* 10(2): 42–68.

Karuka, M. (2019). *Empire's Tracks: Indigenous Nations, Chinese Workers, and the Transcontinental Railroad*. Oakland: University of California Press.

Kimmerer, Robin Wall (2013). *Braiding Sweetgrass: Indigenous Wisdom, Scientific Knowledge, and the Teachings of Plants*. Minneapolis, MN: Milkweed Editions.

King, Tiffany Lethbo (2019). *The Black Shoals: Offshore Formations of Black and Native Studies*. Durham, NC: Duke University Press.

Lee, Robert and Tristan Ahtone (2020). Land-grab universities: expropriated Indigenous land is the foundation of the land-grant university system. *High Country News*, 30 March. https://bit.ly/3xyOvFQ.

McGreevy, Nora (2021). 751 unmarked graves discovered near former Indigenous school in Canada. *Smithsonian Magazine*, 28 June. https://bit.ly/3UdN1Kk.

Mihesuah, Devon A. and Elizabeth Hoover, eds (2019). *Indigenous Food Sovereignty in the United States: Restoring Cultural Knowledge, Protecting Environments, and Regaining Health*. Norman: University of Oklahoma Press.

Parker, Rick (2018). *Equine Science*, 5th edn. Boston: Cengage Learning.

Price, Steve (2017). *America's Wild Horses: The History of the Western Mustang*. New York: Skyhorse Publishing.

Reo, Nicholas James and Kyle Powys Whyte (2011). Hunting and morality as elements of traditional ecological knowledge. *Human Ecology* 40: 15–27. DOI: 10.1007/s10745-011-9448-1.

Rotz, Sarah (2017). "They took our beads, it was a fair trade, get over it": settler colonial logics, racial hierarchies and material dominance in Canadian agriculture. *Geoforum* 82: 158–69.

Rotz, Sarah and Lauren Wood Kepkiewicz (2018). Settler colonialism and the impossibility of a national food system. *Canadian Food Studies* 5(3): 248–58.

Russell, Dale A., Fredrick J. Rich, Vincent Schneider and Jean Lynch-Stieglitz (2009). A warm thermal enclave in the Late Pleistocene of the south-eastern United States. *Biological Reviews* 84(2): 173–202.

Shebala, Rudy (2018). Horses and grazing on the Navajo Indian Reservation. PhD dissertation. Moscow: University of Idaho.

Smith, Linda Tuhiwai. (2012). *Decolonizing Methodologies: Research and Indigenous Peoples*. 2nd ed. London: Zed Books.

Snowshoe, Angela and Noel V. Starblanket (2016). Eyininiw mistatimwak: the role of the first Lac La Croix Indigenous pony for First Nations youth mental wellness. *Journal of Indigenous Wellbeing* 1(2): 60–76.

Solow, Andrew R., David L. Roberts and Karen M. Robbirt (2006). On the Pleistocene extinctions of Alaskan mammoths and horses. *Proceedings of the National Academy of Sciences* 103(19): 7351–3.

Taschereau Mamers, Danielle (2019). Human-bison relations as sites of settler colonial violence and decolonial resurgence. *Humanimalia* 10(2): 10–41.

Tuck, Eve and K. Wayne Yang (2012). Decolonization is not a metaphor. *Decolonization: Indigeneity, Education & Society* 1(1): 1–40.

Weisiger, Marsha (2009). *Dreaming of Sheep in Navajo Country*. Seattle, WA: University of Washington Press.

Whyte, Kyle P. (2017). Indigenous climate change studies: Indigenizing futures, decolonizing the Anthropocene. *English Language Notes* 55(1): 153–62.

Wolfe, Patrick (2006). Settler colonialism and the elimination of the native. *Journal of Genocide Research* 8(4): 387–409.

2

"Red I am": Names for dingoes in science and Story

Rowena Lennox

This chapter considers Western and First Nations epistemologies and ontologies to argue that decolonising white settler knowledge, attitudes towards and discourse around dingoes provides ways to reconfigure relations between the colonial settler state and the diverse cultures of Indigenous Australia. I came to writing about dingoes as a settler Australian who loved my kelpie-cattle dog. Through my research, I learned how ongoing treatment of dingoes parallels the colonial dispossession, killing and marginalisation of First Nations peoples,[1] although, as Driftpile Cree writer Billy-Ray Belcourt notes, "the animal and the Indigenous subject are not commensurable colonial subjects insofar as their experiences of colonisation are different".[2] Analysing white settler epistemology, ontology and actions around dingoes shows how "animal bodies are made intelligible in the settler imagination on stolen, colonised, and re-settled Indigenous lands"[3] and casts a stark light on the ongoing racism and epistemic injustice Aboriginal and Torres Strait Islander peoples experience. As Palawa sociologist Maggie Walter points out, colonisation pervades racial and social hierarchies in settler nations like Australia: racialised discourses define and position

1 See Probyn-Rapsey 2020.
2 Belcourt 2015, 9.
3 Belcourt 2015, 1.

"the Indigenous peoples they [white hierarches] have dispossessed and from whose lands and resources the now-settler nations draw their wealth and identity".[4]

The concept of epistemic injustice used here is theorised by English philosopher Miranda Fricker, who explores how social identity and power affect how knowledge is gained and lost.[5] Fricker is concerned with the ethical and political dimensions of humans' epistemic conduct and defines epistemic injustice as "the wrong done to someone specifically in their capacity as a knower".[6] Fricker's focus on injustice – which, she argues, "is normal" in some spheres of epistemic activity[7] – is a way to think about epistemic justice, which, I contend, is a necessary step towards truth telling[8] and decolonisation. Epistemic injustice can be both testimonial, when one party is not considered credible because of prejudice, and hermeneutical, when, for example, a dominant group has defined how knowledge is constituted so that other forms of knowledge are not able to be articulated or understood as a shared epistemic resource.[9] Attempting to enact epistemic justice as a white person in a colonial context where, as Goenpul sociologist Aileen Moreton-Robinson points out, "invisible, unnamed and unmarked whiteness" is equated with humanity and has shaped knowledge production, demands that I consider how "the dominant regime of knowledge is culturally and racially biased, socially situated and partial".[10]

With this aim, I critically examine knowledge about dingoes constitutive of Western fields of expertise such as biology, ecology and zoology in the sciences, as well as anthropology, cultural studies, history and literary studies in the humanities, with close focus on words, naming and epistemological blind spots. This endeavour requires, as literary scholar Clare Archer-Lean and co-authors write in their analysis of representations of the dingo in literary,

4 Walter 2016, 84.
5 Fricker 2007, vii.
6 Fricker 2007, 1.
7 Fricker 2007, vii.
8 See Davis 2020.
9 Fricker 2007, 1.
10 Moreton-Robinson 2004, 80, 87–8.

anthropological, tourism/geography and scientific discourses, "transdisciplinarity and its close attention to scrutinising the ontological positions (and value assumptions) of the literature itself, rather than assuming the dingo to be the only 'subject' in question".[11] Such examination shows how vocabulary that reflects and reifies hierarchies is essential to scientific and ethnographic ways of knowing and yields insights into colonialist relations and dingoes' experience of colonisation. As education scholar Martin Nakata, from the Torres Strait Islands,[12] argues in his theorising on the Cultural Interface, these fields of expertise, like all systems of knowledge, are "culturally embedded".[13]

This chapter aims to show how, in the still-colonial context, naming can be prescriptive rather than descriptive and functions as an act of possession and domination. In 1770, Lt James Cook and his crew sailed along the east coast of the land mass that is now known as Australia in HMS *Endeavour*. Irene Watson, a Tanganekald and Meintangk Boandik legal scholar, describes Aboriginal political, cultural and linguistic organisation:

> At the time of Cook's coming we had an Aboriginal relationship to this country now called Australia. It was a relationship to land which was shared by hundreds of culturally distinct and different language-speaking first nations peoples. Our lands were held collectively. Individual ownership was a very different concept to an Aboriginal relationship to land. However all Aboriginal relationships to land were deemed by British law to be non-existent.[14]

Cook claimed that he took possession of the east coast of this land for the British Crown from an island in the Torres Strait known to the

---

11 Archer-Lean, Wardell-Johnson et al. 2015, 183.

12 The 274 islands now known as the Torres Strait Islands had names before Spanish navigator Luis Vaez de Torres sailed with Pedro Fernandes de Queirós' expedition through the straits on his way to Manila in 1606. See Pearson 2021.

13 Nakata 2002, 286.

14 Watson 2009, 2.

clan groups of its Indigenous custodians as Tuined, Bedang, Thunadha, Bedhan Lag and Tuidin. The Kaurareg people, traditional owners of Tuined, maintain that Cook did not go ashore on Tuined, or raise the Union Jack there.[15] Nevertheless, Cook renamed Tuined "Possession Island". Cultural studies scholar Katrina Schlunke explains how this renaming of an island, which is already named, is a "distorting falsehood" that becomes part of the unconscious of our white nation.

> The archive shows us Cook knew the land belonged to others as "we" (the white nation) still know it. Through this naming, this "languaging", the nation is granted something like an unconscious (the distorting falsehood) that leads to the national need to confirm our "reality" of possession. This is a daily, naturalised practice, the ordinariness of which belies the uncontrolled, unlawful things it is. A part of the ordinary confirmation of possession is the concomitant domination of the white human over plant, animal, sea and sky through the language that defers an ultimate meaning and orders our knowing into an "us" and "other" through the naming of place.[16]

These names are, as Schlunke puts it, part of the "domination of the white human over plant, animal, sea, and sky". But, as Schlunke points out, within these attempts at "naturalisation" is the knowledge that settler possession of Aboriginal land is "unlawful".

In this chapter, I attempt to decolonise my imagination and expand my capacity to understand dingoes and the networks of relationships with which they are involved with an appreciation of Aboriginal Law and Story.[17] Drawing on insights from Kombu-merri philospher Mary Graham and white anthropologist and ecocritic Deborah Bird Rose,

---

15 The Kaurareg had been warned by smoke signals and messages of the *Endeavour*'s approach and they were prepared to attack if the mariners disembarked (Australian Museum 2021). In 1922, the Kaurareg were forcibly relocated from Tuined to Moa Island. In 1925, the Australian government erected a monument on Tuined to commemorate Cook's alleged landing (Naval Historical Society of Australia 2019).

16 Schlunke 2009, 8.

I re-read texts about Aboriginal dingoes produced by Europeans and settler Australians with attention to Indigenous knowledge and spirituality, including relationship with land, the custodial ethic, autonomy, reciprocity and sentience. I also re-read the dingoes in these texts allusively, including through fire and the colour red. My aims are (1) to position Indigenous dingo knowledge as a possible means for white people to understand the epistemic shifts necessary for structural decolonisation and (2) to enable a nascent consideration of dingoes as cultural mediators and agents of decolonisation.

The Cultural Interface, dingoes and epistemic injustice

To appraise dingoes as both subjects and agents at the intersection of Western and Indigenous knowledge systems, or the Cultural Interface, as Nakata has theorised,[18] I consider how dingoes are conceptualised in "interwoven, competing and conflicting discourses"[19] where "contradiction, ambiguities, conflict and contestation of meanings" cohere (and coagulate) "to inform, constrain or enable what can be seen or not seen, what can be brought to the surface or sutured over, what can be said or not said, heard or not heard, understood or misunderstood, what knowledge can be accepted, rejected, legitimised or marginalised, or what actions can be taken or not taken on both individual and collective levels".[20] Nakata's reference to epistemology, to "what knowledge can be accepted, rejected, legitimised or marginalised", brings me to questions of epistemic injustice. The legal proceedings subsequent to the 1980 disappearance of baby Azaria

17 Regarding the notion of "Story" used here, anthropologist Jim Wafer, via ecocritic and anthropologist Deborah Bird Rose, defines the Arrernte term altyerre (or alchera, altjira) – the word for the concept widely translated in English as the Dreaming – as "story". According to Wafer's interpretation, events that happened in Story create phenomena that we can see today: rocks, mountains, rivers, cave paintings, petroglyphs and other artefacts and natural features (see Rose 1996, 26).

18 Nakata 2007; 2002.

19 Nakata 2002, 285.

20 Nakata 2007, 199.

Chamberlain from her tent in the campground at Uluru puts dingoes and epistemic injustice into the Cultural Interface. On the night Azaria disappeared, her parents, Lindy and Michael, claimed she had been taken by a dingo. That night and the morning after, Aboriginal trackers read and followed pawprints at the Chamberlains' tent, and pawprints and indentations on the nearby sand dune. A week later, when Azaria's jumpsuit, booties and nappy were found four kilometres away near the base of the Rock, the same trackers read and analysed pawprints at that site. But Azaria's body was never found. After two inquests and a trial, Azaria's mother, Lindy, was jailed for murder. A few years later, as the prosecution's evidence was discredited and more evidence came to light, Lindy was released from prison, and in 1986 the Morling Royal Commission of Inquiry into Chamberlain Convictions took place.

In her autobiography, Lindy Chamberlain describes in detail the Morling Royal Commission's adversarial interrogation of Barbara Tjikadu, one of the Anangu Aboriginal trackers who had followed pawprints at the Chamberlains' tent the night Azaria disappeared and at the site where Azaria's jumpsuit was found a week later, through her interpreter, Marlene Cousens.[21] This court room exchange shows how hermeneutical injustice can be compounded by testimonial epistemic injustice,[22] and is an example of how Aboriginal authority "is not respected or is simply disregarded". As a more recent group of researchers into the needs of Aboriginal mothers in prison put it: "We are usually 'experts' under duress and for the benefit of agendas other than our own. These forms of positioning are disrespectful and continually disempowering."[23]

Michael Adams, counsel assisting the Crown, asked Tjikadu about how she knew the tracks that she had followed after Azaria was taken were the tracks of a big male dingo. Tjikadu replied that "male dogs have big tracks".[24] Adams' line of questioning continued to attempt to cast doubt on Tjikadu's tracking expertise and her knowledge of dingo diet and hunting behaviour. She had to repeatedly explain the difference

21 Chamberlain 1990, 634–8.
22 Fricker 2007, 159.
23 Sherwood, Lighton et al. 2015, 186.
24 Barbara Tjikadu quoted in Chamberlain 1990, 635.

between male dingoes' and female dingoes' tracks, between individual dingo tracks, and between mothers' and young dingoes' tracks; she also explained what dingoes ate and how they hunted. When Adams' questioning tried to lead Tjikadu to say that the dingo could have been carrying a joey from the tent, Cousens, Tjikadu's interpreter, responded, "You are talking your way with your ideas and you are talking about lies."[25] When Commissioner Morling intervened to reiterate Adams' question about whether the dingo could have had a joey and not Azaria, Tjikadu retorted, "Was a kangaroo living in the tent?"[26]

This pattern of questioning continued. Adams was questioning Tjikadu about whether it could have been a different dingo at the tent from the dingo at the site where Azaria's jumpsuit was found when Cousens intervened:

> "I would like to tell you something first before you ask questions like that. When Aboriginal people see tracks, they know who it belongs to, what person went there, because they know the tracks, whereas if all these people got out of the courtroom now and walked barefoot, you can't tell, can you?"
> "No," exclaimed Adams.
> The interpreter said, "Aboriginal people can."[27]

I deem that Adams' mode of questioning Barbara Tjikadu is an attempt at "prejudicial exclusion from participation in the spread of knowledge"[28] and demonstrates how "[c]olonization is not just an historical fact; it is a current strategy to exclude Aboriginal ways of knowing, being and doing from mainstream institutions".[29] Tjikadu and Cousens seem to be aware of the work they are doing in the Cultural

25 Marlene Cousens quoted in Chamberlain 1990, 636.
26 Barbara Tjikadu quoted in Chamberlain 1990, 636. The court laughed but according to Chamberlain, Tjikadu's answer was not meant to be funny, and she and Cousens looked offended because, Chamberlain writes, they thought people were laughing at them.
27 Marlene Cousens quoted in Chamberlain 1990, 637–8.
28 Fricker 2007, 162.
29 Sherwood, Lighton et al. 2015, 185.

Interface. As Wiradjuri poet and scholar Jeanine Leane explains, "An Aboriginal person in Australia … can see two epistemologies: the one you are born to – your cultural stance – and the introduced one – the colonial perspective."[30] Tjikadu and Cousens resist the court's attempts to diminish their credibility by educating those present about white people's – not Anangu – lack of hermeneutical resources in this context. As well as calling out and correcting epistemic injustice, Tjikadu and Cousens show that reading tracks is a special form of literacy, as Leane explicates:

> tracking is as much about anticipation as it is following. Tracking is about reading: reading land and people before and after whitefellas. It is about entering into the consciousness of the person or people of interest. Tracking is not just about reading the physical signs; it is about reading the mind. It is not just about seeing and hearing what is there; it is as much about what is not there.[31]

Land, Aboriginal Law and names for dingoes

In reply to one of Adams' questions about dingo diet, Barbara Tjikadu stated, "A dingo is a dingo, and if he wants a feed, he'll kill to eat."[32] Tjikadu's knowledge of dingoes is based on empirical observation[33] and Aboriginal spiritual identity, which posits land as the basis of all meaning.[34] Kombu-merri philosopher Mary Graham writes about the concept of the custodial ethic, achieved through repetitive action, which reveres the land as "*the* great teacher".[35] Land teaches people how to relate to land, and how to relate to each other.[36] Graham explains that Aboriginal Law was not legislated by humans but by Creator Beings,

30 Leane 2014, 2.
31 Leane 2014, 1.
32 Barbara Tjikadu quoted in Chamberlain 1990, 635.
33 See Parker 2006, 122, 239.
34 Graham 2008, 1.
35 Graham 2008, 2 [emphasis in original].
36 Graham 2008, 2.

or spiritual ancestors, during the Dreaming. Like physics, Aboriginal Law is concerned with "the way the real world is perceived to behave" and according to Graham it cannot be "ideologised".[37] Unlike Western scientific laws, which describe physical phenomena, Graham writes, Aboriginal Law describes both physical and spiritual phenomena that "continually interpenetrate each other".[38] In this system, land is the constant: "Aboriginal law is valid for all people only in the sense that all people are placed on land wherever they happen to be, so that the custodial ethic, which is primarily an obligatory system, may be acted upon by anyone who is interested in looking after or caring for land."[39] Graham explains how place-based identity, which "emerges out of the landscape with meaning intact", differs from an ideologically derived "focus of identity" in which "[m]eaning is … moulded to fit [an ideological] framework (rather than emerging intact from a place in the landscape)".[40] This distinction between place-based or "locus" expressions of identity and ideologically focused expressions of identity is evident in Western and Indigenous understandings of dingoes.

Dingoes do not fit easily into settler Australian dichotomies and taxonomies such as wild/domesticated, native/introduced or harmful/beneficial, even though, as Archer-Lean, Wardell-Johnson et al. note, "extreme duality in perceptions of the dingo, even within the 'objective' scientific debates of wildlife ecology", dominates discussion.[41] Dingoes' resistance to categorisation unsettles norms of settler colonialism, which may be one reason why they polarise opinions and arouse strong emotions. Ontological uncertainty about dingoes is reflected in their disputed scientific names. One name, *Canis lupus dingo*, describes the dingo as a subspecies of the wolf, with whom it shares some characteristics, such as living in family groups and breeding once a year (unlike the domestic dog, who can breed twice a year). Another, *Canis familiaris dingo*, denotes that the dingo is a subspecies of the domestic dog. They do look like dogs, sometimes. This name accords

37 Graham 2008, 6.
38 Graham 2008, 5.
39 Graham 2008, 6.
40 Graham 2008, 6.
41 Archer-Lean, Wardell-Johnson et al. 2015, 191.

with one of the current non-Indigenous theories about how dingoes came to Australia: that 3,000 to 5,000 years ago hunter-gatherers from south Sulawesi brought domesticated or semi-domesticated dingoes in boats to the Australian mainland. They may have been food for the voyage.[42] After they were released, or escaped, they formed commensal relationships with Aboriginal people and, according to archaeologist Jane Balme and co-authors, "colonised" the continent.[43]

These scientific names are attempts to describe dingoes' prehistoric genealogy, and they also shape how dingoes are perceived and treated in the present. As animal psychologist Bradley Smith and an interdisciplinary team of co-authors note in their work on dingo taxonomy: "In wildlife conservation and management, using a particular species concept can substantially influence government policy, funding allocations, and management strategies."[44] If the dingo is a subspecies of the domestic dog (*Canis familiaris*) it was once domesticated, but it is now "feral", an invasive animal, a pest, and killable, as animal studies and feminist scholar Fiona Probyn-Rapsey points out.[45] Ostensibly, dingoes are killed because they prey on sheep and calves. Current attempts to eradicate them from large areas of the continent are aided by legislation, government agencies and policies, and financial incentives such as bounties. Spectacular forms of violence, such as hanging dingoes' bodies from fences and trees after trapping, baiting and shooting programs, are common. Dingoes are also killed en masse in national parks with 1080 poison in "conservation" eradication programs aimed at dingoes (who are often called wild dogs in the literature that justifies these killings) and other animals classified as pests, such as foxes and cats. Deborah Bird Rose describes this "man-made mass death" as a form of biocide, to parallel genocide. She observes that this will to destruction involves "imagining a future emptiness and then working systematically to accomplish that

42 Fillios and Tacon 2016.

43 See Balme, O'Connor and Fallon 2018, 2, 3. The employment of the term "colonising" for dingoes in Australia is not explained in Balme, O'Connor and Fallon's article, but it is noteworthy here because it contends, implicitly, that dingoes, like settler Australians, are colonisers.

44 Smith, Cairns et al. 2019, 176.

45 Probyn-Rapsey 2016.

emptiness".[46] Against this killing, some ecologists claim that, as Australia's terrestrial "apex predator" (that is, the top of the food chain), dingoes perform an important role in maintaining biodiversity in fragile Australian ecosystems by suppressing populations of "meso-predators" such as cats and foxes (who are further down the food chain and usually more abundant), and that they may be a key to slowing Australia's accelerating rate of species extinctions. Characterisations of dingoes as either blood-thirsty demons or proxy land managers are based on instrumentalist and normative values that infuse much so-called scientific knowledge about these animals. The language of hierarchy – "apex", "meso", "alpha", "dominant" – is essential to these understandings.

When Barbara Tjikadu tells the Morling Royal Commission, "A dingo is a dingo",[47] I interpret that she is denoting that the dingo is itself, not a cipher for settler ideology. This description accords with a third scientific name, *Canis dingo*, which describes the dingo not as a dog or a wolf but as a unique canid that has lived in Australia in isolation from other canids for millennia.[48] This name is supported by morphological analyses[49] and consideration of taxonomic protocols.[50] But I do not propose the use of this term as some kind of designation of so-called genetic purity.[51]

The names *Canis lupus dingo* and *Canis familiaris dingo* reflect the dichotomy between wild wolf and tame domestic dog, but there is ample documentary evidence that not all dingoes are, or ever have been, wild in the sense of living independently from people. The testimony and culture of First Nations people, and archaeological sources, show that some dingoes have had relationships with Aboriginal and Torres Strait Islander peoples for millennia, at least.[52]

46 Rose 2011, 82.
47 Barbara Tjikadu quoted in Chamberlain 1990, 635.
48 Ardalan, Oskarsson et al. 2012; Balme, O'Connor and Fallon 2018; Cairns, Nesbitt et al. 2017; Cairns and Wilton 2016; Oskarsson, Klütsch et al. 2011; Pang, Kluetsch et al. 2009; Savolainen, Leitner et al. 2004.
49 Crowther, Fillios et al. 2014.
50 Smith, Cairns et al. 2019.
51 Dingo genetics, which I do not have room to discuss here, is another field where ideological agendas inflect knowledge. See Cairns, Nesbitt et al. 2020; Lennox 2021, 16, 221–2; Probyn-Rapsey 2020.

Europeans have recorded a wide variety of relationships between Aboriginal peoples and dingoes.[53] The term "dingo", first published in 1789 in marine Watkin Tench's *Narrative of the Expedition to Botany Bay*,[54] or "tingo", used by midshipman Newton Fowell in a letter home to his family in 1788,[55] is thought to mean "tame" in the Dharug Aboriginal language.[56] Some ethnographers indicate that dingoes were taken from their dens in "the wild" into Aboriginal camps as pups and later they returned to "the wild" as adults and to breed.[57] Smith, Cairns et al. assert that "there is no evidence that dingoes were exposed to domestication or selection pressure by Aboriginal peoples".[58] But anthropologist Norman Tindale claims that "[i]rregularly marked feral dingo pups"[59] or "odd coloured variants"[60] might become camp dingoes. Tindale writes about generations of camp dingoes; his photograph of a "tamed camp dingo" suckling four pups at Warupuju in the Warburton Ranges in 1935 seems to indicate that dingoes did breed in Aboriginal camps.[61] Relationships between Aboriginal people and camp dingoes may "fail to meet the criteria for domestication"[62] in current understandings, but descriptions of camp dingoes that require lexical contortions, such as "tame wild animals",[63] seem to indicate lacunae in English that, possibly, render settler vocabularies incapable

52 Balme and O'Connor 2016; Male Z quoted in Carter et al. 2017, 200; Gollan 1984; Finn Dwyer quoted in Lennox 2021, 171.
53 Bates 1985, 247; Berndt and Berndt 1942, 162; Chewings 1936, 32; Duncan-Kemp 1933, 24–5; Giles 1986, 19–20; Hamilton 1972, 293; Kimber 1976, 143; Meehan, Jones and Vincent 1999, 98; Mitchell, 1965, 347; Mountford 1981, 184–5; Smyth 1972, 147, 190; Tindale 1974, 109 and plate 80.
54 Tench 1789, chapter 11.
55 Fowell 1788, 23.
56 Breckwoldt 1988, 72.
57 Donald Thomson in Dixon and Huxley 1985, 170; Lumholtz 1980, 196; Meehan, Jones and Vincent 1999, 92–3.
58 Smith, Cairns et al. 2019, 186.
59 Tindale 1974, 109.
60 Tindale 1974, caption to plate 79.
61 Tindale 1974, plate 80.
62 Smith, Cairns et al. 2019, 186.
63 Smith, Cairns et al. 2019, 186.

of accurately describing and imagining the relationships between First Nations peoples and dingoes.

While many Aboriginal languages do not distinguish dingoes from domestic dogs, they do distinguish wild-living dingoes and dogs from camp dingoes and dogs.[64] In Butchulla, the language of the traditional custodians of K'gari (Fraser Island), dingoes who live independently from people are called wongari and companion dingoes are called wat'dha.[65] Nineteenth-century accounts record familial relationships between dingoes and Butchulla people on K'gari[66] and dingoes and Gingingbarrah people on the Caloola coast.[67] In interviews conducted in 2015–16, Butchulla people told geographer Jennifer Carter and her co-authors about their long association with the dingoes of K'gari[68] and emphasised "the ways in which dingo treatment was similar to the regulation of Aboriginal people by the settler society throughout colonial histories".[69] Although the Federal Court of Australia recognised the Butchullas' native title rights over K'gari in 2014, contact between all people and all dingoes on the island is prohibited, and dingoes have been routinely killed when they are deemed to pose a safety risk to people. The management of dingoes on K'gari falls under the *Fraser Island Dingo Conservation and Risk Management Strategy*,[70] but, as Carter et al. note, the strategy does not recognise the diversity and individuality of relationships between Butchulla people and dingoes. As one of their Butchulla interview subjects put it: "There are different interactions with dingoes and humans – they are diverse. There are dingoes who are semi tame or in captivity ... They are taking them as aggressive and therefore killing off all dingoes."[71] Public education about dingoes on K'gari emphasises that they are "wild" – that is, wongari. According to a Queensland Parks and Wildlife Service brochure co-authored with a Butchulla ranger, the companion dingoes,

---

64 For a summary see Lennox 2021, 17–19.
65 QPWS 2017.
66 Curtis 1838.
67 Parkhurst 2015, 38; *The Week* 1889, 14.
68 Carter, Wardell-Johnson and Archer-Jean 2017, 200.
69 Carter, Wardell-Johnson and Archer-Jean 2017, 202.
70 Ecosure 2013.
71 Quoted in Carter, Wardell-Johnson and Archer-Jean 2017, 201.

the wat'dha, disappeared as a consequence of colonisation and Aboriginal dispossession: "When the last of our people were taken off the island, all of the dingoes became wild."[72] Butchulla people I spoke with have different views about relationships with dingoes.[73] Ongoing decolonisation of relationships between Butchulla people and dingoes is and will be woven into other aspects of decolonisation across the continent. Epistemic justice and recognition that First Nations sovereignty – "the ancestral tie between the land, or 'mother nature'", and Aboriginal and Torres Strait Islander peoples – has "never been ceded or extinguished"[74] are part of this decolonising process. "How could it be otherwise?" the *Uluru Statement from the Heart* asks. How can it be "[t]hat peoples possessed a land for sixty millennia and this sacred link disappears from world history in merely the last two hundred years?"[75] A similar question could be asked about spiritual and kin relationships between First Nations people and dingoes on K'gari. Do the wat'dha cease to exist because of 200 years of colonisation?

Balnglan

European observers understand relationships of utility between Indigenous peoples and dingoes that are based on warmth (the one-, two- or three-dog night to keep the cold away),[76] water (dingoes as water finders)[77] and food (dingoes as food[78] or dingoes as helpers in procuring food[79]). Balnglan, a dingo from North Queensland, fits into

---

72 QPWS 2017, 2.

73 See Lennox 2021, 93–105, 161–72.

74 NCC 2017.

75 NCC 2017.

76 Hamilton 1972, 292–4; Meehan, Jones and Vincent 1999, 97; Meggitt 1965; Tindale 1974, 109.

77 Tindale 1974, 120.

78 Breckwoldt 1988, 65; Giles 1986, 20; Hamilton 1972, 288–90; Meggitt 1965, 14; Smyth 1972, 148; Tindale 1974, 36, 109. ?

79 Basedow 1925, 119; Bates 1985, 247; Chewings 1936, 32; Gould 1969, 263; Hamilton 1972, 291; Kolig 1978, 91; Meehan, Jones and Vincent 1999, 102; Meggitt 1965, 19; Smyth 1972, 147, 190.

this typology as a renowned hunter of the tree kangaroo, or boongary, as it is called in the Warrgamay language, of the lower reaches of the Herbert River. Without Balnglan, Norwegian ethnographer and naturalist Carl Lumholtz would not have been able to procure specimens of the tree kangaroo that now bears his name – *Dendrolagus lumholtzii*. When Lumholtz published his description of his time in North Queensland with the title *Among Cannibals: An Account of Four Years Travel in Australia and of Camp Life with the Aborigines of Queensland*, he was not the first to sensationally exploit European notions of Indigenous "savagery".[80] As Eualeyai/Kamilaroi writer, film director and legal scholar Larissa Behrendt observes, Europeans' obsession with cannibalism "explains more about the European psyche when vulnerable than it tells us about the cultural practices of Aboriginal people"[81] stories of Aboriginal people's so-called barbarity came to justify colonial settler violence against them and genocide.[82] In much of his narrative, Lumholtz writes with little respect for the First Nations people who were indispensable to his search for the animals he made specimens of, even though towards the end of his book he admits that on Aboriginal country the European "actually is their inferior in many respects"[83] and he feels "deep gratitude" to his guide, Yokkai.[84]

Lumholtz describes close, affectionate and caring relationships between the people of the Herbert River and their dingoes: "The dingo is an important member of the family; it sleeps in the huts and gets plenty to eat, not only meat, but also of fruit. Its master never strikes, but merely threatens it. He caresses it like a child, eats the fleas off it, and then kisses it on the snout."[85] Dingoes who associated with people

80 The Butchulla people who saved Eliza Fraser and other shipwreck survivors on K'gari in 1836 are described in many derogatory ways in John Curtis's *Shipwreck of the Stirling Castle* (Curtis 1838); such descriptions served to justify colonial violence towards Aboriginal people and reinforced for colonial settlers their superiority and the righteousness of their civilising mission. See Behrendt 2016.

81 Behrendt 2016, 193.

82 Behrendt 2016, 119.

83 Lumholtz 1980, 315.

84 Lumholtz 1980, 326.

85 Lumholtz 1980, 195.

could be very useful to their humans. A dingo's keen sense of smell allowed it to trace "every kind of game; it never barks, and hunts less wildly than our dogs, but very rapidly, frequently capturing the game on the run".[86] During his time around the Herbert River in the early 1880s, Lumholtz records Aboriginal people using dingoes to hunt half-grown and old cassowaries (*Casuarius australis*),[87] ground-dwelling yopolo or musky rat-kangaroos (*Hypsiprymnodon moschatus*)[88] and yarri or quolls (*Dasyurus maculatus*).[89] In Lumholtz's narrative, the word "yarri" also refers to the cryptid Queensland tiger, another animal he was keen to find. Lumholtz uses "dog" and "dingo" to describe Balnglan and other camp dingoes. But, once again, Western vocabulary appears to be lacking when it comes to describing the relationships between Balnglan and the people he was close to. In quotes from Lumholtz, I reproduce his terms "owner" and "master", which, aptly, deploy the notions of possession and control that are part of the colonising project. Drawing on Graham's explanation of the custodial ethic, I use the dingo's or Balnglan's "people/person", "family", "kin" and "custodian/s", which I hope in this context can shed connotations of dominance – because it does not seem that Balnglan's human kin dominated him.

The first time Lumholtz saw Balnglan, he was bounding down the mountain ahead of Nilgora, Balnglan's main custodian, and a party of hunters who carried the boongary Lumholtz had been seeking.[90] Lumholtz wanted to joint the hunt for more boongary early the next morning, but Balnglan "was afraid of the white man"[91] so Lumholtz remained in camp. Over ensuing days, Balnglan scented out more boongary, which his custodians caught – five young males and one female in all. Lumholtz was disappointed when Nilgora gave the joey from the young female's pouch to Balnglan rather than to him.[92] Lumholtz wished to continue hunting, but his hosts "tried to convince [him] that there were no more boongary".[93] Traditionally, boongary

86 Lumholtz 1980, 195.
87 Lumholtz 1980, 108.
88 Lumholtz 1980, 192.
89 Lumholtz 1980, 204.
90 Lumholtz 1980, 245.
91 Lumholtz 1980, 250.
92 Lumholtz 1980, 266.

were not their only source of food, and after catching six of them in a short space of time it was clear that Nilgora no longer wished to hunt them. Lumholtz thought his Aboriginal hosts were "tired" of hunting for him and "cannot endure monotony".[94] When he disbelieved their assertion that there were no boongary left, they asked him: "Where is boongary, where? no, no! there is but one in the woods."[95]

Nilgora's resistance to Lumholtz's insistence that they take more boongary is, perhaps, an assertion of the principle of selective harvesting.[96] Anthropologist Deborah Bird Rose's Aboriginal teachers at Yarralin in the Victoria River District of the Northern Territory regarded "their own country as 'good country'", which "amply provides for their needs".[97] According to Rose, in the 1980s, as far as possible, they managed their country by "burning off at the appropriate times, allowing fruits and vegetables to regenerate and to feed other species, and stimulating the reproduction of animal species through selective hunting and through ritual".[98] Lumholtz did not respect Nilgora's decision to stop hunting boongary, but because he could not hunt them without Balnglan and Balnglan's people, in this instance he had no choice.

Another principle that Aboriginal people taught Rose was that of autonomy, in which each part (which might be a group, country and/or species) of a system is "its own 'boss'";[99] no part is subservient to or dominated by another, and each part must pay attention to and respond to other parts.[100] Rose explains:

> From the Aboriginal viewpoint a moral Australia is one which recognises the autonomy of individuals and groups. The key to autonomy is put forth in terms of land. [Before colonisation] all the land was freehold [meaning] that it was both owned and

93 Lumholtz 1980, 263.
94 Lumholtz 1980, 263.
95 Lumholtz 1980, 263.
96 Rose 1996, 10.
97 Rose 1984, 26.
98 Rose 1984, 26.
99 Rose 1984, 37.
100 Rose 1984, 30.

> inalienable. People, too, were free at that time. They were autonomous within their own country, in the sense that no country, or group, was able to dominate others.[101]

In Lumholtz's account, Nilgora appears to respect Balnglan's preference to hunt without the company of the European. Could this be respect for his dingo's autonomy? The dingoes Lumholtz met on the Herbert River were as individual as the people and behaved in different ways. Not all of them were hunters like Balnglan. Yokkai, Lumholtz's guide, had a dingo who "kept faithfully in the footsteps of its master and did not care to chase game".[102]

Eventually, Balnglan took a strychnine bait that Lumholtz had laid in an attempt to catch a large carnivorous yarri (which, in this case, I assume, is the cryptid Queensland tiger). Althouth Lumholtz poured tobacco and water down the dingo's throat to make him vomit up the poison (called "kola" or "wrath" by the local people), Balnglan suffered a seizure and died. Lumholtz blamed Yokkai and another Aboriginal man for Balnglan's taking the bait that he, Lumholtz, had laid. He offered them "two whole sticks of tobacco"[103] for Balnglan's body so he could preserve "its fine black skin with white breast and yellow legs".[104] Balnglan's black, white and yellow colouration is not uncommon for dingoes and would have provided good camouflage for him in the wet sclerophyll forests. Lumholtz records that Yokkai was concerned about Nilgora's anger about Balnglan's death. Lumholtz hoped Nilgora would be compensated for his loss by "giving him his woollen blanket and some tobacco".[105]

---

101 Rose 1984, 38.

102 Lumholtz 1980, 235. Lumholtz also fed another dingo, who had run away from its person, in an attempt to persuade it to go with his party because he thought it might be useful to him. But instead this dingo took food from camp, "stealing the small piece of meat I had left" and disappeared. When this dingo "came stealing" back into camp, Lumholtz writes, his Aboriginal guides convinced him to shoot it (208, 225, 227).

103 Lumholtz 1980, 291.

104 Lumholtz 1980, 289–91.

105 Lumholtz 1980, 291.

In some ways, Balnglan is a cultural mediator between Lumholtz and his (the dingo's) Aboriginal family. Balnglan's role in the Cultural Interface is not fixed, but his story highlights how "particular knowledges achieve legitimacy and authority at the expense of other knowledge".[106] Lumholtz does not (cannot?) hear the principle of selective hunting his hosts are articulating; he does not see his responsibility for Balnglan's death. Lumholtz liked dogs – he took his female Gordon setter with him on his Queensland travels – and his observations of dingoes are, on the whole, more even-handed than his observations of Aboriginal people. Yokkai and Lumholtz met and became associates because of Balnglan: as one of Balnglan's custodians, Yokkai was instrumental in bringing Balnglan to join Lumholtz's hunt for boongary. In their travels Yokkai became "utterly indispensable" to Lumholtz, who "gained much pleasure and entertainment from his company"[107] and acknowledged the "many services he had done me",[108] including saving his life several times.[109] When Lumholtz left Yokkai to return to Norway, he writes, "many emotions crowded upon me". But Yokkai did not reciprocate: "I did not discover the faintest sign of emotion. He gazed at me steadfastly."[110] Yokkai's impassivity on Lumholtz's departure contrasts with the grief he expressed when Balnglan died in his arms: "Yokkai gazed at [Balnglan] for a moment, then turned away and wept bitterly. He sat down and wrung his hands in despair, while large tears rolled down his cheeks."[111]

Lumholtz used bribes of tobacco and the threat of his "double barrelled gun and an excellent American revolver", which his guides called "the baby of the gun", to achieve his aims.[112] Neither Nilgora nor Yokkai had had contact with Europeans before, and Nilgora, like Balnglan, was "very much afraid of the white men".[113] According to Lumholtz, Nilgora, and other locals, developed a taste for "white man's

106 Nakata 2007, 195.
107 Lumholtz 1980, 314.
108 Lumholtz 1980, 326.
109 Lumholtz 1980, 238.
110 Lumholtz 1980, 325.
111 Lumholtz 1980, 290.
112 Lumholtz 1980, 117–18.
113 Lumholtz 1980, 264.

food"[114] – the salt beef, wheat flour and sugar Lumholtz took with him.[115] Lumholtz left the Herbert River with many specimens, including the boongary Balnglan had caught for him and Balnglan's hide. He admits no responsibility for Balnglan's death and remains oblivious to the inequitable exchanges of contact. How does one measure blankets, tobacco, salt beef, wheat flour and sugar against the life of the dingo Lumholtz describes as "the best dog for miles around" and "the most intelligent dingo I have ever seen"?[116]

Ankotarinja/Erintja Ngoolya

Ankotarinja, or Erintja Ngoolya, is not like Balnglan. He does not help men; he hunts them, and women. Nor does he die. He is an Arrernte dingo ancestor or Creator Being from north of Alice Springs in Central Australia. Here I read two versions of his Story – one published in the journal *Oceania* in the 1930s by anthropologist and linguist T.G.H. Strehlow[117] and one published in a book called *The Feathered Serpent*, a collection of "The Mythological Genesis and Recreative Ritual of the Aboriginal Tribes of the Northern Territory of Australia", in the 1950s by poet Roland Robinson.[118] Mary Graham explains how stories are Aboriginal archives, "detailing how Creator Beings from under the earth arose to shape the land and to create the landscape".[119] Before they arose, the Creator Beings slept just under the earth's surface "in a state of potentiality". When they arose from the ground, their "potentiality transformed into actuality",[120] and they interacted with one another, fought, danced, ran around, made love and killed. During this time, humans who were asleep in "various embryonic forms" were awakened. The Creator Beings helped them and gave them "every kind of knowledge they needed to look after the land and to have a stable

114 Lumholtz 1980, 266.
115 Lumholtz 1980, 114.
116 Lumholtz 1980, 289.
117 Strehlow 1933.
118 Robinson 1956, 69–70.
119 Graham 2008, 2.
120 Graham 2008, 2.

society". Afterwards, the Creator Beings returned to the land where they sleep in the eternal sleep from which they awoke at the beginning of time. The places where they sleep are still regarded as sacred sites. The tracks and evidence they left determine the identity of the people, who have "part of the essence" of one of the Beings who formed the landscape. As Graham writes, each Aboriginal person "has a charter of custodianship empowering them and making them responsible for renewing that part of the flora and its fauna"; each human "bears a creative and spiritual identity which still resides in land".[121]

Rose explains how, in Aboriginal thought, the land is sentient and, when people take notice of their country, communication between people and country is two-way.[122] Similarly, animals, trees, rains, sun and moon are sentient and conscious, observing and thinking about human beings. These other beings, like humans, are also concerned with law, which, as Rose defines it, is synonymous with morality.[123] All sentient beings possess and maintain knowledge of their own morality.[124] This morality is, I assume, the knowledge they need to look after the land, which Graham writes about. According to Rose, although no one "person, animal, tree or hill knows everything",[125] and "the purpose of much that exists may remain obscure to others … obscurity, from a human point of view, is not the same as purposelessness. There is a profound sense that this world was not created specifically for human beings."[126]

Sentience and the specificity of who is a legitimate knowledge-holder are part of T.G.H. Strehlow's rendering of what he calls the "myth" of Ankotarinja. Strehlow was the son of Lutheran missionaries and grew up in the early 1900s at Hermannsburg mission, known as Ntaria to its Arrernte custodians, in the MacDonnell Ranges in central Australia, speaking English, German and Arrernte. His interest in the relationship of religion to literature and art[127] is reflected

121 Graham 2008, 2.
122 Rose 1996, 13.
123 Rose 1984, 25.
124 Rose 1984, 29.
125 Rose 1996, 13.
126 Rose 1996, 27.
127 Strehlow 1933, 199–200.

in his commentaries on his transcriptions and translations from Arrernte into English of the songs that are part of the ceremonial performance of this Story, and many others.[128] His version of the Story of "the ancestor of Ankota" starts with the same phrase as the book of Genesis:

> In the beginning there was living at Ankota a man who had sprung from the earth without mother or father. He had been lying asleep in the bosom of the earth, and the white ants had eaten his body hollow while the soil rested on him like a coverlet. As he was lying in the ground a thought arose in his mind: "Perhaps it would be pleasant to arise." He lay there, deep in thought. Then he arose, out of the soft soil of a little watercourse.[129]

The place where Ankotarinja wakes is characterised here as a hospitable place, and the earth is described in detail: soil resting on the Creator Being's body like a coverlet; soil soft because it is in a little watercourse. Place is primary in the version that Tonanga, better known to settler Australians as the landscape painter Albert Namatjira, relates to Roland Robinson. Tonanga was born at Ntaria in 1902, six years before T.G.H. Strehlow, and grew up at the Hermannsburg mission. He was also initiated as an Arrernte man. Robinson describes how, in the presence of Robinson and several mature, responsible Arrernte men, Tonanga re-enacted the Story, called "Erintja the Devil-dog" in Robinson's book: "on his hands and knees in the sand … in the creek-bed under the ghost gums with the purple and violet and ochre-red mountains of Haast's Bluff rising out of the spinifex".[130] Robinson's transcription of Tonanga's version is full of place names, reinforcing anthropologist W.E.H. Stanner's characterisation of the Dreaming as an "everywhen".[131] It begins:

128 Strehlow 1933; 1971.
129 Strehlow 1933, 187.
130 Robinson 1956, x.
131 Stanner 2009, 58.

> Ungortarenga is the name of the place. What the white man calls Burt Well, where there is a well for cattle, lies close to this place. An old-man there has a shield and a boomerang. All the winds that blow, blow back to this one place where that old-man stays. The old-man lies down and the winds from all directions come and cover him up with dust and sand. When a bird calls out from a tree that old-man sits up out of the dust and sand and looks out everywhere. He thinks, he looks round, then lies down again. The winds blow from all directions and cover him up again with dust and sand.
>
> The wind blew from the south. First the nose of the old-man came up out of the dust, then his head and shoulders. He rose on his hands and knees with the dust and the sand sliding off him. On his hands and knees he stretched forward, smelling the wind and looking out in its direction. As the old-man smelled the wind and stretched forwards he changed into the big devil dog Erintja Ngoolya.[132]

In both accounts, Erintja Ngoolya/Ankotarinja (I use both versions of his name in this summary) travels west and eats two tjilpa (Western quoll, *Dasyurus geoffroii*) women who were cooking frogs. He continues, keeping low to the ground, half burying himself when he sees a group of young tjilpa men making a corroboree at Kaimba rrumbulla[133] or Parr' Erultja.[134] There, in a fury of appetite, he eats, one by one, all the young initiates as they sleep in rows. A man from the west comes and – either by throwing a tjurunga (sacred object) at the nape of his neck[135] or by throwing a bull-roarer and cutting the dingo's mouth open from ear to ear[136] – forces Ankotarinja/Erintja Ngoolya to disgorge the men he has eaten. Neither account mentions whether he disgorges the women. Strehlow describes the regurgitated initiates' blithe relief as they "climb up on the rocky hills again, swing

132 Tonanga in Robinson 1956, 69. Although it is unclear how much Robinson has changed and/or paraphrased Tonanga's words, I have referenced this version as Tonanga in Robinson.

133 Tonanga in Robinson 1956, 69.

134 Strehlow 1933, 189.

135 Strehlow 1933, 189.

136 Tonanga in Robinson 1956, 70–1.

the bull-roarers merrily, and decorate their heads with green twigs and wallaby tails".[137] They survive; they've been reborn. Erintja Ngoolya,[138] or just his head,[139] travels underground back to Ungortarenga/Ankota. Like other ancestral beings, he returns to the place he came from. He remains there forever, alive, sentient, conscious and with agency: he hears the birds, he looks, he scents the wind, thoughts occur to him.[140]

Neither version explains the symbolism, morality or significance of Erintja Ngoolya/Ankotarinja's journey and actions in relation to other aspects of Arrernte life. These omissions may reflect Robinson's focus on origin narratives and Strehlow's focus on ritual rather than everyday life[141] and/or sensitivity to Aboriginal protocols about who owns and is authorised to transmit knowledge. According to Strehlow, the Ankotarinja myth, ceremony and song were the property of a small group of northern Arrernte men who once dwelt in the vicinity of Ankota. One of them was a reincarnation of the old ancestor. As Strehlow writes in his foreword to Robinson's book *The Feathered Serpent*, "In Central Australia … the traditions relating to any given totemic ancestor were the private property of the person who was regarded as his reincarnation, or of the heirs of this person."[142] Before he died in Alice Springs, this man told Strehlow the Story. Strehlow explains that the general outlines of a myth might be known by people over a very large area, but the intimate details and traditional designs of the ceremonies are the personal property of a small group.[143]

Strehlow appears to have been more interested in transcribing and textually "saving" myths, songs and rituals than in elucidating the dynamics of how the Ankotarinja Story was transmitted, received and shared by Arrernte people, how it continued and continues to live.[144] This form of "salvage ethnography"[145] risks submerging and

137 Strehlow 1933, 189.
138 Tonanga in Robinson 1956, 71.
139 Strehlow 1933, 189.
140 Strehlow 1933, 189; Tonanga in Robinson 1956, 71.
141 Gibson 2018, 6.
142 Strehlow in Robinson 1956, vi.
143 Strehlow 1933, 198.
144 See Gibson 2018.
145 Gibson 2018, 13.

marginalising Arrernte people who, Nakata points out, "disappear as people at the centre of their own lives as they are co-opted into another history, another narrative that is not really about them but about their relation to it".[146] As Nakata notes in relation to Torres Strait Islanders, using culture to explain "what Islanders once were ... weakens – indeed hijacks – this notion of Islanders' own construction of historical understanding into something apolitical ... lacking the politics of analysis and action and lacking too a reason and logic of its own that is as legitimate as others".[147] Arrernte culture, like Islander culture, has always been "evolving and responding" to new and changing contexts.[148]

The myth that Strehlow's *Oceania* article relates, the ceremony it describes and illustrates, and the song it transcribes and translates into English are not from a textual tradition. Similarly, Robinson transcribed an enacted telling. In his foreword to *The Feathered Serpent*, Strehlow, always finely attuned to language, leaves it to the artistic judgement of the reader to decide whether Robinson has succeeded in "blending certain pidgin English expressions with the higher quality English used normally in his final version".[149] Strehlow devotes a section of his *Oceania* article to describing how the words in the spoken form of the song are "dismembered" and "rearranged" "according to formal and traditional verse patterns" in the chanted form.[150] In both written renderings, the Story appears autonomous and, for this reader, captivating, because it is mysterious, because it does not explain itself to me – but it might be explaining itself perfectly clearly to its intended audience. To me, it appears to rise like the ancestor it animates, independently, with no antecedents. I glean that in Erintja Ngoolya/Ankotarinja, many things are united: the ancestor being of a place, a spirit dingo man, quoll people, anger, hunger, excess, satiation, conflict, place. The spiritual, cultural, biological and ecological knowledge contained in the Story about Erintja Ngoolya/Ankotarinja and the

146 Nakata 2007, 202.
147 Nakata 2007, 203.
148 Nakata 2007, 202.
149 Strehlow quoted in Robinson 1956, vii.
150 Strehlow 1933, 197.

places he travels, hunts and rests, and about relationships between people and animals, is situated, specific and ongoing.[151]

The Story of Erintja Ngoolya/Ankotarinja also offers other, less word-based knowledge. Both renderings convey the dingo ancestor's terrifying power and, implicitly, the need to take this power seriously. But he is not one thing. In Strehlow's translation, the song of Ankotarinja begins:

> 1 Red is the down which is covering me;
> Red I am as though I was burning in a fire.[152]

And ends:

> 18 Red I am, like the heart of a flame of fire,
> Red, too, is the hollow in which I am resting.[153]

In this translation of the song, fire and the colour red are united in this Creator Being. According to T.G.H. Strehlow's father, Pastor Carl Strehlow, red "is the colour of joy and happiness, it is the love-colour"[154] and "the favourite colour" of the Aboriginal people of Central Australia.[155] Carl Strehlow describes how people paint their bodies with

151 Biologist Alan Newsome's (1980) work on integrating Indigenous knowledge with the ecology of the red kangaroo (*Macropus rufus*) is an early example of the increasing interest in integrating Indigenous biocultural knowledge with ecosystem science (see Ens, Pert et al. 2015). Newsome and his team also researched dingoes, but their research on dingo skull morphology, hybridisation between dingoes and domestic dogs, and predator–prey interactions did not take this path. Newsome's dingo research, supported by the CSIRO and the Australian Meat Research Committee and motivated by pastoralists' concerns about dingo predation on livestock, is an example of how the animal body is interpellated as "a colonial subject – that is, as a body subject to settler-colonial (mis)recognition" (Belcourt 2015, 5). As Belcourt argues, this misrecognition forecloses the animal body "within settler-colonial infrastructure of subjecthood and governmentality" (2015, 5).

152 Strehlow 1933, 190.

153 Strehlow 1933, 192.

154 Strehlow n.d., 1505.

155 Chewings 1936, 66.

red designs and daub their sacred objects with red ochre for festivities. The couple to be married are smeared with red ochre to celebrate their wedding. When a widow is daubed with red at the grave of her husband, it is a sign that her mourning time is over.[156] In central and south-eastern Australia, dingo pups were also rubbed with protective red ochre.[157]

Although Ankotarinja gleams "as though [he] was burning in a fire",[158] according to Carl Strehlow, yellow is the colour of fire, the colour of anger, passion and a longing for combat.[159] I extrapolate that Ankotarinja's association with fire and the colour red is important: the colour red for joy and fire for its multifarious life-giving roles, including for cooking and leaching toxins out of certain foods; for warmth and light; in ceremony; to clean up an area before camping; for healing (through warmth and steam using medicinal plants); in warfare; to drive away supernatural beings; for hardening spear points and digging stick points; to drive animals into nets or through a narrow gap or underground (in the case of burrowing animals) and to burn off groundcover so burrowing animals can be dug out; to attract animals to a place where they can be caught; and as a continent-wide system of land management.[160] Fire and smoke are part of rites of passage: birth, initiation, dispute resolution and funerals. People communicate to one another with fire; fire communicates that country is being looked after by people.[161] Fire is a friend.[162]

In another First Nation, dingoes are associated with life and rebirth. Aboriginal people at Yarralin taught Deborah Bird Rose that, unlike other Dreaming beings who walked the earth in human form, "originally Dingo and human beings were one species and their bodily shape was canine".[163] Old Tim Yilngayari told Rose that humans are all descended from canids: "White children out of white

156 Strehlow n.d., 1505.
157 Balme and O'Connor 2016, 777.
158 Strehlow 1933, 190.
159 Strehlow n.d., 1504.
160 Rose 1996, 64; see also Gammage 2012; Pascoe 2014, 115–23.
161 See Rose 1996, 70.
162 Gammage 2011, 278.
163 Rose 1984, 39, n. 4.

dog; Dingo for Aboriginal."[164] As well as being involved in human origins, dingoes are bound up with the way humans die: Daly Pulkara told Rose that instead of being like the moon, which comes back as the new moon after a few days, humans follow the dingo way in that our death lasts forever.[165] But Yilngayari also explained how the Dingo ancestor is also the originator of the Beginning Law, which involves people coming back to life as lizards, kangaroos, birds, crocodiles or other animals after they die.[166] As Rose describes it: "Life wants to live, wants to be embodied, and keeps finding its way back to life. Life is always in a state of metamorphosis, across death into more life, crossing bodies, species, and generations."[167] These "cross-species transformations"[168] keep humans and animals connected across birth and death.

In this chapter I have aimed to show how naming, and its close kin writing, work within Western and scientific epistemologies to possess and dominate land and animals, and to create hierarchies and hierarchical ways of interpreting the world. This project, Leane explains, is a necessary part of nation-building: "you do have to write nation. In contrast, you do not have to write Country because Country is … In Australia, the nation attempts to write over many Countries."[169] As Belcourt argues, the settler colonial nation "re-makes animal bodies into colonial subjects to normalize settler modes of political life (i.e., territorial acquisition, anthropocentrism, capitalism, white supremacy, and neoliberal pluralism) that further displace and disappear Indigenous bodies and epistemologies".[170] Consequently, "decolonization is not possible without centering an animal ethic".[171] A decolonial animal ethic, Belcourt writes, must re-orient animals "within ecologies of decolonial subjecthood" and re-signify them

164 Old Tim Yilngayari quoted in Rose 2000, 47.
165 Daly Pulkara quoted in Rose 2000, 49.
166 Old Tim Yilngayari quoted in Rose 2000, 49.
167 Rose 2011, 137.
168 Rose 2011, 141.
169 Leane 2014, 2.
170 Belcourt 2015, 9.
171 Belcourt 2015, 9.

through "Indigenous cosmologies".[172] Re-orienting knowledge of dingoes according to First Nations epistemology and Law reveals dingoes to be sentient, autonomous, moral beings – both subjects of colonialism and agents of decolonisation; re-signifying Aboriginal dingoes in settler colonial texts grounds and expands my (still partial and occluded) understanding of First Nations cosmologies.

A pragmatic reason for settler Australians to respect Indigenous knowledge about dingoes is that such respect would enable our understanding of dingoes and country to be richer, more accurate and less harmful. Balnglan's story, in which a real dingo dies because a white man wants to catch an imaginary animal, is emblematic of how settler Australians continue to pursue and kill imaginary "wild dogs" and create science based on preconceptions and ideological agendas, not empirical observation. Analysis of settler knowledge about and relationships with dingoes forces settler Australians to address basic and profound issues of justice. In spite of the incommensurate exchanges of contact between white settlers and Indigenous peoples, the myopia of settler epistemologies and ontologies, and the ongoing racism and epistemic injustice experienced by Aboriginal and Torres Strait Islander peoples, First Nations–led initiatives that may offer pathways towards decolonisation, such as the 2017 *Uluru Statement from the Heart*, are optimistic and generous about the two worlds that Indigenous peoples navigate. The *Uluru Statement from the Heart* recognises the legitimacy of the settler state and calls for moderate top-down reform:

> We seek constitutional reforms to empower our people and take a *rightful place* in our own country. When we have power over our destiny our children will flourish. They will walk in two worlds and their culture will be a gift to their country.[173]

My settler colonial understandings are fragmentary and distorted by cultural assumptions and misinterpretations, but it is clear that Balnglan and Ankotarinja/Erintja Ngoolya are complex, conscious,

172 Belcourt 2015, 8.
173 NCC 2017 [emphasis in original].

autonomous beings with their own skills, power, preferences and agency. In different ways their stories show how appetite, cooperation, happiness, vitality and the shared origins, lives and fates of dingoes and people are related.

I would like to thank Rick De Vos and two anonymous reviewers for their insightful comments, which helped me to develop this chapter.

References

Archer-Lean, C., A. Wardell-Johnson, G. Conroy and J. Carter (2015). Representations of the dingo: contextualising iconicity. *Australian Journal of Environmental Management* 22(2): 181–96. https://doi.org/10.1080/14486563.2014.985268.

Ardalan, A., M. Oskarsson, C. Natanaelsson, A.N. Wilton, A. Ahmadian and P. Savolainen (2012). Narrow genetic basis for the Australian dingo confirmed through analysis of paternal ancestry. *Genetica* 140: 65–73. https://doi.org/10.1007/s10709-012-9658-5.

Australian Museum (2021). *Unsettled: Our Untold History Revealed*, Exhibition, curated by Laura McBride and Mariko Smith, 11 October 2021 – 27 January 2022, Sydney.

Balme, J. and S. O'Connor (2016). Dingoes and Aboriginal social organisation in Holocene Australia. *Journal of Archaeological Science: Reports* 7: 775–81. https://doi.org/10.1016/j.jasrep.2015.08.015.

Balme, J., S. O'Connor and S. Fallon (2018). New dates on dingo bones from Madura Cave provide oldest firm evidence for arrival of the species in Australia. *Scientific Reports* 8, article no. 9933. https://doi.org/10.1038/s41598-018-28324-x.

Basedow, H. (1925). *The Australian Aboriginal*. Adelaide: F.W. Preece & Sons.

Bates, D. (1985). *The Native Tribes of Western Australia*. I. White, ed. Canberra: National Library of Australia.

Behrendt, L. (2016). *Finding Eliza: Power and Colonial Storytelling*. St Lucia: University of Queensland Press.

Belcourt, B-R. (2015). Animal bodies, colonial subjects: (re)locating animality in decolonial thought, *Societies* 5(1): 1–11. https://doi.org/10.3390/soc5010001.

Berndt, R.M. and C.H. Berndt (1942). A preliminary report of field work in the Ooldea region, western South Australia (continued). *Oceania* 13(2): 143–69.

Breckwoldt, R. (1988). *A Very Elegant Animal: The Dingo.* Sydney: Angus & Robertson.
Cairns, K.M., S. Brown, B.N. Sacks and J.W.O. Ballard (2017). Conservation implications for dingoes from the maternal and paternal genome: multiple populations, dog introgression, and demography. *Ecology and Evolution* 7: 9787–9807. https://doi.org/10.1002/ece3.3487.
Cairns, K.M., B.J. Nesbitt, S.W. Laffan, M. Letnic and M.S. Crowther (2020). Geographic hot spots of dingo genetic ancestry in southeastern Australia despite hybridisation with domestic dogs. *Conservation Genetics* 21: 77–90. https://doi.org/10.1007/s10592-019-01230-z.
Cairns, K.M. and A.N. Wilton (2016). New insights on the history of canids in Oceania based on mitochondrial and nuclear data. *Genetica* 144: 553–65.
Carter, J., A. Wardell-Johnson and C. Archer-Lean (2017). Butchulla perspectives on dingo displacement and agency at K'gari-Fraser Island, Australia. *Geoforum* 85: 197–205. https://doi.org/10.1016/j.geoforum.2017.08.001.
Chamberlain, L. (1990). *Through My Eyes: An Autobiography.* Port Melbourne: William Heinemann.
Chewings, C. (1936). *Back in the Stone Age: The Natives of Central Australia.* Sydney: Angus & Robertson.
Crowther, M.S., M. Fillios, N. Colman and M. Letnic (2014). An updated description of the Australian dingo (*Canis dingo* Meyer 1793). *Journal of Zoology* 293(3): 192–203. https://doi.org/10.1111/jzo.12134.
Curtis, J. (1838). *Shipwreck of the Stirling Castle.* London: George Virtue.
Davis, M. (2020). Reconciliation and the promise of an Australian homecoming. *Monthly*, July. https://www.themonthly.com.au/issue/2020/july/1593525600/megan-davis/reconciliation-and-promise-australian-homecoming#mtr.
Dixon, J.M. and L. Huxley, eds (1985). *Donald Thomson's Mammals and Fishes of Northern Australia.* Melbourne: Nelson.
Duncan-Kemp, A.M. (1933). *Our Sandhill Country: Nature and Man in South-western Queensland.* Sydney: Angus & Robertson.
Ecosure (2013). *Fraser Island Dingo Conservation and Risk Management Strategy.* Queensland Department of Environment and Heritage Protection.
Ens, E.J., P. Pert, M. Budden, P.A. Clarke, L. Clubb, B. Doran et al. (2015). Indigenous biocultural knowledge in ecosystem science and management: review and insight from Australia. *Biological Conservation* 181: 133–49.
Fillios, M. and P. Tacon (2016). Who let the dogs in? A review of the recent genetic evidence for the introduction of the dingo to Australia and the implications for the movement of people. *Journal of Archaeological Science: Reports* 7: 782–92. https://doi.org/10.1016/j.jasrep.2016.03.001.

Fowell, N. (1788). Letter received by John Fowell, 12 July. State Library of NSW, SAFEMLMSS 4895/1/IE1610008, LF610089. https://bit.ly/3fwdwaU.

Fricker, M. (2007). *Epistemic Injustice: Power and the Ethics of Knowing*. Oxford: Oxford University Press.

Gammage, B. (2012). *The Biggest Estate on Earth*. Sydney: Allen & Unwin.

Gammage, B. (2011). Fire in 1788: the closest ally. *Australian Historical Studies* 42(2): 277–88.

Gibson, J.M. (2018). Listening to T.G.H. Strehlow's recordings of Anmatyerr song. *Artefact* 41: 3–15.

Giles, E. (1986 [1889]). *Australia Twice Traversed*, vol. 2. Lane Cove, NSW: Doubleday.

Gollan, K. (1984). The Australian dingo: in the shadow of man. In Michael Archer and Georgina Clayton, eds. *Vertebrate Zoogeography and Evolution in Australasia*, 921–7. Carlisle: Hesperian Press.

Gould, R.A. (1969). Subsistence behaviour among the Western Desert Aborigines of Australia. *Oceania* 39(4): 253–74.

Graham, M. (2008). Some thoughts on the philosophical underpinnings of Aboriginal worldviews. *Australian Humanities Review* 45: 1–14.

Hamilton, A. (1972). Aboriginal man's best friend? *Mankind* 8(4): 287–95.

Kimber, R.G. (1976). Beginnings of farming? Some man-plant-animal relationships in central Australia. *Mankind* 10(3): 142–50.

Kolig, E. (1978). Aboriginal dogmatics: canines in theory, myth and dogma. *Bijdragen tot de Taal-, Land-en Volkenkunde* 134(1): 84–115.

Leane, J. (2014). Tracking our Country in settler literature. *Journal of the Association for the Study of Australian Literature* 14(3). https://openjournals.library.sydney.edu.au/index.php/JASAL/article/view/10039/9924.

Lennox, R. (2021). *Dingo Bold: The Life and Death of K'gari Dingoes*. Sydney: Sydney University Press. https://dx.doi.org/10.30722/sup.9781743327319

Lumholtz, C. (1980 [1889]). *Among Cannibals: An Account of Four Years Travel in Australia and of Camp Life with the Aborigines of Queensland*. Canberra: Australian National University Press.

Meehan, B., R. Jones and A. Vincent (1999). Gulu-kula: dogs in Anbarra society, Arnhem Land. *Aboriginal History* 23: 83–106.

Meggitt, M.J. (1965). The association between Australian Aborigines and dingoes. In A. Leeds and A.P. Vayda, eds. *Man, Culture and Animals: The Role of Animals in Human Ecological Adjustments* 7–26. Washington, DC: American Association for the Advancement of Science.

Mitchell, T.L. (1965 [1839]). *Three Expeditions into the Interior of Eastern Australia*, vol. 2. Adelaide: Libraries Board of South Australia.

Moreton-Robinson, A. (2004). Whiteness, epistemology and Indigenous representation. In A. Moreton-Robinson, ed. *Whitening Race: Essays in Social and Cultural Criticism*, 75–88. Canberra: Aboriginal Studies Press.

Mountford, C.P. (1981 [1948]). *Brown Men and Red Sand: Journeyings in Wild Australia*. London; Sydney: Angus & Robertson.

Nakata, M. (2007). *Disciplining the Savages: Savaging the Disciplines*. Canberra: Aboriginal Studies Press.

Nakata, M. (2002). Indigenous knowledge and the Cultural Interface: underlying issues at the intersection of knowledge and information systems. *IFLA (International Federation of Library Associations and Institutions) Journal* 28(5/6): 281–9.

National Constitutional Convention (2017). *Uluru Statement from the Heart*, 26 May. https://ulurustatement.org/the-statement.

Naval Historical Society of Australia (2019). Possession Island. https://www.navyhistory.org.au/possession-island/.

Newsome, A.E. (1980). The eco-mythology of the red kangaroo in Central Australia. *Mankind* 12(4): 327–33.

Oskarsson, M.C.R., C.F.C. Klütsch, U. Boonyaprakob, A. Wilton, Y. Tanabe and P. Savolainen (2011). Mitochondrial DNA data indicate an introduction through Mainland Southeast Asia for Australian dingoes and Polynesian domestic dogs. 279(1730): 967–74 *Proceedings of the Royal Society B: Biological Sciences*. https://doi.org/10.1098/rspb.2011.1395.

Pang, J.F., C. Kluetsch, X.J. Zou, A.B. Zhang, L.Y. Luo, H. Angleby et al. (2009). mtDNA data indicate a single origin for dogs south of Yangtze River, less than 16,300 years ago, from numerous wolves. *Molecular Biology and Evolution* 26(12): 2849–64. https://doi.org/10.1093/molbev/msp195.

Parker, M. (2006). Bringing the dingo home: discursive representations of the dingo by Aboriginal, colonial and contemporary Australians. PhD thesis. School of English, Journalism and European Languages: University of Tasmania.

Parkhurst, J. (2015). *The Butchulla First Nations People of Fraser Island (K'gari) and Their Dingoes*. Melbourne: Australian Wildlife Protection Council.

Pascoe, B. (2014). *Dark Emu Black Seeds: Agriculture or Accident?* Broome: Magabala Books.

Pearson, L. (2021). Appropriate terminology for Aboriginal and Torres Strait Islander people – it's complicated. *IndigenousX*, 16 June. http://bit.ly/3P5UTeT.

Probyn-Rapsey, F. (2020). Dingoes and dogwhistling: a cultural politics of race and species in Australia. In K. Struthers Montford and C. Taylor, eds. *Colonialism and Animality: Anti-Colonial Perspectives in Critical Animal Studies*, 181–200. New York: Routledge.

Probyn-Rapsey, F. (2016). Five propositions on ferals. *Feral Feminisms: Feral Theory* 6(Fall): 18–21.

Queensland Parks and Wildlife Service (2017). The dingoes (wongari) of K'gari (Fraser Island): safety and information guide. Queensland Department of National Parks, Sport and Racing. https://bit.ly/3nXFEqK.

Robinson, R. (1956). *The Feathered Serpent*. Sydney: Edwards & Shaw.

Rose, D.B. (2011). *Wild Dog Dreaming: Love and Extinction*. Charlottesville; London: University of Virginia Press.

Rose, D.B. (2000 [1992]). *Dingo Makes Us Human: Life and Land in Australian Aboriginal Culture*. Cambridge: Cambridge University Press.

Rose, D.B. (1996). *Nourishing Terrains: Australian Aboriginal Views of Landscape and Wilderness*. Canberra: Australian Heritage Commission.

Rose, D.B. (1984). The saga of Captain Cook: morality in Aboriginal and European law. *Australian Aboriginal Studies* 2: 24–39.

Savolainen, P., T. Leitner, A.T. Wilton, E. Matisoo-Smith and J. Lundeber (2004). A detailed picture of the origin of the Australian dingo, obtained from the study of mitochondrial DNA. *Proceedings of the National Academy of Sciences of the United States of America* 101(33): 12387–90. https://doi.org/10.1073/pnas.0401814101.

Schlunke, K. (2009). Home. *South Atlantic Quarterly* 108(1). https://doi.org/10.1215/00382876-2008-020.

Sherwood, J., S. Lighton, K. Dundas, T. French, D. Link-Gordon, K. Smith et al. (2015). Who are the experts here? Recognition of Aboriginal women and community workers in research and beyond. *Alternative* 11(2): 177–90.

Smith, B.P., K.M. Cairns, J.W. Adams, T.M. Newsome, M. Fillios, E.C. Deaux et al. (2019). Taxonomic status of the Australian dingo: the case for *Canis dingo* Meyer, 1793. *Zootaxa* 4564(1): 173–97. https://doi.org/10.11646/zootaxa.4564.1.6.

Smyth, R.B. (1972 [1876]). *The Aborigines of Victoria* vol I. Melbourne: John Currey, O'Neil.

Stanner, W.E.H. (2009 [1953]). The Dreaming. In W.E.H. Stanner, ed. *The Dreaming and Other Essays*, 57–72. Melbourne: Black Inc.

Strehlow, C. (n.d.). The Aranda and Loritja tribes in central Australia by Carl Strehlow. Manuscript. C. Chewings, trans. Special Collections, Barr Smith Library (MSS 572.994 S91a.E). University of Adelaide.

Strehlow, T.G.H. (1971). *Songs of Central Australia*. Sydney: Angus & Robertson.

Strehlow, T.G.H. (1933). Ankotarinja, an Aranda myth. *Oceania* 4(2): 187–200.

Tench, W. (1789). *Narrative of the Expedition to Botany Bay: With an Account of New South Wales, Its Productions, Inhabitants, etc*. London: Printed for J. Debrett, opposite Burlington-House, Piccadilly.

Tindale, N.B. (1974). *Aboriginal Tribes of Australia: Their Terrain, Environmental Controls, Distribution Limits, and Proper Names*. Los Angeles; London: University of California Press.

Walter, M. (2016). Data politics and Indigenous representation in Australian statistics. In T. Kukutai and J. Taylor, eds. *Indigenous Data Sovereignty: Toward an Agenda*, 79–98. Canberra: ANU Press.

Watson, I. (2009). Aboriginality and the violence of colonialism. *Borderlands e-journal* 8(1): 1–8. https://ssrn.com/abstract=2476792.

Week (1889). Obituary of James Davis, 11 May. http://www.slq.qld.gov.au/resources/convict-queenslanders/davis#obi1.

3

Reading Toni Morrison close and far: Decolonising literary animal studies

Susan McHugh

Once upon a time, at the end of one of the first large-scale international animal studies conferences, I was sitting at a table in a cafe with a group of new friends, and the conversation turned to the problem that all of the event's several keynote lecturers were white. Around the circle, they all then came out in their various ways as Black, Indigenous and People of Colour (BIPOC). Confirming my whiteness, I gushed about this welcome change of finding myself with a diverse group of scholars and artists, which prompted one to ask: "You've been working in this field for a while now, so maybe you can tell us: is animal studies only for white people?"

I have been carrying that question ever since.

Much has changed for the better since then, as evinced by the 2019 Decolonizing Animals conference in Aotearoa New Zealand, which inspired this volume. But a lot more needs doing, and not just in academia, as witnessed by Black Lives Matter, Idle No More, Rhodes Must Fall, Standing Rock and so many more global movements cultivating more diverse, equitable and inclusive conditions aiming to turn conversations towards justice for all. Looking to my own sub-field of literary animal studies, this chapter reflects on the writing of and about Nobel laureate Toni Morrison as a case study for charting convergences of critical race with animal studies that model decolonisation of scholarly aesthetics.

Walter Mignolo and Rolando Vazquez identify a defining "tic" of the coloniser in the separation and elevation of "aestheTics" (akin to poetics), in order to explain how a powerful counterforce, "decolonial aestheSis [akin to poesis, has become] one sphere where decoloniality is flourishing".[1] Although their interest remains centred on the human, their approach in general helps to explain the relevance of literary studies to decolonial projects. More specifically, I extrapolate from their work that decolonising animals in literary studies requires not just attending to the non-human contents of literary texts but also reckoning with how we come to perceive and value them (or not) by their contributions to the empowerment (or not) of the human. Only, in my reading of Morrison's animals, it has become clear that decolonising animals also entails attending to who and what thereby become excluded in and from representational processes beyond the human, and with what consequences.

Sylvia Wynter's helpful distinction of "Man" as "that which over-represents itself as the human" serves as an important reminder that colonialism proceeds not just through physical means of oppression but also necessarily via conceptual exclusions that limit potentials for imagining even before living social life.[2] Who or what, person or thing, subject or object, animate or lifeless: the hierarchical dualisms represented by Man obscure the continuum of corporeality, personhood, subjectivity and community in which all animate being is practically entangled. For literary animal studies scholars like me, the question becomes: How do writers affirm ways of being human among other animals that undermine or refute Man's colonial legacy? By comparing various strategies of writing and reading Man among animals in discussions of Morrison's writing, I want to suggest some ways in which animal representations, along with their perceptions, map a spectrum of decolonising potentials.

One of the most celebrated contemporary US novelists, Toni Morrison always embraced the label of "black writer", insisting that she was never interested in writing for or about white people, a decision guiding literary scholarship to emphasise her vivid explorations of

1 Mignolo and Vazquez 2013.
2 Wynter 2003, 317.

black American experiences. Much as I have always admired her work, the apparently marginal status of animals in her writing presented an obvious difficulty from the start for the critic interested in questions about the politics of species. In the early 2000s, when a few of us were initially trying to stake the claim that representing animals as animals (and not, say, as symbols for humans) was a legitimate topic for literary studies, it was much easier to make the case that the minor status of non-human beings in fictions like Morrison's proved quite the opposite position.[3] In the last few years, however, several studies have identified how Morrison's inclusions of animals in her stories can be interpreted as purposeful, creative, experimental and otherwise significant interruptions to these longstanding literary patterns. While acknowledging wide variations in both the claims and the methods of the recent scholarship, I piece aspects of it together here to trace the story of how Morrison's animals collectively come to challenge the aestheTics of close reading. Particularly when read non-metaphorically, her writing about more-than-human life, in Mignolo and Vazquez's terms,

> makes the wound[s of colonialism] visible, tangible … [and] at the same time … moves towards the healing, the recognition, the dignity of those aesthetic practices that have been written out of the canon of modern aestheTics.[4]

As I explain later in this chapter, one animal presence in Morrison's novel *A Mercy* (2008) in particular drove home this point for me by encouraging critical self-reflection on the canonicity of close reading in literary criticism.

With long roots in religious exegetical traditions, close reading focuses on details and patterns to claim precise understanding of the

---

3 Attempts to legitimise one of Morrison's most haunting animal characters through alignment with a canonical white male author's "totem animals that radiate an imaginary integrity" (Weinstein 1996, 286) strike me as representative of how and why the originality and complexity of such figures were overlooked by earlier generations of Morrison critics.

4 Mignolo and Vazquez 2013.

relations of meaning and form within a work of literature. Through the turn-of-the-twentieth-century rise of literary studies, it became a central procedure for formal analysis, and subsequently a predominant method taught in literature classrooms. Charged with the modern fervour for scientific precision yet extending faith in transcendent meaning to the literary work, close reading empowered formalist literary scholars to transform the teaching of literature from passive aesthetic appreciation to active critical interpretation, helping shift the gears towards science/technology/engineering/mathematics (STEM) that many now lament as stunting cross-pollinations with the arts and humanities in US educational systems. However, early proponents of the US formalist school of New Criticism like John Crowe Ransom embraced the power play of a STEM-friendly approach to literary studies, arguing that close reading was essential for "sharpen[ing students'] … critical apparatus into precision tools".[5] Practitioners must assume that a truly literary work gains meaning as such through demonstrating internal coherence, and that literature worthy of the name therefore presents a puzzle of clues to be solved only by those who demonstrate masterful reading.

A century later, one marked by unprecedented scales of genocide and extinction, decolonial approaches turned to other strategies – what I term "far reading" methods – that eschew mastery in favour of valuing the different experiences that writers and readers bring to texts. Clarifying the logic of Audre Lorde's prescient line "the master's tools will never dismantle the master's house", Julietta Singh's *Unthinking Mastery: Dehumanism and Decolonial Entanglements* (2018) explains the particular dangers of the masterful aestheTic beyond the realm of Man. While not addressing close reading or Morrison per se, Singh notes how being singled out as

> the master of a language, or a literary tradition … is widely understood to be laudable. Yet, as a pursuit, mastery invariably and relentlessly reaches toward the indiscriminate control over something – whether human or inhuman, animate or inanimate … Mastery, [operating as a destructive force] … across

5 Ransom 1937.

> anticolonial discourse and postcolonial literary texts, also turns inward to become a form of self-maiming, one that involves the denial of the master's own dependency on other bodies.[6]

I would add that, by foregrounding the unequal relations with others that become negotiated through encounters with literary animals, Morrison's writing invites reading practices that engage with the contradictions of mastery in ways that elaborate intercorporeal interdependencies between members of different species. In doing so, her fiction fosters concerns with the complicated legacies of the American history of chattel slavery not just for humans and interhuman relations but also for non-human animals and human–animal relationships.

Cary Wolfe's *Animal Rites: American Culture, the Discourse of Species, and Posthumanist Theory* (2003) seems an inauspicious place to seek support for this argument in literary animal studies, in part because it contains no discussion of animals in Morrison's fictions. Instead, Wolfe focuses on Morrison's lone book of literary criticism, *Playing in the Dark: Whiteness and the Literary Imagination* (1992), in which she explores how "American Africanism", or white people's ideas about blackness, shapes the personae, narrative and idiom of US literature in ways that empower structural racism. For Morrison, American Africanism allows the

> Africanlike … [to] become, in the Eurocentric tradition that American education favors, both a way of talking about and a way of policing matters of class, sexual license, and repression, formations and exercises of power, and meditations on ethics and accountability.[7]

For Wolfe, Morrison's analysis provides one among many illustrations of his overarching thesis: that critical practices that fail to uncouple the discourse of species from the institution of speciesism – which he defines as the systematic discrimination against others based on

---

6 Singh 2018, 10.
7 Morrison 1992.

the generic characteristic of non-human status that in turn fuels a fundamental repression of concerns about human species identity – perpetuate even as they purport to break with humanist epistemologies.

More specifically, Wolfe explores how Morrison's nuanced reading of Ernest Hemingway's *The Garden of Eden* models analysis of interlocking oppressions, but only up to a point. Questioning whether Morrison's charge that Hemingway's "playing in the dark" makes his fiction implicitly racist, Wolfe concedes that isolating Africanist discourse makes it appear to be reproduced in an uncomplicated way. However, by reading the Africanist as "twinned" by Hemingway with species discourse, Wolfe finds a means of antiracist critique "*but not on the terrain of racial discourse itself*, instead using the 'off site' of species discourse to undermine racism's conditions of possibility".[8] Wolfe therefore concludes that it serves as one of many examples of how paying attention to what the animals are doing in (and to) stories compels literary critics to reckon with the legacy of speciesism in fiction writing. Perhaps because so many of us came to literary animal studies through social justice theory, his argument has long been treated within the sub-field as implicitly an extension of antiracist practice.

Yet, over a decade later, Wolfe's treatment of Morrison was pilloried in Alexander Weheliye's *Habeas Viscus: Racializing Assemblages, Biopolitics, and Black Feminist Theories of the Human* (2014) as proof of the racism rampant in animal studies scholarship. Weheliye's overarching point is to show how feminist writers of the black diaspora like Wynter and Hortense Spillers trouble Michel Foucault's, Giorgio Agamben's and other predominantly Eurowhite male scholars' biopolitical framings of the problem of the human. In lieu of engaging all of these thinkers' complicated relationships with anthropocentrist thought, Weheliye dismisses questions of animals and animality tout court by pointing first to Marjorie Spiegel's controversial popular 1989 book *The Dreaded Comparison: Human and Animal Slavery* as evidence that the analogy of human and animal slavery is "frequently … carelessly – and often defensively – brandished about in the field of animal studies".[9]

8 Wolfe 2003, 167 [emphasis in original].
9 Weheliye 2014, 10.

Weheliye's position is conspicuous by its absence from other studies on the topic. Detailing alternative viewpoints through critical analysis of the 2005 People for the Ethical Treatment of Animals (PETA) campaign "Are animals the new slaves?", Claire Jean Kim's *Dangerous Crossings: Race, Species, and Nature in a Multicultural Age* (2015), Lindgren Johnson's *Animal Matters: Fugitive Humanism and African America, 1840–1930* (2018) and Bénédicte Boisseron's *Afro-dog: Blackness and the Animal Question* (2018) all concur that animal rights activists are empowered to make such offensive comparisons not due to any overt encouragement from, but rather as a result of the general absence of any strident positionings taken by, animal studies scholarship on the subject of race. That said, these studies themselves extend discussions of the entangled histories that inform deployments of the concepts of species and race that were initiated much earlier by literary animal studies pioneers, including Marion Copeland, Gerald Vizenor, Helen Tiffin, Robert McKay, Philip Armstrong and of course Wolfe.[10] While not making these connections crystal clear, Wolfe was among the first to make the case for the relevance of literary representations of species difference to enhancing the kind of intersectional approach to analysing differences that Kimberlé Crenshaw has so persuasively argued is essential to black feminism.[11] All of this makes it hard to understand why Weheliye's only citations to support his claim are Speigel's *The Dreaded Comparison* and Wolfe's *Animal Rites*.

Absent this context, Weheliye quotes at length Wolfe's analysis of the absolute power that Morrison characterises as slavery's material condition of possibility, as one that specifically elides race and the power of human freedom, and one that only emerges as such through critique of its faith in total control over all who are excluded in the non-human fold. Weheliye then repudiates Wolfe's interpretation as "spiteful", particularly "[g]iven that Morrison mentions neither the subjugation nor liberation of animals".[12] The question of whether and

10 See Armstrong 2004; Copeland 1983; McKay 2001; Tiffin 2001; Vizenor 1988.

11 Crenshaw 1989.

12 Weheliye 2014, 10. It also strikes me as a strange word choice for repeating, and without reference to, the famous opening line of Morrison's *Beloved*: "124 was spiteful" (1987, 1).

how Morrison's work is misrepresented in this instance returns me to Singh's discussion of how that which "the would-be master yearns to govern over completely", in this case "a body of texts" suffers damage or destruction by virtue of "estranging the mastered object from its previous state of being".[13] Underpinning the dispute of course is the authority with which, in each case, an established academic stakes his claim on Morrison's presumed anthropocentrism. Despite such different readings, Wolfe and Weheliye both set the terms of debate resolutely at the level of structural logics – of race versus species – and at the expense of attending to more specific encounters of particular humans and other animals in and around Morrison's writing.

Searching instead for more nuanced and variable positions has brought me back to the pages of *Playing in the Dark*, where I am struck by how Morrison describes having come to consciousness of the dangerous Africanist game herself by moving interpretation to a different register. Instead of reading as a critic, she approaches the works of Hemingway and others "[a]s a writer reading" and comes to identify the problem thus:

> It is as if I had been looking at a fishbowl – the glide and flick of the golden scales, the green tip, the bolt of white careening back from the gills; the castles at the bottom, surrounded by pebbles and tiny, intricate fronds of green; the barely disturbed water, the flecks of waste and food, the tranquil bubbles travelling to the surface – and suddenly I saw the bowl, the structure that transparently (and invisibly) permits the ordered life it contains to exist in the larger world.

What became transparent were the ways that Americans choose to talk about themselves through and within a sometimes allegorical, sometimes metaphorical, but always structurally limited representation of an Africanist presence.[14] Morrison's perception of the fishbowl thus traces a powerful counter-narrative to Wolfe's and Weheliye's repressions and rivalries of racism and speciesism.

13 Singh 2018, 10.
14 Morrison 1992, 16–17.

Recalling Mignolo and Vazquez's key point that "the modern/colonial project [requires] control over the senses and perception", the writer's attunement to her own aestheSis is what enables Morrison to identify Africanist aestheTics as playing "a key role in configuring a canon, a normativity that enabled the disdain and the rejection of other forms of aesthetic practices [and] other forms of sensing and perceiving".[15]

But why does Morrison characterise her perception in this instance as conditional, "as if [she] has been looking at a fishbowl"? I would add that Morrison's choice to use animal captivity for display – fish in an aquarium – as a metaphor for the paradoxically pervasive invisibility of structural racism in US literature indicates a complex vision of how literary production becomes part of the problem of as well as part of the solution to the paradigm of absolute control.[16] A survey of more recent discussions of Morrison's animals confirms that I am not alone in feeling tempted to follow Morrison into the fishbowl, as it were, to acknowledge the powerful lure of symbolic aspects of animal representations,[17] and at the same time to be inspired by her – especially by thinking of her as the "writer reading" – to be wary of the chokehold on interpretation of literary figures that is imposed by Man and other exclusionary visions of difference. Nevertheless, reviewing

---

15 Mignolo and Vazquez 2013.

16 In turn, I cannot help but perceive something akin to the productive confusion of sentiments diagnosed by Yi-Fu Tuan as linking the bulging-eyed goldfish of today's pet stores to European royalty's history of keeping black African human "pets" in *Dominance and Affection: The Making of Pets* (1984). For Tuan's "narrative-descriptive approach", the point is to forestall "the intellectual assurance of being offered a rigorous explanation" to help "make a reader feel the intellectual pleasure of being exposed to a broad and variegated range of related facts and of understanding them a little better (though still hazily)" (1991, 686), a point illustrated in part through citation of Kenneth Grahame's novel *The Wind in the Willows* (1944).

17 Morrison makes the case that "whiteness as ideology" emerges in Herman Melville's *Moby-Dick* (1851) only by "leav[ing] whale as commerce and confront[ing] whale as metaphor" (1994, 382). Thought-provoking as this approach may be, it obscures the material explanation provided by the novel for the widespread endangerment of most whale species that continues into the twenty-first century, along with the interrelated threats to Indigenous cultures that historically have depended upon whaling. See chapter 3 of McHugh 2019.

how Morrison's fictional animals renew appreciation for her literary genius makes me all the more insistent that far reading should breed suspicion of all analogical "as ifs".

Joshua Bennett's *Being Property Once Myself: Blackness and the End of Man* (2020) reads Morrison as part of a broader

> black aesthetic tradition [that] provides us with the tools needed to conceive of interspecies relationships anew and ultimately to abolish the forms of antiblack thought that have maintained the fissure between human and animal.[18]

Noting the many memorable but minor roles played by non-human animals across Morrison's novels, his chapter on *Song of Solomon* (1977) makes the case that the fleeting "presence, and, more importantly, the *properties*" of birds in that novel anchors a psychoanalytic interpretation of the central human characters in compulsive flight from the weight of black masculinity, from the heavy "duress of everyday life as a perceived threat".[19] A coming-of-age story ostensibly concerned with the growing alienation of a mid-twentieth-century African American man from his community, his family, even himself, *Song of Solomon* thus becomes all the more clearly a meditation on the legacies of beings reduced to properties, broadly writ.

The birdlike ability to fly is the figurative animal property favoured in Bennett's approach. He contrasts the suicidal flight attempt by the character Robert Smith, who jumps off a building while flapping makeshift fabric wings at the start of the novel, with the pivotal later scene in which protagonist Macon "Milkman" Dead and his then friend Guitar Baines spy a white peacock that they assume to be escaped from the nearby zoo. Their initial impulse to catch the peacock gives way to a discussion of his "jive flying"[20] – "no better than a chicken" – and then to what "the bird had set them up" for: their silent, separate, personal visions of the freedom that eludes them.[21] The peacock's "weighted,

18 Bennett 2020, 4.
19 Bennett 2020, 68 [emphasis in original].
20 Morrison 1977, 178.
21 Morrison 1977, 179.

belabored ascension", as Bennett explains, "operates as an evocative stand-in for any number of male characters the reader encounters throughout".[22] Moreover, the bird's leucism makes him a particular puzzle for readers,

> a signifier that comes with a critique of the signified built right in. From the moment the peacock appears, the notion of whiteness as pure transcendence is already unsettled. The white peacock flies no better than [a chicken], and is thus a fraught, imperfect site of aspiration.[23]

Bennett thus identifies how these characters are set up by the peacock not simply to fail to achieve their aspirations: ultimately, Milkman and Guitar are set to fly at each other with love and murderous rage, their desires "complicated to the point of contradiction",[24] not least by the story of Milkman's enslaved ancestor who, as he learns through the course of the novel, legendarily flew like a bird, and back to Africa and, presumably, freedom.

Situating these fictional developments within a broader social context, in which the controversial Moynihan Report of 1965 and Morrison's own comments about writing the novel work together in their different ways to define black masculinity in terms of species difference, Bennett concludes that Morrison invokes animal properties in ways that confront readers with the "seeming paradox" of dominion and escape.[25] In short, Bennett pursues a difficult, compelling argument to take Morrison's "craft problem" seriously, citing her own articulation of her primary aesthetic challenge: "I couldn't use the metaphors I'd used describing [the] women" who take centre stage in her prior novels; instead, she turns to the animal or animal-like property of "flying [as] the central metaphor in *Song*" for black masculinity.[26] While Bennett is clearly following the writer's intention in this instance, I am

---

22 Bennett 2020, 92–3.
23 Bennett 2020, 97.
24 Bennett 2020, 113.
25 Bennett 2020, 101.
26 Morrison quoted in Bennett 2020, 100.

uncomfortable with how metaphorical interpretation opens the possibility for readers to overlook the ethical issues raised by Morrison's representations of human–animal relations throughout the novel: the zoo life from which the peacock presumably escapes, the doe and bobcat hunts through which Guitar and Milkman find dubious affirmations of manhood, even the dairy industry through which Milkman's name circuitously derives. Weheliye's claims about Morrison's disinterest in animal liberation notwithstanding, Bennett's reading of the white peacock as pathetic as well as sympathetic at least implies that her fictions provoke thinking about animals' uneven imbrications in human lives and the consequences for social justice.

Discussions focused on similarly brief but spectacular appearances of individual animals in Morrison's later novels indicate the novelist's more precise interests in the ways in which the properties peculiar to those viewed as property are enlisted in the production of humans, including Wynter's Man. In *Becoming Human: Matter and Meaning in an Antiblack World* (2020), Zakiyyah Iman Jackson focuses on Morrison's best-known novel, *Beloved* (1987), to examine how black masculinity is made to compromise the enslaved man's humanity. Part historical fiction, part ghost story, *Beloved* follows the stories of freed slaves haunted by past violence, introduced in the story through detailed flashbacks. Jackson's analysis focuses primarily on the story of Paul D's at once humiliating, terrorising and enlightening memory of being forced to witness another slave tortured to death while he himself is bound helplessly, even perversely, in restraints that include a bit in his mouth.

The scene is orchestrated by the torturer ominously named Schoolteacher, in order to violently disabuse the slaves of their owner's encouragement to think of themselves as men. But, in Jackson's reading, a particular rooster works his way into the narrative, rather like the peacock in the previous novel, to further unsettle hierarchies. What Paul D's memory returns to is a pivotal encounter with another male bird who happens on the scene, the cock with the menacing name, Mister. Complicating earlier interpretations of the novel as promoting human at the expense of animal liberation,[27] Jackson's deconstruction of this scene cuts across the human–animal divide on the premise that

27 See for instance Ruetenik 2010.

slavery is not a condition of dehumanisation but rather "a technology for producing a kind of human" required of "an imperial racial hierarchy".[28]

Paul D's obsession with the gaze of the rooster settling on him at the height of his distress bears closer scrutiny as provoking or confirming a deep disruption to his sense of himself as a man. Positioning Mister both as material presence and plot device, Jackson's close readings of the descriptions of the cock indicate no mere psychological projection but a distinct animal character, revealed through the exchange of glances between the free-ranging animal and the captive man in irons who covets the bird's freedom. Although at one point pluralised to all five of the plantation's cocks – "[w]alking past the roosters looking at them looking at me"[29] – Paul D's recollections obsessively return to Mister as an individual, different from the rest. For he includes the peculiarly intimate detail that he himself effectively birthed the rooster as a chick, by helping him to hatch out of his shell: "He'd a died if it hadn't been for me."[30] Thus Jackson concludes that the role of the rooster in Paul D's story signals correspondence rather than difference between species, and the co-production rather than ontological certainty of the human–animal divide.

In this case productively sidestepping symbolic interpretations, most obviously of the rooster or cock as phallus,[31] Jackson attends to how "Morrison critically observes the fundaments of animalised representation up close rather than negating them at a distance" and consequently "exposes the complexity and contradictions that produce blackness and animality as proxies, not through the refutation of bestial imagery but rather through its magnification and deconstruction".[32] Her interpretation suggests further how Morrison deeply troubles the analogical reasoning through which Paul D expresses contempt at another slave, Sethe, for having murdered her baby rather than turning

---

28 Jackson 2020, 46–7. The theoretical scaffolding of this point is modelled after Hartman 1997.

29 Morrison 1987, 85.

30 Morrison 1987, 85.

31 On the cock's symbolism in *Beloved*, see Kang 2003. On Morrison's bird symbolism more generally, see González 2000.

32 Jackson 2020, 59.

the child over to the slave-catcher – he tells her, "You got two feet, Sethe, not four"[33] – and helps to explain Sethe's grudging his regret for the terms of his rebuke. For, as Jackson concludes, there are profoundly ethical questions that follow from the ways in which "Morrison's text questions the terms on which we represent and define beasts, human or otherwise".[34]

Jackson's reading of Paul D's primal scene pairs interestingly with the accounts of Sethe's flashback to a similarly traumatic experience developed at greater length in Nathan Snaza's *Animate Literacies: Literature, Affect, and the Politics of Humanism* (2019). In another one of the novel's most haunting scenes, Sethe returns in her mind to overhearing Schoolteacher in the classroom speaking with the children that he allows to sexually assault her. She vividly remembers how he instructed his schoolchildren to write lists that distinguish Sethe's "human characteristics" from "her animal ones".[35] Snaza identifies two ways of reading the encounter: one, as "Schoolteacher's lesson" for the children, namely to see Sethe "as a woman and as a black slave" by perceiving in her a degrading admixture of "both human and animal characteristics"; and another, through Morrison's depiction of the scene itself as "reported speech, relayed by Sethe",[36] which leads to a further "explanation of how Sethe came to be partly human and partly animal"[37] when her owner's wife elaborates "characteristics" as meaning "[a] thing that's natural to a thing".[38]

Like Paul D, when Sethe comes to the conclusion that she is perceived as less than human, she is explicitly depicted in the company of hostile humans and less threatening animals. Snaza's attunement to the non-human actors enlivening the drama of the enslaved woman's growing self-consciousness, including the flies mobbing Sethe's baby, the yard dog licking a pan, even the grass tickling her feet, raises larger questions about whether Morrison's point is simply to draw readers in

33 Morrison 1987, 194.
34 Jackson 2020, 79.
35 Morrison 1987, 228.
36 Snaza 2019, 12.
37 Snaza 2019, 14.
38 Morrison 1987, 230.

close to the details involved in developing a complex character, or also to inspire us to attend to far-reaching effects of the situations that they signify. Snaza elaborates,

> If the literacy event [of the schoolroom scene] in *Beloved* concerns three humans as one teaches the other two how to think about themselves as humans as they read and write, the situation includes the periperformative dehumanising force of the lesson and the direct participation across different scales of a panoply of actants both human and non.[39]

More than just unsettling Sethe's sense of herself as a human being, Snaza's reading underscores that what is at stake is the articulation of "settler humanity" as serving the human at the expense of each and every one of those who, like Sethe, represent "an arrivant whose presence is enabled by the transatlantic slave trade", one that is leveraged via a discursive move that risks "render[ing] the theft of indigenous land and the United State's [sic] genocidal imperialism all but illegible".[40] That he gets there only by attending to the subtleties of Morrison's widening of the frame to encompass a more-than-human ecology of beings invites further inquiry into the way that the objectivity or mastery implicit in close reading is itself troubled by what Snaza frames as his own "much more distant form" of interpretation.[41]

Of the critics discussed so far, Snaza provides the most explicitly decolonial framework for engaging with Morrison's poetics, which inspires me to launch into my own far reading practice that likewise learns from antiracist, feminist and Indigenous studies to consider how different knowledges converge or clash in the making and interpreting of fiction. The point is not to negate but rather to complement what can be learned by close attention to what is in the text with what can be owned up to about what people bring to the text. What is at stake is to find more and better answers to Barbara Christian's long-ago question for black feminists, namely: "For whom are we doing what we are doing

39 Snaza 2019, 17.
40 Snaza 2019, 13.
41 Snaza 2019, 5.

when we do literary criticism?"[42] By bringing into the conversation not just what characters but also what writers and readers know as well as don't know about themselves and others, literary studies could advance decolonialism by practising methods of accounting for the responsibility of responsiveness to Man's necessarily more-than-human social worlds – in other words, by insisting that a world emptied of animality for Man remains a myth, albeit a dangerous one. Working through my own Eurowestern-settler interpretations of scenes featuring horses in Morrison's novel *A Mercy* (2008), I conclude by attempting a reading that respects and values differences among authors, readers and other denizens of the worlds in which we meet.

I am inspired by a line in *A Mercy* that rattled me on the first read. Set in the late-seventeenth-century colony of Virginia, the novel as a whole imagines life in a multiracial plantation community at a time when the distinction between temporary service and lifelong slavery was being legally codified along racial lines. Given Morrison's relentless interrogation of the black experience in America, it seems an important, if one-off, late-career shift in her historical focus, in part because today it is not well known about Colonial America that white people were not always separated and elevated as indentured servants over black slaves, and, as Morrison shows, the genocide of Native Americans also becomes complicated in the transition. As in all of her work, Morrison's primary focus on the historic surrender of moral to capitalist interests plainly concerns the consequences for human history, to which the inclusion of a particular horse in this story provides a strange interruption.

Here is the line that I stumbled over: "She could not decide whether Patrician's accident by cloven hoof was a rebuke or proof of the pudding."[43] The confused person is Florens, a girl of mixed white Portuguese and black African parentage who has been traded in partial payment of a debt by her own mother to a plantation owner. He initially baulks, but, in depicting the process of his ultimately being persuaded to take Florens, Morrison quietly stages the girl's transformation from a person capable of selling her labour to a thing incapable of demanding

42 Christian 1994, 357.
43 Morrison 2008, 94.

wages for work. What Florens' experience figures, in other words, is the historic transition of black people in America from a condition of bonded labour or debt bondage, in which a person pledges themselves or their children against a loan, to chattel slavery, in which a person becomes the personal property of the slaver, or no longer has the full legal personhood characteristic of humanity. Whereas *Beloved* explores the grim choices faced in the nineteenth century by those whose children have long been condemned at birth, in the phrasing of the time, to "follow the condition of the mother" into chattel slavery, *A Mercy* looks back further to consider the different prospects for black servants uncertainly approaching this fate in the 1680s. Consequently, much of the plot concerns fraught mother–child relationships.

Within the scene I question, however, Florens later in life is trying to determine whether to attribute any religious significance to the fact that the only one of her owner's children to survive infancy was subsequently kicked to death by one of his farm animals. The question arises while Florens listens to some "profane" talk by the dead child's mother, Rebecca, who is referred to as the Mistress of the estate. This makes Florens wonder: was the child's death by "cloven hoof" an act of God to punish Rebecca for being a sinner, or proof that Rebecca, as Mistress, was always an instrument of the Devil?[44] Canted perhaps in Eurowestern imaginations by images of satyrs and later Satan with split hooves, there seems a certain poetic justice to the story of the plantation's heir apparent – and a girl named Patrician, at that – as abruptly ended by a goat, sheep or more plausibly cow. After all, Patrician's family's fortune is built on the backs of unpaid labourers, some of whom like Florens only increase the family's wealth when her legal status is reduced to that of farm animals, and further add to their riches when bearing children.

But elsewhere in the story, the animal who kills the girl is explicitly identified as a horse. It is not that such accidents are far-fetched; even today, cows are only marginally more likely to kill you than horses, and horses are the most prominent non-humans in the novel, plausibly as the preferred means of land travel at that place and time. One of the things that attracts Florens' owner, Jacob, to start his plantation

44 Morrison 2008, 94.

is the ease with which a white man can obtain a horse in the New World, without even "a deposit if the man signed a note".[45] And horse ownership is one of the signs that the African blacksmith with whom Florens falls in love is indeed a free man. These realistic depictions of horses make it all the more difficult to understand the reference to the killer horse's "cloven hoof", which makes sense only as an unexplained, severe deformity or injury to the customary closed, bell-shaped structure of an ordinary horse hoof. Nothing within the text accounts for why Florens, who has travelled the countryside living and working as close to the land as it gets, would mistake a horse for being one of the many other farm creatures who, in contrast, are ordinarily born with each of their hooves split into two toes. The more I ponder it, the more the sheer doesn't-add-up-ness of this figure has moved me to question how literary-critical methods contributed to my initial perception of the problem.

Literary criticism's tried-and-true way of accounting for the cloven hoof would identify it as a mistake. Florens' musings do not quite add up to what painter John Ruskin had in mind with what he termed the affective fallacy – designating an aesthetic gesture meant to represent how the world looks askew to a mind in the grip of strong emotion – so it more readily might be written off in the more pejorative sense of Morrison's having favoured figurative speech over factual accuracy in representing natural phenomena. This kind of close reading, however, leads to a lot more questions than answers: does it constitute evidence of an aesthetic failure to match the character's response with the evidence presented – that is, falling short of an internal standard of coherence or "objective correlative" (and by which, according to T.S. Eliot, Shakespeare's *Hamlet* is an utter failure)?[46] Or is the production of internal discord better understood as an effective means of tripping the wire on the whole trap of mastery, what Donna Haraway calls the "god-trick" or "illusion" of objectivity that belies the situatedness of all knowledges?[47] Returning to Mignolo and Vazquez, is the

45 Morrison 2008, 10.
46 See the chapter "Hamlet and his problems" in Eliot 1921.
47 Haraway 1988.

cloven-hoofed horse another indicator of how Morrison's aestheSis challenges the colonising force of aestheTics?

In a novel dramatising the immediate effects of institutionalising racism on the shared living situation of characters variously identified as European, African and Native American, and in a time and place in which freedom was being legislated away from some for the benefit of others, it seems particularly pertinent to think carefully about the contexts conditioning received truths about humans, animals and human–animal relations, not least of which is the literary-critical history that obfuscates them through the strategy of close reading.

More than a century after rising to prominence in literary criticism, close reading persists as a foundational approach in literary classrooms. In part, this is because its methodological appeal transfers easily between schools of criticism, including such strange bedfellows as the formalist new criticism and poststructuralist deconstruction. By contrast, far reading, as a decolonial literary practice, begs reconsideration of several aspects of the emergence of close reading, troubling its persistence in ways that I see as particularly pertinent to the question of Morrison's horse's hoof.

Gaining methodological force in the early decades of the twentieth century, at a time when women, workers and people of colour were making history by earning college degrees as never before, close reading's imperative to imagine literary analysis as objective, dispassionate and detached from anything but literature itself immediately appealed to imperialist agendas. Terry Eagleton historically pinpointed in "the rise of English" at once the academic subject and language of empire to explain how the forces that legitimised teaching literature in the vernacular came to circle their wagons around a selection of literary works that strictly advanced the interests of British rule.[48] "Canon building", as Morrison quips, "is Empire building".[49]

---

48 Eagleton 1983.

49 Morrison 1994, 374. See also Christian (1994), who notes the coincidence whereby Eurowhite theorists advanced Roland Barthes' theory of the death of the author at precisely the historical juncture at which women and BIPOC writers were finding audiences worldwide on a scale never before witnessed.

Among the most prominent early supporters of close reading at that time was a group of academics known as the New Critics, whose membership significantly overlapped with a group of writers calling themselves the Southern Agrarians – including the first US poet laureate, Robert Penn Warren – who in the 1930s became the academic poster-boys for the conservative, agrarian and religious values associated with white power in the antebellum era of slavery, and whose mixed legacy remained influential in the postwar era. The New Critics' laser focus on literary works themselves might be read in this context as weaving a mantle of objectivity around a belief in literature that primarily served what effectively became a white and largely male poets' society. While close reading might not appear to be an obvious or direct tool for oppression, viewed at a distance these associations with plantation history and nostalgia for it compromise any methodological claims to neutrality. So how might a different method – that values the diverse experiences that writers and readers bring to texts – promote understanding that details which at first blush seem incoherent, might be intended and receivable instead as productive inconsistencies?

Situating *A Mercy* as a novel of the twenty-first century helps to foreground its inevitably wide-ranging influence as an imaginative intervention by one of the foremost contemporary writers of the black experience in America. It is important also to understand the novel's wondrous depiction of a portentous horse alongside the marginal yet important and precisely crafted menagerie that emerges through Morrison's fiction as a whole. I suggest further that this particular animal becomes a minor but powerful force in the making and unmaking of characters amid the history of slavery precisely because it sets the trap of mastery off the page and into the very experience of reading. However, interpreting the cloven-hoofed horse in this way requires that I address what I bring to the text, and, more specifically, why it might be that my reading and writing practices are separate from and maybe moving at productive cross-purposes with Morrison's.

As someone who has researched extensively how horse stories came to be characterised by whiteness, femininity and then violence through the twentieth century,[50] I am especially attuned to how

50 See chapter 2 of McHugh 2011.

Morrison's girl-killing equine speaks directly to contemporary anxieties about how the discourses of species enter into gendered, racialised, sexualised and other discursive constructions of settler privilege. The killing is a jarring turn of events because it upsets so many expectations about how horses enhance privilege: the victim of interspecies violence is human, Patrician; she is a minor character who finds no sentimental refuge in the cross-species encounter, let alone any access to an empowering sense of interspecies agency; and, relayed from Florens' perspective, Patrician's story becomes reduced to an object-lesson in the limits of the power and privilege of being human. All of this leads me to question the uncertainty of species identity introduced by the cloven-hoof reference that initially made me wonder about Florens' (and by extension Morrison's) grip on barnyard facts.

That interpretation is all the more plainly shaped by my early scholarly obsessions with representing and reading human–animal relationships, which in turn are hard to separate from perceptions of my own white settler privilege in having spent much of my early life on horse farms. At a distance, I have learned from others, it often is hard to see proximities to horses as not just empowering but also compromising. A theatre scholar writing about staging and performing her up-close-and-personal solo piece, *Horseback Views: A Queer Hippological Performance* (2014), Kim Marra articulates her fraught, multigenerational relationships with British Canadian female relatives and thoroughbred horses in terms of "scarring empowerment":

> My grandfather owned the racehorses but did not ride them; only the women in the family became serious riders. My grandmother suffered memory loss from head injuries incurred in falls from horses in ladies' races, yet she still encouraged her children to ride. My mother did the same for me in spite of her life-altering injury [a compound fracture from jumping off a runaway horse at age 9 that left her with a withered leg]. And when I was kicked in the face by a recalcitrant horse (not one of mine) and lost an eye at age 20, she supported me in continuing to ride and work around horses because I wanted to, and because she knew that riding would help me overcome my injury, as it had helped her.[51]

Among these stories of physical traumas, Marra's *Horseback Views* also works through her mother's homophobia, and how it led Marra away from horses and into academia, where, as she says in her opening line, "I have found it easier to come out as a lesbian than as an equestrian."[52] However, "'Mum,' as she always preferred to be called" – and translated by Marra as "British Canadian for 'Mom'"[53] – saw her queer daughter as more complexly "lost" to her, along with the horses and horse farms that she could no longer afford in her later life.[54] Echoing *A Mercy*, Marra's story of horses, women and girls drawn into dangerous proximities highlights the powers and problems of settler colonialism.

Also writing in the genre of queer personal criticism, Elspeth Probyn identifies in *Outside Belongings* (1996) that a major difficulty for taking human–horse relationships seriously is the concept of English or "British horsiness", which for so long has operated as both motive and mechanism of ethnic, racial and class exploitation, with consequences not only for the subsequent cultural devaluation of equine subjects but also for "British colonisation (of lands and girls)".[55] Her childhood memories of the thrills and chills that followed from her Canadian mother's scrappier realisation of her dreams of "the upper class hunts of the south of England"[56] resonate deeply with my own past experiences with people seemingly psychically affirmed even as they were so often materially and otherwise hurt for it – people who almost always were Eurowhite women and girls building lives with, then without, horses.

Although my admittedly brief surveys of Morrison's other writing and biographical accounts of her life have yielded little evidence that she, like me, elected to spend a lot of time with the kinds of animals that she wrote about,[57] her equine girl-killer in *A Mercy* resonates deeply with my sense of horses as anything but vehicles of mastery. This is likely because my experience of the actuality of non-masterful

---

51 Marra 2012, 503. For the full text of the performance, see Marra 2014.
52 Marra 2012, 489.
53 Marra 2014, 116.
54 Marra 2012, 493.
55 Probyn 1996, 55.
56 Probyn 1996, 39.
57 For a rare biographical account of Morrison's sometime affinity for wild birds, see Guzmán 2020.

horse-knowing connects deeply with the catachrestic portrayal in *A Mercy*. To return to Singh's analysis, the weirdly cloven-hoofed horse asserts instead "a promise of stalling mastery", whether in the story for Florens' owner, whose plantation-master legacy is forestalled by the deadly kick, or around it for the writer and her readers, "whose position[s] in relation to the 'natural' world remain haunted by both the force of Enlightenment thought and those other 'conceptions' of subjectivity that it has repressed".[58]

The foregoing belaboured attention to the seeming physiological error in *A Mercy* thus opens out to questions about literary and critical practices as negotiations of authoritative understandings of humans and other animals. Animal studies scholarship abundantly clarifies that attunement to knowledges of non-human life is never neutral, so I would not want to claim that interpretation is ever a matter of "just the facts" of internal coherence regarding non-human life in literary fiction. Rather, it suffices the needs of far reading just to ponder how my initial confusion at Morrison's cloven-hoofed horse marks different ways of knowing the world in its complexities that can emerge through histories and experiences of human–animal proximities. With the help of all the critics cited above and more, I have come to appreciate that it is not despite but precisely because of those differences that I learn so much about the potentials for identifying as well as disidentifying with animals from reading Morrison's work.

Gaining distance from Weheliye's and Wolfe's contested readings, Morrison's animals are inspiring critical reflection on the complicated ways in which the discourses of race and species intersect in her storyworlds. While respecting their differences, Bennett, Jackson and Snaza together persuade me that Morrison's writing requires critics to reckon with the imbrication of these discourses. But I want to clarify that my point is not about reading for critical winners or textual mistakes: the purpose of far reading is to reckon with why there inevitably needs to be different and conflicting answers to Christian's question: For whom are we doing what we are doing when we do literary criticism? Paying close attention to distancing details, that is, the particularities that do and do not resonate with direct or textual

58 Singh 2018, 161.

experiences with the more-than-human world, is a practice that follows from acknowledging how different privileges and interests – also even lack thereof – shape the foregoing examples of how Morrison's novels are read as profound and lasting critiques of settler colonialism. Attending to the humans, animals and human–animal relations in and around literary texts can position us to appreciate the multiplicity of contexts through which we come to perceive what and who we value in literary texts, and clue us in to how often we do so in proximity to – and ideally not at the expense of – so many others. Far reading thus offers a way of decolonising animals and – or rather, as – ourselves.

References

Armstrong, Philip (2004). "Leviathan is a skein of networks": translating nature and culture in *Moby-Dick*. *ELH* 71(1): 1039–63.

Bennett, Joshua (2020). *Being Property Once Myself: Blackness and the End of Man*. Cambridge: Harvard University Press.

Christian, Barbara (1994). The race for theory. In Angelyn Mitchel, ed. *Within the Circle: An Anthology of African American Criticism from the Harlem Renaissance to the Present*, 348–59. Durham, NC: Duke University Press.

Copeland, Marion (1983). *Black Elk Speaks* and Leslie Silko's *Ceremony*: two visions of horses. *Critique* 24(3): 158–72.

Crenshaw, Kimberlé (1989). Demarginalising the intersection of race and sex. *University of Chicago Legal Forum* 1: 139–67. http://bit.ly/3Il8Y6m.

Eagleton, Terry (1983). *Literary Theory: An Introduction*. London: Blackwell.

Eliot, T.S. (1921). *The Sacred Wood*. New York: Knopf. https://www.bartleby.com/200/sw9.html.

González, Susana Vega (2000). Broken wings of freedom: bird imagery in Toni Morrison's novels. *Révista de Éstudios Norteamericanos* 7: 75–84.

Guzmán, Sandra (2020). Remembering Toni Morrison, the bird whisperer. *Audubon Magazine*, 5 August. http://bit.ly/3EOA6J5.

Haraway, Donna (1988). Situated knowledges: the science question in feminism and the privilege of partial perspective. *Feminist Studies* 14(3): 575–99.

Hartman, Saidiya (1997). *Scenes of Subjection: Terror, Slavery, and Self-making Nineteenth-century America*. Oxford: Oxford University Press.

Jackson, Zakiyyah Iman (2020). *Becoming Human: Matter and Meaning in an Antiblack World*. New York: New York University Press.

Kang, Nancy (2003). To love and be loved: considering black masculinity and the misandric impulse in Toni Morrison's *Beloved. Callaloo* 26(3): 836–54.

Marra, Kim (2014). Horseback views: a queer hippological performance. In Una Chaudhuri and Holly Hughes, eds. *Animal Acts: Performing Species Today*, 111–30. Ann Arbor: University of Michigan Press.

Marra, Kim (2012). Riding, scarring, knowing: a queerly embodied performance historiography. *Theatre Journal* 64(4): 489–511.

McHugh, Susan (2019). *Love in a Time of Slaughters: Human-Animal Stories against Extinction and Genocide*. University Park: Pennsylvania State University Press.

McHugh, Susan (2011). *Animal Stories: Narrating across Species Lines.* Minneapolis: University of Minnesota Press.

McKay, Robert Ralston (2001). Getting close to animals with Alice Walker's *The Temple of My Familiar. Society & Animals* 9(3): 253–71.

Mignolo, Walter and Rolando Vazquez (2013). Decolonial aestheSis: colonial wounds/decolonial healings, *Social Text Online*, 15 July. https://socialtextjournal.org/periscope_article/decolonial-aesthesis-colonial-woundsdecolonial-healings/.

Morrison, Toni (2008). *A Mercy*. New York: Knopf.

Morrison, Toni (1994). Unspeakable things unspoken: the Afro-American presence in American literature. In Angelyn Mitchel, ed. *Within the Circle: An Anthology of African American Criticism from the Harlem Renaissance to the Present*, 368–98. Durham, NC: Duke University Press.

Morrison, Toni (1992). *Playing in the Dark: Whiteness and the Literary Imagination*. Cambridge: Harvard University Press.

Morrison, Toni (1987). *Beloved.* New York: Knopf.

Morrison, Toni (1977). *Song of Solomon.* New York: Knopf.

Probyn, Elspeth (1996). *Outside Belongings.* New York: Routledge.

Ransom, John Crowe (1937). Criticism, inc. *VQR* (Autumn). https://www.vqronline.org/essay/criticism-inc-0.

Ruetenik, Tadd (2010). Animal liberation or human redemption: racism and speciesism in Toni Morrison's *Beloved. ISLE: Interdisciplinary Studies in Literature and the Environment* 17(2): 317–26.

Singh, Julietta (2018). *Unthinking Mastery: Dehumanism and Decolonial Entanglements.* Durham, NC: Duke University Press.

Snaza, Nathan (2019). *Animate Literacies: Literature, Affect, and the Politics of Humanism*. Durham, NC: Duke University Press.

Tiffin, Helen (2001). Unjust relations: animals, the species boundary, and postcolonialism. In Greg Ratcliffe and Gerry Turcotte, eds. *Compr(om)ising*

Postcolonialism(s): Challenging Narratives and Practices, 30–41. Sydney: Dangaroo Press.

Tuan, Yi-Fu (1991). Language and the making of place: a narrative-descriptive approach. *Annals of the Association of American Geographers* 81(4): 684–96.

Tuan, Yi-Fu (1984). *Dominance and Affection: The Making of Pets*. New Haven: Yale University Press.

Vizenor, Gerald (1988). *Fugitive Poses: Native American Scenes of Absence and Presence*. Norman: University of Oklahoma Press.

Weheliye, Alexander (2014). *Habeas Viscus: Racializing Assemblages, Biopolitics, and Black Feminist Theories of the Human*. Durham, NC: Duke University Press.

Weinstein, Philip M. (1996). Mister: the drama of black manhood in Faulkner and Morrison. *Faulkner and Gender* 1994: 272–96.

Wolfe, Cary (2003). *Animal Rites: American Culture, the Discourse of Species, and Posthumanist Theory*. Chicago: University of Chicago Press.

Wynter, Sylvia (2003). Unsettling the coloniality of being/power/truth/freedom: towards the human, after Man, its overrepresentation – an argument. *CR: The New Centennial Review* 3(3): 257–337.

4

Mass extinction and responsibility

Katarina Gray-Sharp

1. Te oha

Ripiripia! Haehae!
Ripiripia! Haehae!
Tuakina!
Paranitia te ūpoko o te ngārara kaitangata!

Ue hā

He aha te tohu o te ringaringa?
He kawakawa
Tuku ki raro ki a hope rā
He korokio
Ko te whakatau o te mate

Ue hā
Ue hā.

Anei rā te mihi i whakawhiti mai Te Moana Tāpokopoko a Tāwhaki hei pōhutuhutu i ngā wai o Te Pāpaka a Maui. E ngā kiri gadi, kiri gurgi, kiri waratah, tēnā kautau. Huri noa ki ngāi mōrehu kua tae pākoro mai: e tau rā ki te māhau nei. Ko te roimata, ko te aroha, ko rāua rāua. E ngā kōhengi o te rangi, e ngā peka o ngā tūpuna awa, tēnā kautau tātau katoa.

I was raised on the hills and speak the language of my paternal grandfather's People, Ngāti Rangi. As an adult, I made home by a stream of my maternal grandfather's People, Ngāti Kauwhata. I have grown life in these places, mourned death in these places. To live as tangata whenua – the human form of land – is to know identity is a responsibility for another.

Such calls me to recognise this chapter as travelling far from source to its publication site at the University of Sydney. It crosses Te Moana Tāpokopoko a Tāwhaki (known by some as the "Tasman Sea") to splash in the waters of Te Pāpaka a Maui (oft-called "Australia"). Hence, I acknowledge the Gadigal People of the Eora Nation as custodians of that unceded place, where my thoughts become marks on a page. You are the People who stand like epidermides (kiri) to the gadi,[1] gurgi (rarauhe)[2] and waratah.[3,4] I thank you for continuing to give voice to the land and for hosting my words.

This chapter is based on a conceptual and methodological inquiry into my responsibility in the face of mass extinction.[5] Following its foundation in Māori and Indigenous studies, the work proffers various ways of researching the structure of anthropogenic mass extinction. The techniques presented here include scientific, etymological and conceptual analyses. Such an approach prioritises ethics: to affirm life and support survival, all methods will be considered.

The chapter is in four main sections. In the first section, a replication study of the 2015 study by Gerardo Ceballos, Paul R. Ehrlich and others is presented using 2018 data.[6] The replication study, like the research on which it is based, confirms the continuation of the anthropogenic mass extinction. While such confirmation is not

1 *Xanthorrhoea* spp.
2 *Pteridium esculentum*.
3 *Telopea* spp.
4 Troy 1994; 2019.
5 Gray-Sharp 2021.
6 Ceballos, Ehrlich et al. 2015a; 2015b.

determinative, acknowledgement of both the phenomenon and our position in a web of connections provokes responsibility. The etymology of responsibility as an agential construct is considered in the second section. In the third, mātauranga Māori is applied as a tool for thinking to reveal mass extinction as a structural violence. In the final section, suggestions are made for a non-agential responsibility fed by the place where mātauranga Māori and Levinasian ethics meet.

2. Mass extinction

According to Chris Park and Michael Allaby, extinction is the "permanent disappearance of a species throughout its entire range, caused by the failure to reproduce and the death of all remaining members".[7] In a related sense, Robert Hine and Elizabeth Martin define extinction as the "irreversible condition of a species or other group of organisms having no living representatives in the wild, which follows the death of the last surviving individual of that species or group".[8] An expected phenomenon, taxons are classed as "Extinct when there is no reasonable doubt that the last individual has died".[9] Due to data "uncertainties", extinctions are quantified as fractions versus "absolute numbers".[10] For example, there is an accepted background rate of between 0.1 and 1 extinctions per million species-years (0.1–1 E/MSY).[11] This means that at the higher rate, if there were one million species, one species would become extinct each year as a normal part of the evolutionary process.

Mass extinctions are extinctions of the greatest magnitude, occurring "when many diverse groups of organisms become extinct over short periods of time".[12] In November 2017, 15,372 scientists declared a consensus:

7 Park and Allaby 2017c.
8 Hine and Martin 2015, para. 1.
9 International Union for Conservation of Nature and Natural Resources, Species Survival Commission 2012, 14.
10 Pimm, Jenkins et al. 2014, 1246752-1.
11 Ceballos, Ehrlich et al. 2015a; Lamkin and Miller 2016.
12 Condie 2011, 250.

- mass extinctions have occurred at least five times in the past;
- a sixth mass extinction has begun;
- humans are the cause of the latest episode.[13]

However, "the oft-repeated claim that Earth's biota is entering a sixth 'mass extinction' depends on clearly demonstrating current extinction rates are far above the 'background' rates".[14]

The research team led by Ceballos and Ehrlich gathered 2014 data from the International Union for Conservation of Nature and Natural Resources (IUCN).[15] The IUCN Red List of Threatened Species is "a checklist of taxa that have undergone an extinction risk assessment using the IUCN Red List Categories and Criteria".[16] It does not cover the whole tree of life, only a sample. Currently, the Red List hosts data on species from four kingdoms: Fungi, Plantae, Animalia and Chromista. The IUCN classifies evaluated species with adequate data into extinction risk categories from Least Concern to Extinct.[17]

Ceballos and Ehrlich's team developed current extinction rates for five Chordata (or vertebrate) groups: mammals, birds, reptiles, amphibians and fishes.[18] As indicated in Table 4.1, the authors present two current extinction rates based on IUCN categories. The "highly conservative rate" (shown in the table shaded in grey) only includes species that have been categorised by the IUCN[19] as Extinct.[20] The "conservative" or combined rate (shown in the table in white) includes

13 Ripple, Wolf et al. 2017.

14 Biota are "all of the living organisms (including animals, plants, fungi, and micro-organisms) that are found in a particular area", in this case Earth (Park and Allaby 2017a). Ceballos, Ehrlich et al. 2015a, 1.

15 Ceballos, Ehrlich et al. 2015b.

16 International Union for Conservation of Nature and Natural Resources 2019, para. 1.

17 International Union for Conservation of Nature and Natural Resources Species Survival Commission 2012.

18 Like "mammals" is the plural of mammal species, "fishes" is the plural of fish species. Ceballos, Ehrlich et al. 2015a.

19 International Union for Conservation of Nature and Natural Resources 2018.

20 Ceballos, Ehrlich et al. 2015a, 2.

Table 4.1 Comparison of extinct only and combined extinction rates

	Ceballos, Ehrlich et al. (2015)	**Gray-Sharp (2021)**
Extinct only	Extinct (EX)	Extinct (EX)
Combined	Extinct (EX)	Extinct (EX)
	Extinct in the Wild (EW)	Extinct in the Wild (EW)
	Critically Endangered – Possibly Extinct (PE)	Critically Endangered – Possibly Extinct (CR[PE])
		Critically Endangered – Possibly Extinct in the Wild (CR[PEW])

these extinct species alongside species declared Extinct in the Wild[21] and a "subcategory of Critically Endangered", the Possibly Extinct.[22]

2.1 Method

I collected data for the same taxonomic groups as Ceballos and Ehrlich[23] for all publication years available in 2018 (including 2015, 2016, 2017 and 2018) from the IUCN website. I also collected unspecified data for all listed taxonomic groups, including invertebrates and plants. Like Ceballos and Ehrlich's group,[24] I collected for two rates. The first was under the assessment category Extinct. The second was for a combined rate. Due to a change in IUCN categories between 2014 and 2018, my combined rate includes two new Critically Endangered subcategories: Critically Endangered (Possibly Extinct) and Critically Endangered (Possibly Extinct in the Wild).

21 Ceballos, Ehrlich et al. 2015a, 2.
22 Ceballos, Ehrlich et al. 2015a, 2; 2015b, 1.
23 Ceballos, Ehrlich et al. 2015a.
24 Ceballos, Ehrlich et al. 2015a; 2015b.

I analysed all data following the method outlined in Ceballos, Ehrlich et al.[25] Although other methods are available,[26] I found none as clear in their description. I expressed the method as an equation:

$$\textit{current rate} = \frac{\textit{observed extinctions}}{\left(\frac{\textit{number of evaluated species}}{10{,}000}\right) \mathbf{x} \left(\textit{background rate x number of centuries}\right)}$$

It includes the same background rate used by the authors. That rate is the higher, mammalian background extinction rate rounded upward to two extinctions per 10,000 species per century[27] (or 2 E/MSY).[28] This rate reflects the taxa under study and allows for "a more conservative assessment of differences between current and past extinction rates for the vertebrates as a whole".[29] A simplified version of the equation might be expressed as:

$$G = F / \left(\frac{x}{10{,}000}BC\right)$$

25 Ceballos, Ehrlich et al. 2015b.
26 Pimm, Jenkins et al. 2014
27 From 1.8 E/MSY.
28 Ceballos, Ehrlich et al. 2015a, 2.
29 Ceballos, Ehrlich et al. 2015a, 2.

Table 4.2 Comparing background and current extinction rates (2018)

	[x]	[A]	[B]	[C]	[D]	[E]	[F]	[G]
Taxonomic Group	Number of IUCN Evaluated Species	Species 10,000	Background Extinction of 2 E/MSY	Centuries since 1500	Expected Background Extinctions (BxC)	Expected Extinctions since 1500 (AxD)	Observed extinctions	Extinction Rates relative to Expected (F/E)
Mammals	5677	0.57	2	5.18	10.36	5.88	81	13.77
Birds	11,122	1.11	2	5.18	10.36	11.52	156	13.54
Reptiles	6669	0.67	2	5.18	10.36	6.91	28	4.05
Amphibians	6682	0.67	2	5.18	10.36	6.92	32	4.62
Fishes	16,406	1.64	2	5.18	10.36	17	64	3.77
Vertebrates	**46,556**	**4.66**	**2**	**5.18**	**10.36**	**48.23**	**361**	**7.48**
All Taxonomic Groups	93,577	9.36	2	5.18	10.36	96.95	872	8.99

2.2 Results

Table 4.2 shows the equation in application for vertebrates that have been categorised by the IUCN as Extinct across all publication years available in 2018. On the left are the taxonomic groups. Column [x] is the number of evaluated species. Column [A] shows that number in a per 10,000 species per century ratio. For example, the total number of vertebrates is divided by 10,000 for a rounded ratio of 4.66. Column [B] is the rounded mammalian background extinction rate of 2.0, and [C] is the number of centuries since 1500. Columns [B] and [C] are multiplied to provide the expected background rate for the given timeframe as shown in Column [D]. Columns [A] and [D] are multiplied to render the expected extinctions since 1500 shown in Column [E]. For vertebrates, this number is 48.23. Column [F] lists the actual observed extinctions. In the case of vertebrates, that is 361. When the observed extinctions of [F] are divided by the expected of [E], the extinction rate is the quotient. When the observed extinctions of [F] are divided by the expected of [E], the extinction rate is the result (or quotient). For vertebrates, the quotient is 7.48. For all taxonomic groups, the quotient is 8.99.

Figure 4.1 compares the 2014 and 2018 results for vertebrates classified as Extinct. The black arrow indicates the background mammalian extinction rate of 2.0. My analysis of the 2014 data finds a current rate for Extinct-only vertebrates of 8.38. The 2018 data suggests a fall to 7.48. This is still higher than the background rate. The report does not improve when classes are considered. As the most highly studied animal groups, mammals and birds continue to lose ground in the Extinct-only rates. The improvement in fishes' extinction rate is likely due to an increase of almost 4,000 evaluated species.

Figure 4.2 displays both extinct-only and combined rates of extinction. The black arrow indicates the background mammalian extinction rate of 2.0. The off-black bar shows the 2014 rate of extinction for all vertebrates classified as Extinct, Extinct in the Wild, and Possibly Extinct. At 14.86, it compares positively with the 2018 combined data (to the right in light-grey) of 14.20. I draw your

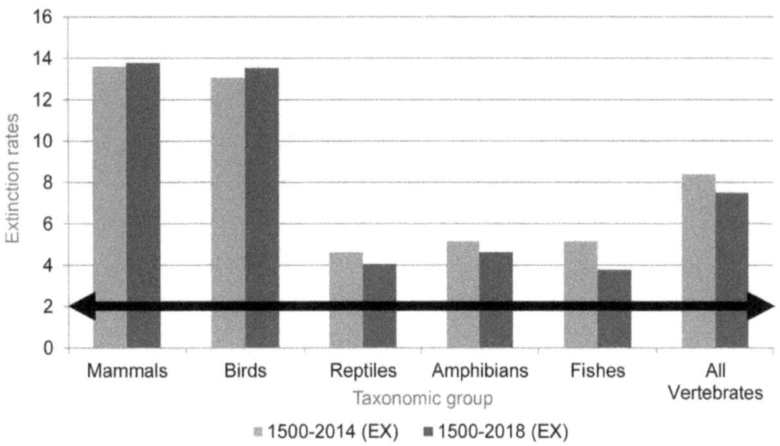

Figure 4.1 Comparison of extinct-only and combined rates (2014 and 2018)

attention to the tallest bars in this figure. Although their Extinct-only assessments are lower, amphibians appear the most at risk. The combined category extinction rate for amphibians was 22.14 in 2014. In 2018, it was 23.40. In summary, the current rates range between 1.9 and 11.7 times higher than the background rate of two extinctions per million species-years. The results confirm the continuation of the current mass extinction.

2.3 Discussion

There were differences between my results and those of Ceballos and Ehrlich's group.[30] My analysis of the data provided by the authors in the supplementary material produces a lower number of observed extinctions for 2014 in the Extinct in the Wild and Possibly Extinct categories. I found 18 fewer vertebrate species: 4 mammals, 5 birds, 1 reptile, 2 amphibians and 6 fishes. Hence, my 2014 calculated rate of current extinction in the combined categories for mammals is 18.88

30 Gray-Sharp 2021.

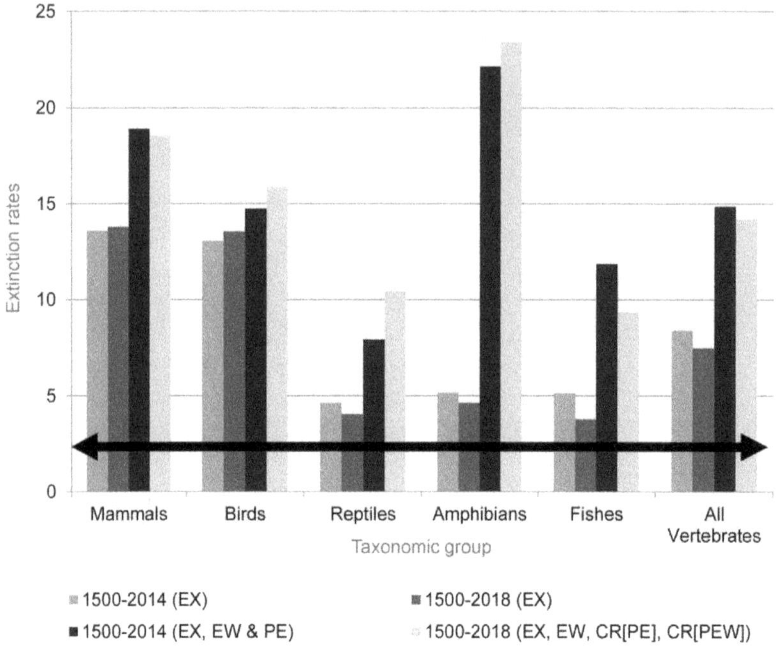

Figure 4.2 Results for extinct-only and combined categories (2014 and 2018)

versus the original 19.59. I outline this and other differences in my thesis.[31]

The current extinction rate is accepted in the literature as a range between 100 and 1,000 times greater than the background rate.[32] That range is calculated on a much lower background rate than my replication study and the paper upon which it is based.[33] Both these results show a range at least 10 times lower than that given in the literature. Nevertheless, "an exceptionally rapid loss of biodiversity" is still revealed, "indicating that a sixth mass extinction is already under way".[34]

31 Ceballos, Ehrlich et al. 2015a; 2015b.
32 Lamkin and Miller 2016; Pimm, Jenkins et al. 2014.
33 Ceballos, Ehrlich et al. 2015a.

Such revelation, in itself, is not determinative; subsequent action has multiple influences. As tangata whenua (people of the land), for example, a whakapapa[35] construction of identity provokes us to respond. Frequently glossed over as "genealogy",[36] whakapapa is relational, "inherently non-hierarchical in structure and purpose, serving to link all facets of creation in a complex web that extends in all directions and into infinity".[37] It provides for multiple paths, whether scientific or otherwise. Epistemologically, whakapapa can be seen as "a way of thinking, a way of learning, a way of storing knowledge and a way of debating knowledge".[38] As such, it is "an analytical tool that … is both vehicle and expression of mātauranga Māori".[39]

Whakapapa gifts us with identity. This identity is sourced and sent elsewhere, offering a means for fulfilling our obligations to those with whom we share the world. In the acknowledgement of our position in a web of connections rebuilt daily, we act as responsible subjects.

3. Historicising responsibility

The development and divergence of specific concepts (including the production and reproduction of associated terms and predicates) can influence subsequent action. For example, I have found differences of opinion between some members of the ecological and palaeontological communities over the existence of the anthropogenic extinction. Both groups accept evidence of a process, that "current [extinction] *rates* would produce Big-Five-magnitude mass extinctions in the same amount of geological time that we think most Big Five extinctions spanned".[40] However, palaeontological metrics require a sixth mass

34 Ceballos, Ehrlich et al. 2015a, 1.

35 "Whakapapa" can mean "to place upon one upon another, as a stack of boards" (Williams 1852, 212), to "lie flat" or "place in layers" (Williams 1957, 259). As Ani Mikaere states, "The word 'whakapapa' literally means to build one layer upon another" (Mikaere 2010, para. 24).

36 Smith 1999, 181; Te Aho 2007, 10.

37 Mikaere 2010, para. 24.

38 Mead 1996, 210.

39 Pihama 2015, 8; see section 4 of this chapter.

extinction to "approach … Big Five mass extinction *levels*, which are characterized by an estimated 75–96% loss of known species".[41]

Though both metrics are comparative, those who predicate mass extinction on *rates* (a metric for measuring speed or frequency of change) identify a current phenomenon. Those who predicate mass extinction on *levels* (a metric that states a particular variable's value at a certain point) perceive an impending disaster. How an idea is defined, how the words that name it are elected, have impact. This section considers the definition and etymology of a different term: responsibility.

3.1 Definitions

Responsibility is related to the Proto-Indo European etymon **spend-*, meaning execution of ritual[42] and offering.[43] Such acts can be seen in the ceremonies of libation, where one remembers the dead in the pouring of drink. Current conceptions of responsibility reflect this promise of respectful conduct while emphasising agency.

According to the *Oxford Dictionary of English*, responsibility has two definitions that are relational and one that is agential.[44] First, responsibility is defined as a duty or an obligation for something. Second, responsibility is "the state or fact of being accountable or to blame for something".[45] Third, it is a characteristic of agency, an "opportunity or ability to act independently".[46]

Agency is "the degree to which a subject is able to determine the course of their own actions".[47] Agency is posed conceptually in opposition to structures that may affect that degree, such as the institutions of democracy, heterosexuality and paid employment. In

40 Barnosky, Matzke et al. 2011, 55 [author's emphasis].
41 Barnosky 2014, 160 [author's emphasis].
42 Harper 2020c. All Proto-Indo European (PIE) etyma begin with an asterisk to indicate the (re)constructed nature of the language.
43 Linguistics Research Centre 2014.
44 Stevenson 2015a.
45 Stevenson 2015a.
46 Stevenson 2015a.
47 Buchanan 2018.

this third definition of responsibility, the agent has the possibility or capacity for autonomous action. Indeed, an agent is characterised by the degree to which this is true.

Adjectives can be added to further elucidate responsibility as a term. For instance, a person has *causal* responsibility if they were the direct or indirect cause of something. *Legal* responsibility is an "accountability under the law", as either a legal obligation or a penalty for an offence.[48] *Moral* responsibility links two notions: "(i) the having of a moral obligation and (ii) the fulfilment of the criteria for deserving blame or praise (punishment or reward) for a morally significant act or omission".[49] *Role* responsibility is likely the most practically significant in its articulation of duties. For example, "a job, or profession, or social role will be partly defined in terms of the responsibilities it involves".[50]

While the legal and moral elucidations host a relational form, all four conceptions offer opportunity to choose and are, therefore, agential. Responsibility thusly posed is "a feature of agency" that at times is "used to denote an action or sphere of action which is part of someone's duty".[51] It is an expression of individuality, liberty and self-rule. However, this interpretation of responsibility is a construct of particular circumstances.

3.2 Etymology

Responsibility is a noun derived from the adjective "responsible".[52] Like its derivative, "responsible" is about obligation, answerability, blame, credit and duty.[53] It has no equivalent in Old English. The term did not arrive in the language until the 1590s, as "answerable", via the Latin and French.[54]

48 Klein 2005, para. 1.
49 Klein 2005, para. 2.
50 Blackburn 2016.
51 Scruton 2007, para. 1–2.
52 Harper 2020a.
53 Stevenson 2015b.
54 Harper 2020b.

The Latin sources contain elements present in later reflexes. They begin with *sponsis* (meaning "an ancient formula of prayer") and *spondĕo* meaning "in bargains, covenants, treaties, etc, *to promise solemnly* … [or] *to promise* for another, *to become security* for a person".[55] With the addition of the prefix "re-" (back), the verb *rē-spondĕo* is "*to promise* a thing *in return* for something else; *to offer* or *present in return*".[56] Its present active infinitive, *respondēre*, appears as the point when responsibility attained legal ramifications, specifically in the development of common law and judicial hierarchies.

Respondēre was an instrument of law development, interpretation and comment that operated for over 600 years, from the Roman Republic through to the rule of Emperor Hadrian.[57] There was a custom in the Republic of pontiff magistrates giving legal rulings as an act of service.[58] Seeking stability, Emperor Augustus and the early Principate maintained the custom as *responsa prudentium*, opinions given without remuneration by jurists to those seeking interpretations of law.[59] *Ius respondendi* was the right granted to favoured jurists by Augustus to give *responsa* "by special Imperial authority or patent".[60] Later systemic amendments added qualification of expertise and remuneration. The change in responsibility from a reciprocal arrangement to a legal one can be understood in terms of Roman bureaucracy. The legal aspect was reinforced and its structures redesigned as a consequence of the French influence on English.

French began as a dialect of Latin. Attested as distinct from the ninth century, Old French was a literate language within 200 years.[61] The adoption of responsibility's legal sense from Latin is evidenced within 500 years. The noun *responsaule* (meaning a type of vassal in the feudal system, the man who must pay in perpetuity a lord the rent of an ecclesiastical fief[62]) is attested from 1284 and the adjective *responsable* (meaning who answers, who is guarantor[63]) from 1304.[64] The adjective

55 Lewis and Short 1891, 1745.
56 Lewis and Short 1891, 1581.
57 Chroust 1955, 547.
58 Berger 1953, 681; Chroust 1955, 554.
59 Berger 1953, 681.
60 Chroust 1955, 542.
61 Matthews 2014.

indicates an ability to respond (as in "response-able") and has been defined as "responsive responding, corresponding".[65]

Its first appearance in English, in the late sixteenth century, as "'answerable' (to another, for something)" indicates a shift from a promise to an imperative.[66] Moral judgement is attested from 1766 with a letter to the Third Duke of Grafton, Augustus FitzRoy, from the exiled Member of Parliament John Wilkes. Republished the following year, it concerns Grafton's message that Wilkes should contact the Earl of Chatham and Lord Privy Seal William Pitt. Wilkes' response declares Chatham's new office (functionally that of Prime Minister) "neither important, nor responsible".[67]

Unlike "responsible", "responsibility" first appears as a term in Late Modern English. Though attested from 1787 as the "condition of being responsible",[68] an agential rendering appeared a few years earlier "with regard to the degree of responsibility belonging to the offices of cashier and accountant".[69] Agency is even clearer in the translated 1793 declaration of vicomte de la Platière and French Minister of Interior Jean-Marie Roland. On 21 January, Louis XVI of France was executed. Two days later, Roland stated:

> I have done my duty, and I will not shrink from the responsibility attached to the deliberations in which I have taken part: but I declare, that I will not sign the general account of the state of the nation, to be presented by the executive council on the 1st of February.[70]

62 "Subst. *responsaule* «homme ayant la charge à vie de payer à un seigneur la rente d'un fief ecclésiastique»" (Centre National de la Recherche Scientifique 2012 – author's translation).
63 "*Responsable* adj. «qui répond, qui est garant»" (Centre National de la Recherche Scientifique 2012 – Google Translate).
64 Centre National de la Recherche Scientifique 2012 – translated.
65 Hoad 2003.
66 Harper 2020b.
67 Wilkes 1767, 165.
68 Harper 2020a.
69 Parliamentary History, 1783, 287.
70 Affairs of France, 1793, 129.

He resigned instead. The translation of Roland's declaration may be interpreted as an example of a political origin for responsibility. As Garrath Williams states, "in all modern European languages, 'responsibility' only finds a home toward the end of the eighteenth century ... within debates about representative government".[71] However, in the translation of Roland's words the seeds of contemporary conceptions can also be seen.

Roland accepts the promise he has made as representative: he fulfils his legal, moral and role responsibilities. The promise is refined in the translation through a claim to autonomous action and free will ("I will not shrink from the responsibility"). His resignation is an example of rational action, which is defined by Bauman as "guided by motives and purposes, amenable in principle to conscious scrutiny and correction" and consisting of "decision-making and choice".[72] That claim to autonomy and rational action expresses the "revolution taking place in the European mentality ... the new feeling of self-reliance and self-assurance, readiness to seek and try unorthodox solutions to any current trouble and worry, belief in the ascending tendency of human history and growing trust in the capacity of human reason".[73] Roland's translator is presenting a completely modern conception of responsibility.

Current agential conceptions of responsibility likewise reproduce this tendency towards individual freedom and rationality. The move from a spiritual to a legalistic interpretation reflected the expansion of bureaucracy in the Roman Empire's colonial project.[74] Equally, the emphasis on agency in current definitions reflects the norms of modernity. Hence, responsibility mediates "the development of a new fabric of selfhood rooted in concepts of individuality, autonomy, and freedom".[75] It allows the site of control to be localised. As such, it becomes mātauranga, something that can (but need not) rest in me.

71 Williams 2009, para. 4.
72 Bauman 2004, para. 12.
73 Bauman 2004, para. 3.
74 Berger 1953; Chroust 1955.
75 Calhoun 2002.

4. Mātauranga Māori: a tool for thinking

According to Linda Tuhiwai Smith,

> decolonisation is a process which engages with imperialism and colonialism at multiple levels. For researchers, one of those levels is concerned with having a more critical understanding of the underlying assumptions, motivations and values which inform research practices.[76]

I approach research aware that the solutions I pose must reclaim history, must "centr[e] our concerns and world views" as Indigenous peoples so that we may develop our own theoretical and research approaches "for our own purposes".[77] An "explicit, codified and externalised" form of knowledge, mātauranga, offers an initial basis for this approach.[78]

Mātauranga is a transferable, active structure that sometimes takes the form of a "wise and knowledgeable person".[79] Mātau means "know … understand … be certain of", the suffix "-tanga" deriving a noun.[80] It is shared knowledge, "'ma' and 'tau' … said to be attained when it is held or comes to rest within us".[81] An example of mātauranga is the replication study in the second section of this chapter.

When an inherited erudition, it is *mātauranga Māori*. Such "responds to the three great questions of life, namely: Who am I? What is this world that I exist in? What am I to do?"[82] However, mātauranga Māori "is not like an archive of information but rather is like a tool for thinking, organising information, considering the ethics of knowledge, the appropriateness of it all and informing us about our world and our place in it".[83] An example of mātauranga Māori are the responses that arise from that calculation.

---

76 Smith 1999, 20.
77 Smith 1999, 39.
78 Royal 2005, 137.
79 Royal 2005, 139.
80 Williams 1957, 191.
81 Smith 2015, 51.
82 Royal 2012, 35.
83 Mead 2003, 306.

4.1 Mātauranga Māori and extinction

Mātauranga Māori offers a perspective on extinction. William Williams lists a number of verbs in the reo (Māori language) for extinction as it relates to fire: "*kétokéto*", "*kéwa*",[84] "*ngio*"[85] and "*weróku*".[86] Closer to the contemporary meaning is the concept of "**whare ngaro**" (literally, hidden house), where genealogical lines are without offspring and "become extinct".[87]

Tikanga is "responsibility; those rules, which demarcate what is correct to a specific context".[88] Such exists for the prevention of extinction among humans, including child-rearing by others (whāngai or taurima) and re-partnering for barren pairs (punarua). Among the People of Ngātokowaru, a place of our female line west of Punahau (Lake Horowhenua), the actions of Te Whatanui towards Muaūpoko may be considered another strategy.[89] Extinction is constructed as a preventable state.

Like People in other places, my father's People of Whanganui have an idiom ("pērā ki te moa") for the idea that something has become extinct "like the moa".[90] Indeed, the moa[91] has become the extinct version of the "kiwi",[92] mourned at international conservation events to affirm nationhood.[93] This is because, when compared to others, the moa's life is constructed as grievable.[94]

For example, the team of Priscilla Wehi and Murray Cox displays the predominance of moa in ancestral proverbs (whakataukī) via a figure comparing the number of whakataukī with the number of

84 Williams 1852, 47.
85 Williams 1852, 95.
86 Williams 1852, 199.
87 Williams 1957, 489 (bold in original).
88 Gray-Sharp 2021, 57.
89 Ballara 1990; Kernot 1981.
90 Mead and Grove 2003, 286; Te Iwi Māori o te Rawhiti 1874, 267; Wikiriwhi 1955, 41.
91 Order Dinornithiformes.
92 *Apteryx* spp.
93 Young 1983.
94 Butler 2003.

archaeological sites evidence found.[95] A note to the figure states: "Birds represented in blue (i.e. moa and pouakai) became extinct prior to European arrival – but other extinct birds do not occur in the *whakataukī* and are thus not shown."[96]

A review of supplementary evidence shows six other extinct avifauna with proverbial reference.[97] All are represented in the figure like the extant species (for example, kereru[98]). Whakataukī about these birds are not stated in the text (in most cases, the sole mention is in the figure). All birds were made extinct post-settler colonisation.

The identification of the moa as the "poster species" and "hashtag" for extinction in New Zealand has consequences.[99] It allows the timing of extinction to be isolated to a time before settler colonialism. Like a prehistoric dinosaur, the narrative of the biodiversity crisis becomes one with the past, incapable of resolution. It allows attribution of blame to pre-European social formations. Avowing Indigenous savagery is a standard strategy for Unsettler nation-building. Further, #moa confirms the role of conservation science as an archive of obituaries. It is "the means by which a life becomes, or fails to become, a publicly grievable life, an icon for national self-recognition, the means by which a life becomes noteworthy".[100]

Hence, in the #moa's shadow, the vulnerability – the very existence – of other species (extinct and extant) is made unreal. "They cannot be mourned because they are always already lost or, rather, never 'were,' and [those that survive] must be killed, since they seem to live on, stubbornly, in this state of deadness."[101] I think this is why Wehi and Cox's team could not recognise the extinction of the koreke,[102] the hakuwai,[103] the moho,[104] the piopio,[105] the whekau[106] and the huia.[107] I also think adherence to mātauranga Māori's ethical imperatives may have resulted in a different outcome.

95 Wehi, Cox et al. 2018.
96 Wehi, Cox et al. 2018, 466.
97 Wehi, Cox et al. 2018.
98 *Hemiphaga novaeseelandiae*.
99 Wehi, Whaanga and Cox 2018, para. 15.
100 Butler 2003, 23.
101 Butler 2003, 22.
102 *Coturnix novaezelandiae*.

4.2 Structuring the sixth mass extinction

As a contributor to Kaupapa Māori research,[108] I use a variety of mātauranga Māori approaches and sources in my work. For example, I conducted an exegesis on *Ripiripia* (the traditional funeral chant that opened this chapter) to help me understand a research problem.[109] Electing a waiata over other mātauranga Māori sources reflected that project's methodology, in that song embodies the creative source of all mana ("te toi o ngā mana") that is mana motuhake.[110] The exegesis of *Ripiripia* described a tool for thinking and unearthed a structure of relevance to mass extinction research.

Structure could be described as a "recurring pattern", and in social settings "the ordered interrelationships between the different elements of a social system".[111] It may appear in iterations, sedimentary layers built as a river carves a bed, carves a valley. As an "institutionalized social arrangement", a structure can appear as "the rules that underlie and create the outward features of a society; the social relations that underpin these superficial features".[112] Structure, thus, may be posed as oppositional to agency in that it can limit autonomous action.[113] As a category, structure "prioritizes the logic of relations over the logic of substance".[114] Hence, it is useful for identifying connections with neither apparent agent nor aim.

The extinction crisis can be seen as an "outward feature of [a] society" structured by the long-established dominance of humans over

---

103 Incorrectly identified as *Coenocorypha iredalei* in Table S1, the binomial for the hakuwai is stated correctly in Table S2 as *Coenocorypha barrierensis* (Wehi, Cox et al. 2018).

104 *Porphyrio mantelli*.

105 *Turnagra* spp.

106 *Sceloglaux albifacies*.

107 *Heteralocha acutirostris*. Wehi, Cox et al. 2018.

108 Pihama 2015; Royal 2012; Smith 1999.

109 See Gray-Sharp 2021.

110 Black 2000, 289.

111 Scott 2015, para. 1.

112 Kent 2007.

113 Brown, McLean and McMillan 2018.

114 Sandywell 2011, para. 2.

our non-human kin. It follows a paradigm of exceptionalism where "humans are different from all other organisms, all human behaviour is controlled by culture and free will, and all problems can be solved by human ingenuity and technology".[115] It extends to a worldview "that sees humans as the source of all value, since the concept of value itself is a human creation, and that sees nature as of value merely as a means to the ends of human beings".[116] That worldview is anthropocentrism.

In Western philosophy, this human-centredness can be traced from Protagoras' "man as measure"[117] to Aristotle's *scala naturae*[118] and hylomorphism.[119] It is classically maintained in modernity by Kantian ethics, where rationalism marks personhood "and the rest of nature [is defined] as a sphere of things devoid of intrinsic moral value or worth in themselves".[120] It can be seen in Alexandre Kojève's interpretation of Georg Wilhelm Frederich Hegel and onwards.[121]

The Darwinian revolution of 1859 was meant to abolish such anthropocentrism.[122] No longer accompanied by divinity, humankind would finally understand itself as "part of the evolutionary stream".[123] Instead, Victorian Darwinists worried that "close similarities between man and the rest of the animal world destroyed any purpose of human existence other than that which all animals have".[124] In the "survival of the fittest", "the overall purpose of existence is the necessity of reproduction. Sexuality therefore becomes the most important motivation for human behaviour."[125] The emphasis on genetics and speciation over extinction in evolutionary circles, and the impact of *Roe*

115 Park and Allaby 2017b.
116 Park and Allaby 2017a.
117 Iannone 2001.
118 Ross 1995.
119 Balz 1918.
120 French 2008, para. 7.
121 Kojève 1969.
122 Mayr 1972; see United Nations Educational, Scientific and Cultural Organization 1950, 17.
123 Mayr 1972, 988.
124 Diniejko 2010, para. 3.
125 Diniejko 2010, para. 3.

v. Wade in US society, gain additional meaning. Instead of destroying the paradigm of human exceptionalism, Darwinism birthed it anew.

4.3 The structural violence of the sixth mass extinction

In addition to being structured by human exceptionalism and anthropocentrism, the current mass extinction is a recurring pattern of relations that underpins features we experience in the everyday. By this, I tender an argument that the extinction crisis is itself a structure. Like narrative (and, in this case, language), the sixth mass extinction is "a network of interrelated units, the meaning of the parts being specifiable only with reference to the whole".[126] The untimely death of an individual,[127] the unfortunate extirpation of a population,[128] and the unexpected extinction of a species[129] are interconnected acts of a narrative. The broader meaning of these acts cannot be comprehended without reference to the structure of anthropogenic mass extinction. The crisis provides the social arrangements by which the independent units can be understood.

The narrative is one of violence. Expanding on the humanism of sociologist Johan Galtung, I recognise the sixth mass extinction as "*the cause of the difference between the potential and the actual*".[130] There is a significant gap "between what could have been and what is".[131] The *potential* rate of one (maximum) extinction per million species-years is *actually* exceeded almost nine times over. The "ultimate cause" of the disparity is human activity.[132] Our actions and inactions are a violence against our non-human kin.

I identify the sixth mass extinction as a form of structural violence. The violence is "built into the structure", in that a personal subject remains undefined.[133] Instead, the collective noun of "humanity" is

126 Crystal 2008.
127 Wilcox 2019.
128 Charlie Mitchell 2018; Wright 2011.
129 Manaaki Whenua – Landcare Research 2019.
130 Galtung 1969, 168 [emphasis in original].
131 Galtung 1969, 168.
132 Ladle and Malhado 2013, para. 2.

invoked, concealing "the vast inequalities of harm and suffering that attend global patterns of ecological rupture".[134] This is a meaningful composition in two ways.

First, "by conjuring a homogenous figure of humanity", causal responsibility is avoided.[135] Agency is no longer assigned, particularly to those who benefit from the anthropogenic drivers of "industrialization, international trade, global economic growth and resource extraction".[136] This is because agentive descriptions influence the attribution of blame and punishment, which would likely be costly. Instead, drivers are identified as "the *unintended* outcome of '*human* development'", allowing attribution to be shared equally.[137] In this case, inequality is more equitable. Of utility, a weakness is made visible: "ethical systems directed against *intended* violence will easily fail to capture structural violence in their nets".[138]

Second, the anthropogenic order that distributes the right to classify is maintained. Extinct species are not the primary object of the structure but "collateral damage". Such "collateral" is, of course, an intentional outcome, for otherwise it would be prevented. Its creation is an example to those who may resist. As may be attested by survivors of the Christchurch mass murder of 15 March 2018, the consequences of being classified as anything less than "fully human" are untenable.[139] No matter one's rank in the hierarchy of humanity, it is better to be in that hierarchy than not.

The ensuing violence is both physical and psychological. In the physical form, it lowers "somatic capacity" to the point of death.[140] Like the structural violence of mass human incarceration, it also constrains movement. Ironically, both climate change and conservation efforts (for example, reservations, captive breeding programs) disrupt the range

133 Galtung 1969, 171.
134 Audra Mitchell 2018, 6.
135 Audra Mitchell 2018, 6.
136 Audra Mitchell 2018, 5.
137 Audra Mitchell 2018, 5 [author's emphasis].
138 Galtung 1969, 172.
139 Al Jazeera 2019.
140 Galtung 1969, 169.

of various species. As psychological violence, it reduces our ability to perceive and respond to it.

The structural violence of the sixth mass extinction is both negative and positive. In the negative mode, existing populations, species and relationships are eliminated. In the positive mode, "elimination is an organizing principle … rather than a one-off (and superseded) occurrence".[141] For example, adaptation allows vulnerable populations (human and non-human) to contribute to the new relation through (for example) ecological services. Hence, mass extinction is the negation of life in order to establish and maintain exogenous domination with expropriated resources, including the bodies of the dead and the labour of their survivors.

5. A non-agential responsibility

I wish to make some suggestions towards a non-agential responsibility informed by, first, mātauranga Māori and, second, Levinasian ethics. The suggestions are made in the context of research conducted outside of the natural sciences into the current mass extinction. They are intended to be generative and protective for those who are called to the vocation of (what I term) mass extinction studies. I would like to help keep safe any researchers who are drawn in without will.

Mātauranga Māori is "an indigenous body of knowledge that arises from a worldview based upon kinship relationships between people and the natural world".[142] It offers tools for thinking about the consequences of currentextinction rates. These include exegetical analyses that make visible the episode's structural violence. Mātauranga Māori also poses questions about the ethical consequences of such knowledge. If we have evidence that our non-human kin (and, indeed, our own offspring) are being "*deprive*[d] *of life* or *strength*", what is our responsibility?[143] Levinasian ethics offers some suggestions towards answering this question.

141 Wolfe 2006, 388.

142 Royal Society Te Apārangi 2017, para. 2.

143 Lewis and Short 1891, 704 [emphasis in original].

Informed by the work of philosopher and Talmudic scholar Emmanuel Levinas, Levinasian ethics would propose a "calling-into-question of the ego" such that subjectivity "start[s] from the other", revealing a "figure … in the shape of [my] responsibility for" them.[144] This subjectivity is *a priori*, an unchosen obligation, which assumes me "before the responsibility of freedom".[145] Neither "memorisable" nor refutable, here subjectivity is not conditional on choice: "it constitutes *me* even before *I* begin to choose".[146] Thus, the mastery that is my will is subjected.

A form of non-agential responsibility in research that references Levinasian ethics would begin with an awareness of our incarnate subjectivity, "a recurrence to oneself out of an irrecusable exigency of the other, a duty overflowing my being, a duty becoming a debt".[147] When that indebtedness is viewed through mātauranga Māori, we find it is first to whakapapa as a "non-hierarchical" layering of relationships linking "all facets of creation in a complex web that extends in all directions and into infinity".[148]

My initial suggestion towards a non-agential responsibility draws from this whakapapa through two lines in the chant *Ripiripia*. The first line is a question: "He aha te tohu o te ringaringa?" (What is the sign of the hand?) Frequently representative of whole persons, hands are actors for command in the reo.[149] As even non-human actors may have subjectivity – our mountain ancestor of Ruapehu, for example, is an *ego* (Latin for "I"), as is the family cat – hands can justifiably substitute.[150] But the *Ripiripia* hand also has a "tohu" of its own.

The tohu is a "sign", "a token of remembrance" and the act of "protecting, watching over".[151] In its presence we find not a singular metaphor but a "series of metonymies".[152] Metonymy "replaces the

144 Zarka 2011, 118.
145 Zarka 2011, 118.
146 Zarka 2011, 118.
147 Levinas 1989, 99.
148 Mikaere 2010, para. 24.
149 Biggs 1998, 66–7.
150 Levinas 1989.
151 Tregear 1891, 524.
152 Derrida 1998, 21.

name of one thing with the name of something else closely associated with it, e.g. *the bottle* for alcoholic drink, *the press* for journalism".[153] The tohu represents the hand that substitutes the person.

The second line names the tohu: "He kawakawa!" Kawakawa (*Macropiper excelsum*) is a plant used to treat different ailments. Metaphorically, the herb denotes the beginning and ending of life; different parts of the plant can be used as an aphrodisiac, "to ensure conception", and "as a symbol of grief".[154] However, in metonymy the hand is displaced[155] to lend its meaning to the leaf it holds in contiguity. In my non-agential responsibility, we are each a oneself, a rau kōtahi, a single leaf re-placing those for whom we stand as tohu, a whole kawakawa tree of ancestors and descendants, of cousins, human and otherwise. Thus substituted, the researcher's subjectivity may be found in the plant's caress: desire, joy and sorrow.

A second suggestion for a non-agential responsibility, "tae pākoro", considers an indeclinable submission and is based on an idiom of my paternal grandfather's People. "Tae pākoro" describes someone as arriving heavily laden. In arriving somewhere newly laden with and aware of one's own sorrow, we can see it in others. As Alphonso Lingis notes, "Suffering is a bond with others. One does not suffer without understanding that others suffer, understanding how others suffer."[156]

I came to my research burdened, a widow seeking to both give meaning to my sorrow and re-create for others the comfort I had received in my grief. Compassion is from the Latin *compati*; *-pati* means "to suffer", and *com-* "with". Tae pākoro is the sense that overtook me, an unwilled suffering, a generative compassion. I am bonded to and suffer with our cousins, the human and more-than-human. But it is a trial in terror.

I experienced ideation after the calculations of my doctoral thesis' third chapter. I was suicidal after the sixth. Subsequent to describing some of the structures of the current extinction crisis, my own death appeared logical. I felt tricked into staying alive and resented our

153 Baldick 2015 [emphasis in original].
154 Gray 2012, 2.
155 Colman 2015.
156 Lingis 2000, 110.

children for justifying my survival. This obligation to my children – this compassion for Beloveds who already have lost one parent – is also something I arrived with to this work. Indeed, their presence was a belongingness that made it possible.

A feeling of belonging – to long for and to be longed for – is a sensation of proximity that keeps the researcher safe. Following Levinas, the sensation is an "obsession … irreducible to consciousness"[157]: "in responsibility for the other for life and death, the adjectives unconditional, undeclinable, absolute take on meaning".[158] Life here is a sensuality that undercuts the realm of thought. Life here is felt as "divine", reflecting its etymological relation "to shine … sun … [and] deity".[159] Complementary to the mystery of death, "life is orā, shining in the sun".[160]

Where tae pākoro disturbs, my third suggestion, the māhau, gives space for acknowledging our burdens. A māhau is a verandah that provides shelter before and after entering a house, giving space to remove and replace footwear. In my People's architecture, the māhau demarcates boundaries between inside/outside, tapu/noa, life/death. As a kaikaranga (first voice), I have called bereaved visitors to the māhau and sat with them. They arrived as substitutes, a Beloved's face visible in their crumpled form. For a while, what is carried may be laid down.

There are agential practices to protect the mass extinction researcher – a month off upon completion of each major piece of writing, active engagement with our loved ones, regular alone time making music. In order to do this work, to meet one's obligations, I advocate for space away from it. However, as evidenced by my mental health crises, these agential acts have not always been sufficient.

The māhau, then, is a calling and an acceptance when agency fails. In my case, it was both a voice inside my head that sent me to, and the actuality of, my mother. Like footprints made by me barefoot on grass, the voice was a call by a first speaker. It was someone beyond myself who waited for me, who dreamed of me, who knew me before

157 Levinas 1989, 91.
158 Levinas 1989, 113.
159 Linguistics Research Centre 2020.
160 Gray-Sharp 2021, 66.

I knew myself. Strangely, it also felt like my husband during the birth of our third child, patiently leading me to second stage. It was a call I responded to without will.

My mother, comparatively, has a unique gift of non-judgement and applies our nanny's listening techniques with great skill. It meant I could sit on her porch talking until I came to my own conclusion. The māhau offers a controlled transition so that we may carry on. The call and acknowledging our burdens are its process.

My non-agential responsibility conforms with relational forms. There are still duties and the possibility of being held to account. However, it is absent of liberty, particularly the ability to choose. Such "freedom is a form of rule and *rank* relative to others".[161] It "produces not only self-rule, but also the *self as ruler*".[162] Maintenance of such a position requires a concept of exceptionalism – for who is more exceptional than he who rules – alongside a worldview that finds oneself as the source of all value. Beyond its generative and protective factors, a non-agential responsibility actively denies the structures that underpin the mass extinction crisis.

6. Kupu whakatepe

Kāti i kōnei. Tēnā kautau tātau katoa.

This work is an output from doctoral research conducted by Katarina Gray-Sharp under the supervision of Professors Brendan Hokowhitu and Linda Tuhiwai Smith at Te Pua Wānanga ki te Ao (University of Waikato, New Zealand). The author acknowledges the support of the University of Waikato Doctoral Scholarship and Te Ati Hau Trust Robin Murphy-Peehi Scholarship.

161 Kautzer 2014, 114.
162 Kautzer 2014, 114.

References

Affairs of France (1793). *Universal Magazine of Knowledge and Pleasure* 92: 128–33. London: W. Bent. http://bit.ly/3EkSSIK.

Al Jazeera (2019). Mosque shooter brandished material glorifying Serb nationalism. 16 March. https://www.aljazeera.com/news/2019/03/zealand-mosque-gunman-inspired-serb-nationalism-190315141305756.html.

Anderson, Atholl (1991). Current research issues in the study of moas and moa-hunting. In Bruce McFadgen and Phillip Simpson, comp. *Research Directions for Conservation Science? Five Papers Presented at the Science & Research Division Department of Conservation 1990*, 63–74. https://www.doc.govt.nz/globalassets/documents/science-and-technical/sr37.pdf.

Baldick, Chris (2015). Metonymy. In *The Oxford Dictionary of Literary Terms*, 4th edn. Oxford: Oxford University Press. https://doi.org/10.1093/acref/9780198715443.001.0001.

Ballara, Angela (1990). Te Whatanui. In *Dictionary of New Zealand Biography, Te Ara – the Encyclopedia of New Zealand*. https://teara.govt.nz/en/biographies/1t86/te-whatanui.

Balz, Albert G.A. (1918). Dualism and early modern philosophy II. *Journal of Philosophy, Psychology and Scientific Methods* 15(9): 225–41. http://www.jstor.org/stable/2940452.

Barnosky, Anthony D. (2014). Palaeontological evidence for defining the Anthropocene. In Colin N. Waters, Jan A. Zalasiewicz, Mark Williams, Michael A. Ellis and Andrea M. Snelling, eds. *A Stratigraphical Basis for the Anthropocene*, 149–65. Geological Society, London, Special Publications 395. Geological Society of London. https://doi.org/10.1144/SP395.6.

Barnosky, Anthony D., Nicholas Matzke, Susumu Tomiya, Guinevere O.U. Wogan, Brian Swartz, Tiago B. Quental et al. (2011). Has the Earth's sixth mass extinction already arrived? *Nature* 471(7336): 51–7. https://doi.org/10.1038/nature09678.

Bauman, Zygmunt (2004). Modernity. In Joel Krieger, ed. *The Oxford Companion to Politics of the World*. Oxford: Oxford University Press. https://doi.org/10.1093/acref/9780195117394.001.0001.

Berger, Adolf (1953). *Encyclopedic Dictionary of Roman Law*. Philadelphia: American Philosophical Society. http://bit.ly/3IhMHGi.

Biggs, Bruce (1998). The imperative with universals. In *Let's Learn Maori: A Guide to the Study of the Maori Language*, 65–68. Auckland: University of Auckland Press.

Black, Taiarahia (2000). Kāore te aroha … te hua o te wānanga. Doctoral thesis, Massey University. http://hdl.handle.net/10179/1117.

Blackburn, Simon (2016). Responsibility. *The Oxford Dictionary of Philosophy*. Oxford: Oxford University Press. https://doi.org/10.1093/acref/9780198735304.001.000.

Brown, Garrett, Iain McLean and Alistair McMillan, eds (2018). Structure. In *The Concise Oxford Dictionary of Politics and International Relations*. Oxford: Oxford University Press. http://doi.org/10.1093/acref/9780199670840.001.0001.

Buchanan, Ian (2018). Agency. In *A Dictionary of Critical Theory*. Oxford: Oxford University Press. https://doi.org/10.1093/acref/9780198794790.001.0001.

Butler, Judith (2003). Violence, mourning, politics. *Studies in Gender and Sexuality* 4(1): 9–37. https://doi.org/10.1080/15240650409349213.

Calhoun, Craig, ed. (2002). Modernity. In *Dictionary of Social Sciences*. Oxford: Oxford University Press. https://doi.org/10.1093/acref/9780195123715.001.0001.

Ceballos, Gerardo, Paul R. Ehrlich, Anthony D. Barnosky, Andrés Garcia, Robert M. Pringle and Todd M. Palmer (2015a). Accelerated modern human-induced species losses: entering the sixth mass extinction. *Science Advances* 1(5): 1–5. https://doi.org/10.1126/sciadv.1400253.

Ceballos, Gerardo, Paul R. Ehrlich, Anthony D. Barnosky, Andrés Garcia, Robert M. Pringle and Todd M. Palmer (2015b). Supplementary materials for "Accelerated modern human-induced species losses: entering the sixth mass extinction". *Science Advances* 1(5): 1–5. https://www.science.org/doi/10.1126/sciadv.1400253.

Centre National de la Recherche Scientifique (2012). Responsable, adj. et subst. *Centre National de Ressources Textuelles et Lexicales*. http://www.cnrtl.fr/etymologie/responsable.

Chroust, Anton-Hermann (1955). Legal profession in ancient imperial Rome. *Notre Dame Lawyer* 30(4): 521–616. https://scholarship.law.nd.edu/cgi/viewcontent.cgi?article=3652&context=ndlr.

Colman, Andrew M. (2015). Displacement. In *A Dictionary of Psychology*, 4th edn. Oxford University Press. https://doi.org/10.1093/acref/9780199657681.001.0001.

Condie, Kent C. (2011). Mass extinctions. In *Earth as an Evolving Planetary System*, 250–9. Oxford, UK: Elsevier.

Crystal, David (2008). Structure. In *Language Library: A Dictionary of Linguistics and Phonetics*. Hoboken, NJ: Wiley. https://search.credoreference.com/content/entry/bkdictling/structure/0.

Derrida, Jacques (1998). From Adieu à Emmanuel Levinas. *Research in Phenomenology* 28(1): 20–36. https://doi.org/10.1163/156916498X00029.

Diniejko, Andrzej (2010). Charles Darwin's theory of evolution and the intellectual ferment of the mid- and late Victorian periods. *The Victorian Web*. http://www.victorianweb.org/science/darwin/diniejko.html.

French, William C. (2008). Ecoethics: Western anthropocentrism. In Lester R. Kurtz, ed. *Encyclopedia of Violence, Peace and Conflict*. Elsevier Science & Technology. https://search.credoreference.com/content/entry/estpeace/ecoethics/0.

Galtung, Johan (1969). Violence, peace, and peace research. *Journal of Peace Research* 6(3): 167–91. http://www.jstor.org/stable/422690.

Gray, Kelly (2012). Expectorant plants. In *The Use of Rongoā Contemporary Physiotherapy: An Exploratory Study*, 2–4. Auckland: AUT University. https://bit.ly/3KlJbNW.

Gray-Sharp, Katarina (2021). My responsibility in the face of mass extinction. Doctoral thesis, University of Waikato. https://hdl.handle.net/10289/14209.

Harper, Douglas (2020a). Responsible (adj.). In *Online Etymology Dictionary*. https://www.etymonline.com/word/responsible.

Harper, Douglas (2020b). Responsibility (n.). In *Online Etymology Dictionary*. https://www.etymonline.com/word/responsibility.

Harper, Douglas (2020c). Spondee (n.). In *Online Etymology Dictionary*. https://www.etymonline.com/word/spondee.

Hine, Robert and Elizabeth Martin (2015). Extinction. In *A Dictionary of Biology*. Oxford University Press. https://doi.org/10.1093/acref/978019874378.001.0001.

Hoad, Terry F, ed. (2003). Respond. In *The Concise Oxford Dictionary of English Etymology*. Oxford University Press. https://bit.ly/3EoLiN1.

Iannone, A. Pablo (2001). Anthropocentrism. In *Dictionary of World Philosophy*. London; New York: Routledge. https://search.credoreference.com/content/entry/routwp/anthropocentrism/0.

International Union for Conservation of Nature and Natural Resources (2019). *Raw Data to Red List*. https://www.iucnredlist.org/assessment/process.

International Union for Conservation of Nature and Natural Resources (2018). Table 9: Possibly extinct and possibly extinct in the wild species. *The IUCN Red List of Threatened Species*. https://www.iucnredlist.org/statistics.

International Union for Conservation of Nature and Natural Resources Species Survival Commission (2012). *IUCN Red List Categories and Criteria*. version 3.1, Gland, Switzerland: IUCN. https://portals.iucn.org/library/node/10315.

Kautzer, Chad (2014). Antiracism and the Whiteness problem. In *Radical Philosophy: An Introduction*. London; New York: Routledge. http://bit.ly/3UgoUuc.

Kent, Michael (2007). Structure. *The Oxford Dictionary of Sports Science & Medicine*. Oxford: Oxford University Press. https://doi.org/10.1093/acref/9780198568506.001.0001.

Kernot, Bernie (1981). An artist in his time. *Journal of the Polynesian Society* 90(2): 157–70. http://www.jps.auckland.ac.nz/document/?wid=3911.

Klein, Martha (2005). Responsibility. In Ted Honderich, ed. *The Oxford Companion to Philosophy*. https://doi.org/10.1093/acref/9780199264797.001.000.

Kojève, Alexandre (1969). In place of an introduction. In Kojève, Alexandre, *Introduction to the Reading of Hegel*, Allan Bloom, ed., James H. Nichols, Jr, trans. 1–29. http://bit.ly/3EMSsKh.

Ladle, Richard J. and Ana C.M. Malhado (2013). Biodiversity and extinction: theoretical background. In Christopher G. Bates and James Ciment, eds. *Global Social Issues: An Encyclopedia*. London; New York: Routledge. https://bit.ly/3YKc9vg.

Lamkin, Megan and Arnold I. Miller (2016). On the challenge of comparing contemporary and deep-time biological-extinction rates. *BioScience* 66(9): 785–9. https://doi.org/10.1093/biosci/biw088.

Levinas, Emmanuel (1989). *The Levinas Reader*. Seán Hand, ed. Oxford: Basil Blackwell.

Lewis, Charlton T. and Charles Short (1891). *A New Latin Dictionary*. New York: Harper & Brothers. http://bit.ly/3IdQaWn.

Lingis, Alphonso (2018). A hard and brutal mysticism. *Mosaic* 51(4): 47–53. https://muse.jhu.edu/article/714501.

Lingis, Alphonso (2000). To die with others. *Diacritics* 30(3): 106–13. https://www.jstor.org/stable/1566346.

Linguistics Research Center (2020). PIE etymon and IE reflexes: Pokorny etymon: 1. dei-, deiʔə-, dī-, diʔā- "to shine, glitter; day, sun; god, deity." In *Indo-European Lexicon*. https://lrc.la.utexas.edu/lex/master/0322.

Linguistics Research Center (2014). PIE etymon and IE reflexes: Pokorny etymon: spend- "to offer a libation". In *Indo-European Lexicon*. http://bit.ly/3Klz3EJ.

Manaaki Whenua – Landcare Research (2019). Huia louse: extinct before being discovered! *Insects and Spiders*. https://www.landcareresearch.co.nz/resources/teaching/Insects-and-spiders/fantastic-facts/huia-louse-extinct-before-being-discovered!.

Matthews, Peter H. (2014). French. In *The Concise Oxford Dictionary of Linguistics*. Oxford: Oxford University Press. https://doi.org/10.1093/acref/9780199675128.001.0001.

Mayr, Ernst (1972). The nature of the Darwinian revolution. *Science* 176(4038): 981–9. https://science.sciencemag.org/content/176/4038/981.

Mead, Hirini Moko (2003). *Tikanga Māori: Living by Māori Values*. Wellington, New Zealand: Huia.

Mead, Hirini Moko and Neil Grove (2003). *Ngā Pēpeha a Ngā Tīpuna: The Sayings of the Ancestors*. Wellington, New Zealand: Victoria University of Wellington.

Mead, Linda T.T.R. (1996). Kaupapa Maori research. In Nga aho o te kakahu matauranga: the multiple layers of struggle by Maori in education, 196–225. Doctoral dissertation, University of Auckland. http://www.rangahau.co.nz/kaupapa-maori-articles/185/.

Mikaere, Ani (2017). Matiu Dickson: the measure of the man. *Waikato Law Review: Taumauri* 25: 100–6. https://search.informit.com.au/documentSummary;dn=998515054325481;res=IELHSS.

Mikaere, Ani (2010). Māori critic and conscience in a colonising context – law and leadership as a case study. Paper presented at the 27th Annual Conference of the Law and Society Association of Australia and New Zealand, Victoria University of Wellington, December.

Mitchell, Audra (2018). Revitalizing laws, (re)-making treaties, dismantling violence: Indigenous resurgence against "the sixth mass extinction". *Social and Cultural Geography* (October): 1–16. https://doi.org/10.1080/14649365.2018.1528628.

Mitchell, Charlie (2018). What happened here. *Stuff*. http://bit.ly/3Z5PdXc.

Park, Chris and Michael Allaby (2017a). Biota. In *A Dictionary of Environment and Conservation*. Oxford: Oxford University Press. https://doi.org/10.1093/acref/9780191826320.001.0001.

Park, Chris and Michael Allaby (2017b). Catastrophism. In *A Dictionary of Environment and Conservation*. Oxford: Oxford University Press. https://doi.org/10.1093/acref/9780191826320.001.0001.

Park, Chris and Michael Allaby (2017c). Extinction. In *A Dictionary of Environment and Conservation*. Oxford: Oxford University Press. https://doi.org/10.1093/acref/9780191826320.001.0001.

Park, Chris and Michael Allaby (2017d). Extirpation (local extinction). In *A Dictionary of Environment and Conservation*. Oxford: Oxford University Press. https://doi.org/10.1093/acref/9780191826320.001.0001.

Parliamentary History (1783). *London Magazine* 1(October): 281–8. https://archive.org/details/londonmagazine00unkngoog/page/n298.

Pievani, Telmo (2014). The sixth mass extinction: Anthropocene and the human impact on biodiversity. *Rendiconti Lincei* 25(1): 85–93. https://doi.org/10.1007/s12210-013-0258-9.

Pievani, Telmo (2009). The world after Charles R. Darwin: continuity, unity in diversity, contingency. *Rendiconti Lincei* 20(4): 355–61. https://doi.org/10.1007/s12210-009-0064-6.

Pihama, Leonie (2015). Kaupapa Māori theory: transforming theory in Aotearoa. In Leonie Pihama, Sarah-Jane Tiakiwai and Kim Southey, eds. *Kaupapa Rangahau: A Reader*, 5–15. Hamilton, New Zealand: Te Kotahi Research Unit. http://www.waikato.ac.nz/rangahau/publications-and-resource-hub/ebooks.

Pimm, Stuart L., Clinton N. Jenkins, Robin Abell, Thomas M. Brooks, John L. Gittleman, Lucas N. Joppa et al. (2014). The biodiversity of species and their rates of extinction, distribution, and protection. *Science* 344(6187): 1246752-1–10. https://doi.org/10.1126/science.1246752.

Ripple, William J., Christopher Wolf, Thomas M. Newsome, Mauro Galetti, Mohammed Alamgir, Eileen Crist et al. (2017). World scientists' warning to humanity: a second notice. *BioScience*, bix125: 1–3. https://doi.org/10.1093/biosci/bix125.

Ross, William David (1995). Biology. In *Aristotle*, 72–82. London; New York: Routledge.

Royal, Te Ahukaramū Charles (2012). Politics and knowledge: kaupapa Māori and mātauranga Māori. *New Zealand Journal of Educational Studies* 47(2): 30–7.

Royal, Te Ahukaramū Charles (2005). Exploring Indigenous knowledge. In Joanna Kidman, Joseph Te Rito and Wally Penetito, eds. *Proceedings of the Indigenous Knowledges Conference: Reconciling Academic Priorities with Indigenous Realities*, 133–47. http://www.maramatanga.ac.nz/sites/default/files/TKC%202005.pdf.

Royal Society Te Apārangi (2017). *Mātauranga Māori in Modern Day Research*. https://bit.ly/3ElIjVx.

Sandywell, Barry (2011). Structure. In *Dictionary of Visual Discourse: A Dialectical Lexicon of Terms*. Surrey, UK; Burlington, VT: Ashgate Publishing. https://search.credoreference.com/content/entry/ashgtvd/structure/0.

Scott, John, ed. (2015). Structure (social structure). In *A Dictionary of Sociology*. Oxford: Oxford University Press. https://doi.org/10.1093/acref/9780199683581.001.0001.

Scruton, Roger (2007). Responsibility. In *Palgrave Macmillan Dictionary of Political Thought*. Basingstoke, UK; New York: Macmillan Publishers.

Smith, Linda T. (2015). Kaupapa Māori research – some kaupapa Māori principles. In Leonie Pihama and Kim Southey, eds. *Kaupapa Rangahau: A Reader*,

47–53. Hamilton, New Zealand: Te Kotahi Research Unit. http://hdl.handle.net/10289/9531.

Smith, Linda T. (1999). *Decolonizing Methodologies: Research and Indigenous Peoples*. London: Zed Books.

Stevenson, Angus, ed. (2015a). Responsibility. In *Oxford Dictionary of English*. Oxford: Oxford University Press. https://doi.org/10.1093/acref/9780199571123.001.0001.

Stevenson, Angus, ed. (2015b). Responsible. In *Oxford Dictionary of English*. Oxford: Oxford University Press. https://doi.org/10.1093/acref/9780199571123.001.0001.

Te Aho, Linda (2007). Tikanga Māori, historical context and the interface with Pākehā law in Aotearoa/New Zealand. *Yearbook of New Zealand Jurisprudence* 10: 10–14. https://www.waikato.ac.nz/__data/assets/pdf_file/0014/32801/Yearbook-of-NZ-Jurisprudence-Vol-10-2007-print.pdf.

Te Iwi Māori o te Rawhiti (1874). He wharangi tuwhera. *Waka Maori* 10(21): 267–8. https://paperspast.natlib.govt.nz/newspapers/WAKAM18741020.2.17.

Tregear, Edward (1891). *The Maori-Polynesian Comparative Dictionary*. Wellington, New Zealand: Lyon & Blair. http://nzetc.victoria.ac.nz/tm/scholarly/tei-TreMaor.html.

Troy, Jakelin (2019). Trees are at the heart of our country – we should learn their Indigenous names. *Guardian*, 1 April. http://bit.ly/3kghWJN.

Troy, Jakelin (1994). Plants. In *The Sydney Language*, 59–62. Canberra: Panther.

United Nations Educational, Scientific and Cultural Organization (1950). Summary report of the first plenary session of the international technical conference on the protection of nature. In *International Technical Conference on the Protection of Nature, Lake Success, 22–29 – VIII – 1949: Proceedings and Papers*, 15–23. https://unesdoc.unesco.org/ark:/48223/pf0000133578.

Wehi, Priscilla, Murray Cox, Tom Roa and Hēmi Whaanga (2018). Human perceptions of megafaunal extinction events revealed by linguistic analysis of Indigenous oral traditions. *Human Ecology* 46(4): 461–70. https://doi.org/10.1007/s10745-018-0004-0.

Wehi, Priscilla, Hēmi Whaanga and Murray Cox (2018). Dead as the moa: oral traditions show that early Māori recognised extinction. *Conversation*, 6 September. http://bit.ly/3ihoc2K.

Wikiriwhi, Hirone Te Mokai (1955). Proverbial and popular sayings of the Maori: nga whakatauki me nga pepeha Maori. *Te Ao Hou: The New World*, 1 December. http://teaohou.natlib.govt.nz/journals/teaohou/issue/Mao13TeA/c21.html.

Wilcox, Christie (2019). Lonely George the tree snail dies, and a species goes extinct. *National Geographic*, 8 January. http://bit.ly/3xAWl1V.

Wilkes, John (1767). A second letter to His Grace the Duke of Grafton, First Commissioner of His Majesty's Treasury. *A Complete Collection of the Genuine Papers, Letters, &c. in the Case of John Wilkes, Esq: Late Member for Aylesbury, in the County of Bucks*, 160–91. Paris, France: Chez J.W. Imprimeur. https://archive.org/details/acompletecollec01wilkgoog/page/n173.

Williams, Garrath (2009). Responsibility. *Internet Encyclopedia of Philosophy*. http://www.iep.utm.edu/responsi/.

Williams, Herbert W. (1957). *A Dictionary of the Maori Language*. Wellington, New Zealand: Government Printer. http://nzetc.victoria.ac.nz/tm/scholarly/tei-WillDict.html.

Williams, William (1852). *A Dictionary of the New Zealand Language, and a Concise Grammar; To Which is Added a Selection of Colloquial Sentences*. London: Williams & Norgate. https://archive.org/details/adictionarynewz01willgoog.

Wilson, Che (2010). *Nga hau o tua, nga ia o uta, nga rere o tai*. Whanganui, New Zealand: Te Puna Matauranga o Whanganui.

Wolfe, Patrick (2006). Settler colonialism and the elimination of the Native. *Journal of Genocide Research* 8(4): 387–409. https://doi.org/10.1080/14623520601056240.

Wright, Michael (2011). Rare snails die in storage mishap. *Stuff*. http://bit.ly/3XI2eFg.

Young, Venn (1983). Address at the opening of the 15th session of the IUCN general assembly. In *15th Session of the General Assembly of IUCN and 15th IUCN Technical Meeting, Christchurch, New Zealand, 11–23 October 1981*, 78–82. Gland, Switzerland: International Union for the Conservation of Nature and Natural Resources. https://portals.iucn.org/library/efiles/documents/GA-15th-009.pdf.

Zarka, Yves Charles (2011). Levinas: humanism and heteronomy. Edward Hughes, trans. *British Journal for the History of Philosophy* 19(1): 111–20. https://doi.org/10.1080/09608788.2011.533014.

5

Crypsis, discovery and subjectivity: Unsettling fish histories

Rick De Vos

I write this chapter in the wake of the challenges presented by animal studies scholars who have engaged with fish as beings with whom we live, benefit from and exploit, and from whom we face ethical demands. Jonathan Balcombe has argued that fish deserve our moral concern in the light of clear evidence that they are autonomous, sentient individuals living sophisticated lives, evidence constantly occluded by restricting stereotypes.[1] Dinesh Wadiwel has challenged those of us who address fish in our research, given the obstacles to fish welfare prompted by an unprecedented rise in global fish consumption, to consider resistance as a generative model for thinking about the agency of fish; to consider it in relation to the instrumentation of the violence visited upon them, and how that resistance has sometimes been forgotten or ignored, and at other times used against them.[2] Zoe Todd, in arguing that the bodies and movement of fish have mobilised and articulated resistance to colonial dispossession in northern Canada, has challenged us to recognise and relate to fish as kin with whom we share a past, and as cohabitants within the context of an oceanic consciousness where oceans and waterways are our familiars and not a frontier or other space.[3]

---

1 Balcombe 2017.
2 Wadiwel 2016.
3 Todd 2017; 2018.

These are challenges I read and feel as immediate and personal. I have had a lifelong interest in fish, enthralled by stories and descriptions in children's science books, hours spent watching the tropical fish in my father's fish tanks in Perth, Western Australia, and visiting aquarium shops with him, listening to him talk about his memories of fish during his childhood in Sri Lanka and comparing them to those he saw in Perth aquariums. Visits to beaches filled my head with questions about the fish present beyond and under the waves, and of whom I knew so little. I was unaware that many humans and fish lived lives that were tied to and entangled with one another, physically and culturally, and had done so for many thousands of years. The documentaries presented by Jacques Cousteau about his oceanic explorations were part of my favourite television viewing, the underwater footage of sea life suggesting a different way of being and seeing. In my reading I was captivated by accounts of life in the Devonian period, the "Age of Fishes", between 300 and 400 million years ago, and the prehistoric fish that dominated the oceans at that time. One particular fact that stayed with me was that two groups of fish who lived in the Devonian period, lungfish and coelacanths, had survived to the present day. In this chapter, I examine and question the colonial histories of these fish, along with that of New Zealand longfin eels, in order to consider their ways of seeing and knowing, their pre-colonial lives, their relationships with local Indigenous people and European settlers, and their potentials for resisting and evading colonial subjectivity and surveillance.

Dala

Dala, or Queensland lungfish,[4] are endemic to the Mary and Burnett rivers in south-east Queensland, Australia. Fossils found in northern New South Wales indicate that lungfish have lived for over 100 million years in rivers in eastern Australia, witnessing and adapting to dramatic changes in their environment, and in the courses and flows of the rivers they inhabited. Dala are distinct from other lungfish species in a

4 Dala are also known as Australian lungfish.

number of ways.[5] They have only one lung and breathe air only when forced to do so. Their gills are fully formed, enabling them to live totally in fresh water. In the warm waters of the Moocooboola or Mary River in south-east Queensland, Dala live in small groups in areas sheltered by either tree roots or submerged logs and branches, preferring the deeper, slower flowing reaches of the river. At night they hunt for small fish, frogs and aquatic invertebrates. Living in small social groups, Dala have over millions of years passed on knowledge of how to live, eat, avoid predators and find mates. While they seek to spend all their time in the waters of the Moocooboola, they are able to use their single lungs to supplement their respiration during times of extreme heat when oxygen levels in the water fall or in times of drought when water levels in the river drop. Their strong, fleshy fins are utilised in aiding them to move over shallows in order to find areas with sufficient water.

Gubbi Gubbi people, for whom the Moocooboola is country, recognise Dala as kin, eliciting an ethical demand for respect and protection. For Gubbi Gubbi, humans and Dala are both part of the natural environment, and as such are connected to one another. They share country, and Gubbi Gubbi people do not eat lungfish. Their close spiritual and familial relationship was highlighted by Gubbi Gubbi elder and Queensland University of Technology academic Dr Eve Fesl in a 2007 statement to the Australian Parliament opposing a proposed water project, the Traveston Crossing Dam, the construction of which would have dammed a large section of the Moocooboola, posing very serious threats to Dala and other endemic or vulnerable species living in the river.

> I am an Elder of the Gubbi Gubbi (Indigenous Australian) People whose traditional lands encompasses the Mary River … My mother and many of my ancestors were born near the banks of the river when the area was covered in dense rainforest. We were known by many other Indigenous Groups as the "Dala People".
>
> The reason for this name is that we hold sacred "Dala", the Queensland Lung Fish (*Neoceratodus forsteri*). For thousands of years the duty of our people has been to care for this creature. As

5 Allen, Midgley and Allen 2002, 54–5.

> small children we were taught not to kill or eat it and to protect it and its breeding places from harm. This has been part of our cultural duty …
>
> [T]hrough their edicts and directives to protect Dala, over thousands of years, my people have always recognised the uniqueness of Dala through their knowledge of anatomy, physiology, and breeding habitats of creatures – knowledge which was necessary for survival in a world reliant on hunting skills. It has only been recently that we learned of its importance to the rest of the world.[6]

Dala and the Moocooboola are familiars to Gubbi Gubbi people, and not separate from them. Knowledge is shared and connected in this context. The presence of Dala means that certain stories and the knowledge held within them can continue to be told. The Moocooboola is also, however, since 1847, the Mary River, and has been utilised historically by colonial settlers for rafting logs, as a site for panning for alluvial gold and as a source of water for irrigating crops and servicing dairy farming. In these practices the river as a source of cultural connection and knowledge was recast as a colonial resource in the face of a violent regime, settlement and economic demands.

Audrey Appudurai argues that different cultural histories of lungfish reveal different frames of knowledge, different methodologies, and different ways of making meaning, where science can be seen as a cultural tool reflecting the society in which it operates. Inasmuch as they are capable of breathing in both air and water, and thus suggest a liminal subjectivity, Appudurai suggests that lungfish provide a meaningful way of comparing different cultural approaches to understanding non-human life.[7]

The introduction of lungfish to Western science was shaped by nineteenth-century debates in Europe over the validity of Charles Darwin's theory of evolution. In 1837, the Austrian zoologist Leopold Fitzinger described two lungfish specimens collected some years earlier by his compatriot Johann Natterer from a river in the Amazon

6 Fesl 2007a; 2007b.
7 Appudurai 2016, 81–2.

rainforest in Brazil.[8] Of particular significance was the fact that the specimens each had what appeared to be a pair of lungs, with anecdotal evidence suggesting the animals were breathing air through them. Natterer classified them as amphibious reptiles. While their evolutionary and taxonomic relationship remains unresolved, Natterer's description led to conjecture about the transition of vertebrates from water to land. In 1839, the influential biologist, paleontologist and Fellow of the Royal Society Richard Owen described a lungfish specimen collected from the Gambia River in West Africa, classifying the specimen as a fish and arguing that the lungs were vestigial.[9] Owen was a steadfast critic of theories of evolution, and his pronouncement of the specimen as a fish without questioning the presence of lungs was regarded as a way of allaying suspicions that lungfish were indeed a transitional species providing evidence of an evolutionary link between fish and reptiles.

Queensland lungfish were introduced to Western science by zoologist and director of the Australian Museum Gerard Krefft in 1870. Krefft had been alerted to the existence of the fish in the Burnett River some years earlier by the former parliamentary leader of the Colony of New South Wales William Forster. Forster was previously a pastoral squatter in Queensland, with control of several leases near the Burnett River, and during this time had helped to organise a retributive raid and massacre of Taribelang people on Paddy Island on the Burnett River.[10] Despite dismissing earlier claims by Forster that the fish he had found possessed lungs, Krefft eventually examined a specimen, and was both amazed and confounded by the fish's single lung. Krefft immediately called for more specimens to be collected. His subsequent report, published initially in the *Sydney Morning Herald* and later that year in the journal of the Zoological Society of London, described the lungfish as an amphibian, related to the South American and West African species, and, without a trace of irony, expressed surprise that although the fish had been commonly seen by locals, they had not

8 Machado, Wellendorf and Brito 2010, 57.

9 Carneiro, Dutra et al. 2021, 760.

10 Coffey 2006; Laurie 1952.

come to the attention of natural historians.[11] Krefft named the lungfish *Neoceratodus forsteri*. He unequivocally claimed the fish as an Australian species rather than a British one, and positioned his findings squarely within the context of Darwin's theory of evolution. Peter Kind has described the announcement of the new species as sparking excitement and fervour in the scientific community, attracting large numbers of scientists to Australia.[12] Despite requests from the Royal Society that it send specimens to London, amid fears that colonial subjects would almost certainly kill them all, the Australian Museum refused to defer to Britain as zoological authority. As Appudurai argues, "This time, the new Australian immigrants 'colonised' the unique animals of the continent to establish their hold on the land ... It had to be 'rediscovered' to the Western world by Western colonists."[13]

The enunciation of Dala as *Neoceratodus forsteri* marks a merging of colonial, scientific and national interests. A group of fish with a history of many millions of years was re-presented as a new species, re-articulated and subjectified within a more recent taxonomic and colonial order that denied the history of Dala and Gubbi Gubbi people and imposed itself as prior or first knowledge. Their different conditions of subjectivity meant that Dala were separated from Gubbi Gubbi by the new colonial order, which ignored and discounted the ongoing relationships of care, protection and reciprocity that had existed for thousands of years.

Appudurai suggests that lungfish's respiratory fluidity provides a point of tension for a colonial scientific order in a way that it does not for Indigenous people living with the fish.[14] Gubbi Gubbi people's understanding of Dala as being able to breathe both air and water precedes Western knowledge of lungfish, and reinforces a conception of amorphousness in animal forms and shapes. The world of Gubbi Gubbi and Dala encompasses both water and land, with both the river and the surrounding lands constituting shared country, with humans and

11 Krefft 1870a; 1870b.
12 Kind 2011, 64.
13 Appudurai 2016, 95.
14 Appudurai 2016, 84.

fish sharing a past in which they inhabited both land and water. The struggles of colonial taxonomists can be seen as attempts to incorporate the discovery and enunciation of the fish into an existing imperial narrative, reproducing it as a sign of authority. In Australia, as was the case in South America and Africa, lungfish became a colonial animal and a subject. Their otherness was aligned with that of Indigenous subjects, both groups constituting a problem of knowledge and of authority. While Gubbi Gubbi people saw Dala as belonging to country, the lungfish were transformed by the colonial gaze into commodities. Many lungfish were captured and shipped to zoos and museums to be displayed. In 2017, the Shedd Aquarium in Chicago announced the death of Granddad, a Queensland lungfish estimated to be over 90 years old, who at the time was the oldest fish in any public zoo or aquarium in the world. He was one of a pair of lungfish that had been sent to be displayed at the 1933 World's Fair in Chicago before being moved to the aquarium.[15]

Gombessa

Gombessa, or coelacanths, are large fish that grow to between 1.5 and 1.8 metres in length and weigh between 60 and 100 kilograms. Coelacanths have lived in the oceans for at least 400 million years, with fossils from the early Devonian period found in Australian waters.[16] Two species are known to survive today: the Western Indian Ocean coelacanth and the Indonesian coelacanth. Western Indian Ocean coelacanths live along a section of the south-east African coast, with the largest group believed to live in the vast system of underwater caves beneath the steeply eroded volcanic slopes of the Comoro Islands, at depths of between 200 and 700 metres. They are sociable fish and often congregate in their caves, possibly returning to the same home cave each day.[17] The coastal waters in this area experience strong currents, and coelacanths are able to make use of oceanic upwellings and

15 Johnson 2017.
16 Johanson, Long et al. 2006, 443.
17 Fricke, Schauer et al. 1991, 281.

downwellings to move around and hunt fish in open waters, and to expertly negotiate the crevices and narrow passages of the underwater caves with their numerous muscular pairs of fins and by electro-perception. Comorian fishermen have shared the coastal waters with Gombessa, as coelacanths are locally known, since at least the sixth century, avoiding catching them, as they were recognised as not good to eat.

The story of Western science's introduction to modern coelacanths is well known, and provides perhaps the best-known example of what has been described as a Lazarus taxon, a group of living beings believed to be extinct but later discovered to be still alive or to have survived to a significantly later date. In *Old Fourlegs: The Story of the Coelacanth*, James Leonard Brierley Smith, a South African chemistry professor and part-time ichthyologist, provides an account of how he became aware of the fish's continued existence.[18] He had received a letter and a sketch from schoolteacher and part-time curator of the East London Museum Marjorie Courtenay-Latimer asking for help in identifying what she believed to be a coelacanth, caught off the South African coast near the Chalumna River in December 1938. Smith visited the museum in February 1939, confirming that the specimen was indeed a coelacanth. In June 1939, Smith released a scientific paper announcing the discovery of the coelacanth, naming the species *Latimeria chalumnae* after the museum curator and the river where the fish was found. Smith's account of the discovery in *Old Fourlegs* details the capture of the fish, the fishing boat captain Hendrik Goosen's decision to contact Courtenay-Latimer, the curator's attempts to get the unwieldy specimen back to the museum, the lack of ice or refrigeration in the general vicinity and the decision to stuff and mount the specimen, the contacting of Smith and his suspicion of the unlikely identity of the specimen, the enforced delay before Smith could travel to East London and, as a climax, the moment when he first came into the presence of the specimen:

> [T]he caretaker ushered us into the inner room and there was the – Coelacanth, yes, God! Although I had come prepared, that first

---

18 Smith 1956, 27–43.

> sight hit me like a white-hot blast and made me feel shaky and queer, my body tingled. I stood as if stricken to stone. Yes, there was not a shadow of a doubt, scale by scale, bone by bone, fin by fin, it was a true Coelacanth. It could have been one of those creatures of 200 million years ago come alive again.[19]

Each incident leading up to this encounter is related as the outcome of miraculous chance but also of destiny, reconnecting prehistoric time with modern time. Catching, identifying, transporting, mounting and classifying specimens are presented as extraordinary events, removed from the pattern of everyday life, represented as events of historic importance. If reviewed in the light of the political and social context of the Union of South Africa in 1938, however, what is framed as a miracle seems less impressive. Despite comprising an ethnically and linguistically diverse country, legislation in the Union had formalised racial segregation and disenfranchised all black South African adults. The 1923 Native Urban Areas Act introduced residential segregation and provided cheap labour for industry led by white people, while the 1926 Mines & Works Amendment Act, also known as the Colour Bar Act, prevented anyone black from practising skilled trades.[20] The labour involved in effecting the catching, identifying, transporting, mounting and classifying of the coelacanth specimen, and the regime enforcing the social hierarchy that privileges the enunciated and enunciating historical agents while silencing subalterns, are sublimated in Smith's account and in subsequent re-presentations. The colonial order is assumed and justified in such a translation of the encounter. Despite the political context in which this event was enunciated, the narrative of historic discovery has persisted to the present day, colouring the memories of those who read about or were taught about the coelacanth and the fish's presentation as a first, referential specimen.

The scientific monumentality of the event and the celebration of the coelacanth as a South African fish, were subsequently brought into question by the identification of another coelacanth specimen in the

19 Smith 1956, 41.
20 O'Malley 2021a; 2021b.

Comoro Islands in 1952. Since 1946, the islands had been recognised as a French Overseas Territory, with French colonial forces having had a presence there for a century beforehand. Smith had posted a reward for any coelacanth specimen found since the 1938 discovery, and was immediately informed of the 1952 find. He made a covert trip to the islands to collect the specimen and hand over the reward, an event narrated in heroic detail in *Old Fourlegs*.[21] The French government soon discovered the incident and banned the taking of coelacanth specimens immediately afterwards, as well as forbidding expeditions by foreign scientists near the Comoros coastlines. Over the next decade, the French government launched an intensive research campaign of its own in the Comoros, only then learning that Comoran fishermen had been aware of Gombessa for many generations. Several subsequent specimens have been caught off the islands of Grand Comoro and Anjouan in what is now the Union of the Comoros.[22]

In 1998 another coelacanth discovery was announced, this time on the northern tip of Sulawesi in Indonesia. A Canadian visitor, Arnaz Erdmann, had seen what looked like a coelacanth in a fisherman's cart while at a fish market the previous year, and had pointed the fish out to her husband, ichthyologist Mark Erdmann. Erdmann had immediately recognised the fish as a coelacanth and excitedly took some photographs and briefly interviewed the fisherman, who sold the fish soon afterwards. Erdmann was able to obtain a coelacanth specimen the following year from an Indonesian fishing crew. He observed the fish's last hours of life, and arranged for the body to be deep frozen and for tissue samples to be taken. The announcement of the capture and preservation of a living coelacanth almost 9,000 kilometres from the Comoros appeared as a cover story by Erdmann and colleagues in the journal *Nature*, and the discovery was also featured in electronic and print media around the world.[23] *Discover* magazine listed the discovery as one of the top science stories of 1998. Again, local fishermen had long been aware of the fish, which they

21 Smith 1956.
22 Bruton and Coutouvidis 1991, 375.
23 Erdmann 1999.

called *Rajah Laut*, meaning “king of the sea”, but had not pursued them, as their flesh was considered to be very unpleasant in taste.[24]

Smith’s and Erdmann’s stories of discovery take the form of narratives that open up the possibility of miraculous chance. They constitute a step away from an objective scientific description and move towards the realm of wonder. It is in that moment/movement that their accounts become open to reinterpretation. It is in these stories’ claims to primacy, in presenting a time and space as a first instance, that an event is made open to contestation. Other perspectives are suggested, other subjectivities are brought into contact with that of the narrator, and the authoritative nature of the story is brought into question.

Both the Western Indian Ocean and the Indonesian coelacanth populations have a restricted range due to water temperature and food sources. Climate change is seen as a major threat to their survival in the future. In addition, they have become more vulnerable to capture as fishermen seek to sell specimens to scientists.[25] No coelacanth has ever survived capture. As a result of these factors, the coelacanth populations are considered to be critically endangered, and conservation measures have been launched to attempt to protect them from extinction.

Tuna kuwharuwharu

Tuna kuwharuwharu, or New Zealand longfin eels, are the only endemic freshwater eel species in Aotearoa New Zealand, and the largest freshwater eels in the world. They live the great majority of their lives in rivers and lakes, and when they reach a certain size and age they migrate to the open ocean between early April and late May, to breed and then to die. Where precisely they go remains unknown. The fertilised eggs develop into tiny see-through creatures called leptocephalus. These drift on currents back towards the New Zealand coast, developing into glass eels along the way. Between July and

24 Erdmann, Caldwell and Moosa 1998.
25 Fricke 1997, 12.

November, large numbers of the tiny glass eels enter waterways, where about a week later they develop dark skin pigment and become elvers. Elvers can climb straight up wet rock faces and other obstacles as they move inland.[26]

Female tuna can grow up to 2 metres in length, weigh in excess of 20 kilograms, and live up to 100 years. Males are shorter in length and lead shorter lives. Historically, they have been the top predators of Aotearoa river systems, occupying concealed places near riverbanks, rocks and logs during daylight hours and emerging at night to hunt insect larvae, snails, fish and crayfish and to take advantage of dead animals and birds in the river.

Tuna kuwharuwharu hold a significant place in Māori cultural history, with many stories, artefacts and songs dedicated to them. They are also important nutritionally and economically, and an indicator of the health of rivers and of water quality. Māori and eels have traditionally shared knowledge, time and space. The researcher and writer Joseph Potangaroa has discussed the way Māori knowledge of tuna was built up and passed on through careful and patient observation, coming to an understanding of habitats, life cycles and migration patterns, including the ages at which female and male tuna migrated. The knowledge gained helped Māori to determine a sustainable number of eels to take for food, a practice undertaken at certain times according to lunar cycles and other environmental indicators.[27]

Tuna kuwharuwharu numbers have decreased in Aotearoa since the middle of the nineteenth century due to a variety of settler activities, including the clearing of native forests, the draining of swamps, the diversion of rivers and the establishing of irrigation schemes. The introduction of trout and salmon as sport fish, initially by individual settlers and later by acclimatisation societies, also proved disastrous to eels, as thousands of adults were killed both to make room for, and to eradicate what was viewed as a potential predator of brown trout.[28] Acclimatisation societies were established in the latter half of the nineteenth century with the purpose of facilitating colonial

26 Hoyle and Jellyman 2002, 887–8.
27 Potangaroa 2010, 10.
28 Jellyman 2014.

settlement by introducing familiar plants and non-human animals to New Zealand and other British colonies.[29] Local or native fauna were seen to be lacking something and indeed hindered settlers from feeling "at home". Trout and salmon were perceived as familiar, "settling" and promising sport in the form of recreational fishing. Conversely, tuna kuwharuwharu were perceived as strange, dangerous and startling: they were literally unsettling to settlers. It is interesting to note that these perceptions endure in Aotearoa today, with many people still choosing to avoid swimming in rivers with tuna populations, and stories of eel encounters often portraying them as monstrous and fearsome.[30]

In more recent times, the increasing threats to tuna have included water poisoning from lead shot used by hunters, pollution from sewage, dairy runoff and industrial chemical discharges, and the consequent loss of oxygen in the water. The building of dams and culverts has restricted access to the waterways traditionally used by eels on their migration journeys. Ninety percent of pre-European wetlands have now been drained, and thousands of hectares of forest have been cut down. At the same time, the past 50 years have seen a steady increase in commercial fishing.[31] While Māori have customary take rights for cultural events, as well as a portion of the commercial take, some iwi [Maori nations] have stopped or minimised harvesting eels, concerned by their dwindling numbers.

In contrast to Māori knowledge of tuna kuwharuwharu, European knowledge has been comparatively recent and scarce. They were observed by the German-born surgeon and naturalist Ernst Dieffenbach between 1839 and 1841, while he was working for the New Zealand Company, a chartered British company that sought to establish a business model based on property and labour organisation that would expedite the systematic colonisation of Aotearoa. A specimen of the eel was collected by members of the Ross expedition as they returned after their Antarctica voyage in 1842. The species received the scientific name *Anguilla dieffenbachia*.[32]

---

29 McDowall 1991, 394–5.
30 Hunt 2021.
31 Potangaroa 2010, 14.
32 Dieffenbach 1843.

One of the problems in considering tuna kuwharuwharu as a subject of Western science is the shape and pattern of their lives. While being born, entering the river and eventually leaving the river to spawn and die can be described and partly documented, the everyday lives of these eels, their knowledge and behaviour, evade closer surveillance. In addition, like many other groups of eels, the movement of tuna kuwharuwharu in the open ocean is also largely unknown. David Righton and co-authors, in a 2012 article in the *Journal of Fish Biology*, argued that eel migration continued to remain largely a mystery. Despite the use of marine remote sensing, genetic analysis, computer modelling and electronic tagging, clear knowledge about eel movements in the open ocean still eludes scientists.[33] A long series of questions continues to baffle researchers. How do the eels achieve such incredibly long migrations? How do they metamorphose? What do they do all day long? Where do they spawn, and why there? How do they deal with changes in temperature, and with hydrostatic pressure when swimming at great depths?

Longfin eels, because of their size and relative visibility, have been electronically tagged, although these tags have eventually dropped off during the course of their migration. They have suggested, however, a partial route, past the north-east of New Caledonia, and a rate of migration – 20 to 25 kilometres a day – but without a clear indication of spawning grounds.[34] While Māori knowledge of tuna life and relationships, their seasonal movement and their ecological and cultural importance has increased over generations, a Western scientific focus on taxonomy, hierarchy and fish biology has prevented a fuller sense of how eels live and their relationships with others.

Discovery, collecting and subjectivity

Notions of scientific and zoological discovery do not just assume a previously unknown animal or group of animals; they also assume an unknown space. The narrations of and within such spaces reinforce

33 Righton, Aarestrup et al. 2012, 366.
34 Righton, Aarestrup et al. 2012, 371.

a sense of time that allows, or prepares its readers, for a sense of "newness" free from the determination of local or traceable history. Western enunciations of new species take place in a discursive space that is justified by scientific rigour and peer review but separated from the colonial contexts, and from the cultural and historical conditions, that enable them to operate as official and referential. The colonial violence enacted in enforcing the authority of colonial regimes and settlement in Australia, South Africa and Aotearoa is separated and erased in stories of zoological discovery, an oppressive political order concealed by a more abstract taxonomic order.

The term "collecting" as used in historical accounts of scientific discovery, works to flatten out social hierarchies and erase the labour of Indigenous and colonial subjects exploited in the obtaining of fish and other animals as scientific specimens, and to mask the violence preceding and facilitating each act of collection. Such violence does not merely exploit labour, however. Collecting as a historical sign is always also the exploitation of Indigenous knowledge, prior knowledge of the animals in question, knowledge informing where, when and how collecting can occur, and which must be written over in order to represent imperial knowledge as authoritative. For non-human animals, collecting does not simply mean a denial of agency, knowledge and history. It is always lethal. The history of Western biological discovery and taxonomy is always a history of killing, a celebration and lauding of power and knowledge written on the dead bodies of animals. Acquiescence and subservience are not options. Non-human animals serve the colonial order and facilitate settlement by their deaths: by their absence as living beings and by their presence as specimens or commodities. This fate is not confined to a few individual animals who are killed as exemplars or exhibits, but rather marks a change in the fortunes of larger or entire populations. Stories of colonial discovery have a strong correlation with an increased vulnerability and endangerment for endemic species. Dala, Gombessa and tuna kuwharuwharu populations all face serious threats to their continued survival as a consequence of their discovery by Western science.

Sea Country and fish places

The three colonial histories of which I have provided short accounts suggest that what problematises official narratives of discovery as authoritative, referential historic moments is a tension around time, space and the completeness of subjectivity. As Patrick Wolfe has argued, settler colonialism works perpetually towards the erasing of Indigenous people and culture, establishing structures and organising principles that facilitate the process of erasure.[35] In Australia, for example, it works to replace conceptions of an ancient, settled space with that of a "young and free"[36] white space, one which enables nature to be whitewashed as *terra nullius*. Within the context of this project, the idea and principles of Sea Country – as it is understood, practised and lived differently by different Aboriginal and Torres Strait Islander groups in Australia – disturb colonial time and space, in part by incorporating knowledges and practices on land now beneath the ocean and in water now reclaimed – that is, in spaces and times preceding and exceeding the historical and geographical borders of the nation.[37] This concept is particularly important in countering the disconnection and disorientation caused by forced relocation either away from coastal areas or to coastal areas that were not traditional country and where culture and ceremony could not be practised. Sea Country remembers specific sites of active, coastal engagement between human and non-human animals, and specific moments of meaning-making in which coastal inhabitants gained knowledge of, and bore witness to, the lives of one another. It is an idea that provokes and encourages us to imagine other stories and other perspectives, including those of fish who also precede and exceed us. Whitehouse, Watkin Lui et al. argue that Sea Country provides a context for addressing a new consciousness and a new way of learning and knowing, disrupting public discussions of conservation and the

35 Wolfe 2006.

36 From 1 January 2021, the words of the second line of the Australian National Anthem were amended from "For we are young and free" to "For we are one and free". See Australian Government, Department of the Prime Minister and Cabinet 2021.

37 See e.g. National Oceans Office 2002; Rist, Rassip et al. 2019; Whitehouse, Watkin Lui et al. 2014; Yunupingu and Muller 2009.

environment, where Western science and Eurocentric concepts tend to be privileged and settler colonial perspectives foregrounded.[38] Reference to Sea Country in Indigenous land claims, community consultations and coastal and marine management plans in Australia is often made in response to political and cultural demands regarding the ownership and use of waterways and coastal spaces, and, as exemplified by Dr Eve Fesl's statement opposing the planned building of the Traveston dam, in response to the continuation of modern and colonial expansion.

In working to place fish and people together as central actors in the political landscape of northern Canada, Zoe Todd challenges us to consider every space as a fish place:

> Every place is tended to by waters that cycle through the earth's hydrological systems and make their way back continuously to the ocean. And these watery arteries link us explicitly to the oceans that cover the majority of the globe. It is crucial, in times of environmental/socioecological upheaval, to underscore and impress the interconnectedness of lands, waters, space, people, and time ... [39]

While Todd's call for us to be more aware of the interrelatedness of all life, non-human and human, and to see the connections between terrestrial and aquatic ecologies, is grounded in Métis legal traditions and cosmology, the notion of collective reciprocal responsibilities and the recognition of kinship can clearly be seen in Gubbi Gubbi people's relationships with Dala and Moocooboola, and in Māori cultural relationships with tuna kuwharuwharu. It is in the light of these ancient, ethical and familial relationships that we gain an insight into the consequences of colonial settlement and the effect of separation and subjectivity on human and non-human kin.

38 Whitehouse, Watkin Lui et al. 2014.
39 Todd 2017.

Crypsis, subjectivity and settlement

To the colonial gaze, lungfish, coelacanths and eels are strange, nonconforming, unsettling fish. Their inscrutable histories provoke us to ask: How long have they known about us? How have they eluded and how do they continue to elude us? In each of the cases presented, groups of fish have been transformed into colonial subjects through their incorporation into specific and selective histories. As part of this subjectification, lungfish, coelacanths and longfin eel have experienced targeted violence in forms that include increased commercial or trophy fishing, specimen hunting, predation by introduced species and habitat degradation as a result of plant and animal agriculture. In each example, power has been exercised in controlling the way in which fish are perceived, made sense of and experienced.

Kathryn Yusoff challenges us to pay attention to non-human animals inhabiting insensible worlds, subjects whom we cannot meet on an even footing, and life that does not cooperate or cohabitate with us. Yusoff works on the premise that our modes of attention, discourse and ethics are shaped through aesthetic representational practices, arguing that human–non-human encounters are underpinned by a prior relation with representation.[40] Discrete, authoritative acts of representation, including nomenclature, speciation and archivisation, subject non-human animals to the sovereignty of biological sciences:

> The represented nonhuman subject is a thing caught between two worlds; as a life held in a space in which it cannot be held. In giving subjectivity, we take sovereignty. The thing is not as it would be on its own terms.[41]

Humans, particularly where and when they enter new and foreign spaces, are the least cryptic species, trumpeting and inscribing their presence as they impose themselves on the environments around them. They leave signs before and after their incursions. It is difficult for us to imagine ourselves as the objects of interspecies surveillance and

40 Yusoff 2012, 582.
41 Yusoff 2012, 583.

awareness. Cryptic animals, however, by resisting surveillance and detection, also resist representation. They are given to non-representational acts. By moving away from formal scientific description into the realm of anecdotal narrative, stories of discovery come into contact with alternative perspectives. The context in which each group of fish discussed became a subject of colonisation is significant and revealing. Discovery as a historic sign foregrounds specific actors, rendering them authorised and decisive, and specific events, recasting them as wondrous or miraculous, while concealing the social, cultural and political relations that enabled the actors and events to be represented in that way. The political contexts in which Gerard Krefft obtained his lungfish specimen, in which Marjorie Courtney-Latimer and James Leonard Brierley Smith lay claim to the resurrection of the coelacanth, in which Ernst Dieffenbach was able to describe and classify longfinned eels, and in which members of the Ross expedition obtained a specimen for the British Museum, are not remembered as spaces, times and social orders produced by colonial violence, despite that violence being germane to establishing the social order that enabled the historic moment to be produced. They are, however, spaces of silencing as much as they are spaces of enunciation. The historic is simultaneously the quotidian, and the unremarkable. In enunciations that seek to produce knowledge as authority, as controlling, and as settled, contact with colonial subjects reveals competing versions of knowledge, other relationships and other conceptions of time and space, knowledges and relationships, both human and non-human, that precede and contain these enunciations.

Inasmuch as we, as animal studies scholars, tell animal stories motivated by care and attention, Yusoff calls for us to acknowledge the violence we have inherited in our relations with non-humans, arguing that shifting the visual or conceptual frame of ecological care, ethical concern, welfare and conservation allows us to keep in mind our material connections with non-human animals. Distancing violence allows us as narrators not to be implicated in that violence despite it being a primary mode of engaging and of the obtaining of knowledge. The degree to which biotic subjects are subjectified is influenced by what is seen or unseen, and how subjectivities are made and disclosed.

What is described and narrated as a mystery, as part of the cryptic nature of some animals, suggests something other than merely surprisingly delayed or deferred discoveries. It is the all-too-likely possibility that coelacanths and lungfish saw us thousands of years before we saw them. Crypsis does not simply signify an ability to evade or an inability to be detected or observed; it marks an excess in perception and experience. While longfinned eels, lungfish and coelacanths are indeed nocturnal, and to varying degrees camouflaged and lead subterranean or deeply submerged lifestyles including periods of dormancy, they each possess heightened sensory perception and awareness. Coelacanths and lungfish are both electroreceptive, possessing the ability to sense even minute changes in the electrical fields generated by oceanic currents. Like lungfish, longfinned eels have an excellent sense of smell, which in their case is enhanced by tubular nostrils that stick out in front of their noses to help in hunting. They also have sensors on their sides, taste buds on their heads, and highly sensitive skin, allowing them to sense what is around them in waterways. More-than-human awareness of human presence provides a problem for colonial histories, suggesting a starting point that precedes colonisation and settlement, foregrounding the generational achievements of species that have survived for millions of years in the face of countless threats.

The names "Dala", "Gombessa" and "tuna kuwharuwharu" denote more than Indigenous names for known species. They not only mark a different body of knowledge shaped by different people, spaces and times, but also posit a sense of specificity and connection that highlights and questions the colonial demands inherent in scientific narratives that seek to define and classify fish within a universal regime of knowledge. Western science has a specific cultural history that is very much entangled with a colonising project. Settling and securing spaces that are already inhabited and that already hold significance compel the coloniser to also settle and fix meanings and knowledge. For those seeking to assume and reinforce such an order, the cryptic lives of Dala, Gombessa and tuna kuwharuwharu, their ancient histories and diverse relationships, continue to prove unsettling.

References

Allen, Gerald R., Stephen H. Midgley and Mark Allen (2002). *Field Guide to the Freshwater Fishes of Australia*. Perth: Western Australian Museum.

Appudurai, Audrey (2016). The lungfishes from a historical perspective: how humans see the other. *Otherness: Essays and Studies* 5(2): 79–110.

Australian Government, Department of the Prime Minister and Cabinet (2021). Australian National Anthem. Canberra: Commonwealth of Australia. https://www.pmc.gov.au/honours-and-symbols/australian-national-symbols/australian-national-anthem.

Balcombe, Jonathan (2017). *What a Fish Knows: The Inner Lives of Our Underwater Cousins*. New York: Farrar, Straus and Giroux.

Bruton, Michael N. and Sheila E. Coutouvidis (1991). An inventory of all known specimens of the coelacanth *Latimeria chalumnae*, with comments on trends in the catches. *Environmental Biology of Fishes* 32: 371–90.

Carneiro, Jeferson, Guilherme Moreira Dutra, Rodrigo Moreira Nobre, Luiz Marcelo de Lima Pinheiro, Pedro Andrés Chira Oliva, Iracilda Sampaio et al. (2021). Evidence of cryptic speciation in South American lungfish. *Journal of Zoological Systematics and Evolutionary Research* 59(3): 760–71.

Coffey, Renee (2006). Frontier violence in Gin Gin: a history of murder, massacre and myth. Honours thesis, School of History, Philosophy, Religion & Classics, University of Queensland.

Dieffenbach, Ernst (1843). *Travels in New Zealand: With Contributions to the Geography, Geology, Botany and Natural History of That Country*. London: J. Murray.

Erdmann, Mark V. (1999). An account of the first living coelacanth known to scientists from Indonesian waters. *Environmental Biology of Fishes* 54(4): 439–43.

Erdmann, Mark V., Roy L. Caldwell and M. Kasim Moosa (1998). Indonesian "king of the sea" discovered. *Nature* 395: 335.

Fesl, E. 2007a. *Submission to the Senate Standing Committee on Rural and Regional Affairs and Transport*. https://www.aph.gov.au/~/media/wopapub/senate/committee/rrat_ctte/completed_inquiries/2004_07/traveston_dam/submissions/sub60_pdf.ashx.

Fesl, E. 2007b. A bid to save "Dala" the Queensland lungfish. http://www.savethemaryriver.com/_mgxroot/page_10786.html.

Fricke, Hans (1997). Living coelacanths: values, eco-ethics and human responsibility. *Marine Ecology Progress Series* 161: 1–15.

Fricke, Hans, Jurgen Schauer, Karen Hissmann, Lutz Kasang and Raphael Plante (1991). Coelacanth *Latimeria chalumnae* aggregates in caves: first observations on their resting habitat and social behaviour. *Environmental Biology of Fishes* 30: 281–5.

Hoyle, Simon D. and Don J. Jellyman (2002). Longfin eels need reserves: modelling the effects of commercial harvest on stocks of New Zealand eels. *Marine and Freshwater Research* 53(5): 887–95.

Hunt, Ellie (2021). A creature of mystery: New Zealand's love-hate relationship with eels. *Guardian*, 24 April. http://bit.ly/3SfH4xa.

Jellyman, Don J. (2014). Freshwater eels and people in New Zealand: a love/hate relationship. In K. Tsukamoto and M. Kuroki, eds. *Eels and Humans*, 143–53. Tokyo: Springer. https://doi.org/10.1007/978-4-431-54529-3_10.

Jellyman, Don J. (2007). Status of New Zealand fresh-water eel stocks and management initiatives. *ICES Journal of Marine Science* 64(7): 1379–86.

Johanson, Zerina, John Long, John A. Talent, Philippe Janvier and James W. Warren (2006). Oldest coelacanth, from the early Devonian of Australia. *Biology Letters* 2(3): 443–6.

Johnson, Steve (2017). Australian lungfish "Granddad," the oldest zoo animal in Chicago, dies. *Chicago Tribune*, 6 February. https://bit.ly/3lQ0o81.

Kemp, A. (1986). The biology of the Australian lungfish, *Neoceratodus forsteri* (Krefft 1870). *Journal of Morphology* S1: 181–98.

Kind, Peter K. (2011). The natural history of the Australian lungfish *Neoceratodus Forsteri* (Krefft, 1870). In Jorden Morup Jorgensen and Jean Joss, eds. *The Biology of Lungfishes*, 61–97. Boca Raton: CRC Press.

Krefft, Gerard (1870a). Letter to the editor. *Sydney Morning Herald*, 18 January: 5. https://trove.nla.gov.au/newspaper/title/35#.

Krefft, Gerard (1870b). Description of a giant amphibian allied to the genus *Lepidosiren* from the Wide-Bay district, Queensland. *Proceedings of the Zoological Society of London* 16: 221–4. https://www.biodiversitylibrary.org/part/71832.

Laurie, Arthur (1952). Early Gin Gin and the Blaxland tragedy. *Journal of the Royal Historical Society of Queensland* 4(5): 709–17.

Machado, Lucio Paulo, Helmut Wellendorf and Paulo M. Brito (2010). On the type material of *Lepidosiren paradoxa* Fitzinger, 1837 (Sarcopterygii, Dipnoi). *Comptes Rendus Biologies* 333: 56–60.

McDowall, Robert M. (1991). Freshwater fisheries research in New Zealand: processes, projects, and people. *New Zealand Journal of Marine and Freshwater Research* 25(4): 393–413.

National Oceans Office (2002). *Sea Country – An Indigenous Perspective: The South-east Regional Marine Plan Assessment Reports.* Hobart: Marine Parks Branch, Parks Australia.

O'Malley, Padraig (2021a). 1923. Native Urban Areas Act no 21. https://omalley.nelsonmandela.org/omalley/index.php/site/q/03lv01538/04lv01646/05lv01758.htm.

O'Malley, Padraig (2021b). 1926. Mines & Works Amendment Act no 25. https://omalley.nelsonmandela.org/omalley/index.php/site/q/03lv01538/04lv01646/05lv01763.htm.

Potangaroa, Joseph. 2010. *Tuna Kuwharuwharu: The Longfinned Eel.* Wellington: Rangitane O Wairarapa Inc., Greater Wellington Regional Council and Te Papa Atawhai Department of Conservation.

Righton, D., K. Aarestrup, D. Jellyman, P. Sébert, G. van den Thillart and K. Tsukamoto (2012). The *Anguilla* spp. migration problem: 40 million years of evolution and two millennia of speculation. *Journal of Fish Biology* 81: 365–86.

Rist, Phil, Whitney Rassip, Djalinda Yunupingu, Jonathan Wearne, Jackie Gould, Melanie Dulfer-Hyams et al. (2019). Indigenous protected areas in Sea Country: Indigenous-driven collaborative marine protected areas in Australia. *Aquatic Conservation: Marine and Freshwater Ecosystems* 29(S2): 1–14. https://doi.org/10.1002/aqc.3052.

Smith, James Leonard Brierley (1956). *Old Fourlegs: The Story of the Coelacanth.* London: Longmans, Green and Co.

Todd, Zoe (2018). Refracting the state through human-fish relations: fishing, Indigenous legal orders and colonialism in north/western Canada. *Decolonization: Indigeneity, Education & Society* 7(1): 60–75.

Todd, Zoe (2017). Protecting life below water: tending to relationality and expanding oceanic consciousness beyond coastal zones. *American Anthropologist*, 17 October. https://www.americananthropologist.org/deprovincializing-development-series/protecting-life-below-water.

Wadiwel, Dinesh (2016). Do fish resist? *Cultural Studies Review* 22(1): 196–242.

Whitehouse, Hilary, Felecia Watkin Lui, Juanita Sellwood, M.J. Barrett and Philemon Chigeza (2014). Sea Country: navigating Indigenous and colonial ontologies in Australian environmental education. *Environmental Education Research* 20(1): 56–69.

Wolfe, Patrick (2006). Settler colonialism and the elimination of the native. *Journal of Genocide Research* 8(4): 387–409.

Yunupingu, D. and S. Muller (2009). Cross-cultural challenges for Indigenous Sea Country management in Australia. *Australasian Journal of Environmental Management* 16(3): 158–67.

Yusoff, Kathryn (2012). Aesthetics of loss: biodiversity, banal violence and biotic subjects. *Transactions of the Institute of British Geographers* 37(4): 578–92.

6

Speculative shit: Bison world-making and dung pat pluralities

Danielle Taschereau Mamers

Figure 6.1 *Good-Bye, Uncle Sam, I Am a Subject of the King.* N.A. Forsyth.

A single bison is driven up a narrow wooden chute into a waiting freight car, emblazoned with white letters: Northern Pacific N.P.R. Men in suits and felt hats stand atop the car overseeing those in work shirts leading the animal. A boy leans over the corral fence and stares directly into the camera. Identifying the stereograph, the photographer's caption is typewritten below: "Good-Bye Uncle Sam, I Am a Subject of the King." Taken by settler journalist Norman A. Forsyth in 1907 at the round-up of the last free-ranging bison herd in North America, the photograph is a scene of settler colonial alienation in action. As Anna Loewenhaupt Tsing describes, alienation is the process of tearing things from lifeworlds and making them into objects of exchange.[1] Alienation is a process of transformation, a central component of what Tsing explains as the translation machine of capital, which works "across living arrangements, turning worlds into assets".[2] The bison led up the wooden chute and onto the waiting boxcar was marched out of her lifeworld, and out of a landscape shared with her herd, other species and Indigenous peoples in the verdant Flathead Valley of what is currently called Montana. The alienating removal of bison from the valley and translation of the herd into objects of consumption are characterised by what Goenpul scholar Aileen Moreton-Robinson diagnoses as the possessive function of whiteness. White possessiveness, Moreton-Robinson argues, is a system in which white supremacist racial hierarchies are anchored in the dispossession of Indigenous lands and the disavowal of Indigenous sovereignties and relationships that "exist outside of the logic of capital".[3] The alienation of bison is at once an imposition of colonial logics of capital and possession, as well as the active repudiation of lifeworlds beyond capital. Removing bison was one act within processes of asserting white possession in the Flathead Valley and across the continent.

The critical methods of settler colonial studies, visual studies or critical history offer one avenue for analysing this image and the historical moment it depicts. Such an analysis would pay careful attention to the men, the rail and fence infrastructures they had built, and their alienating work conducted in the name of colonial states. Indeed, the men atop the boxcar and their captured bison are the intended subjects of the image. Forsyth, a photographer based in Butte,

1 Tsing 2015, 121.
2 Tsing 2015, 133. It is crucial to note that human bodies were also subject to alienation under settler colonisation, including the violent processes of enslavement, indentured labour, and confinement to reserves and reservations. For analyses of these processes, see Bandhar 2018; Daschuk 2013; Day 2016.
3 Moreton-Robinson 2015, 191.

Montana, travelled 250 kilometres north-west to Ravalli to document the round-up of the last free-ranging bison herd on the continent. Forsyth's stereographs are a visual record that celebrated the success of a state-run conservation effort – an effort made necessary by state-sanctioned bison extermination across the continent and state-ordered dispossession of the Flathead Valley through federal allotment policy. Forsyth sold the "Good-Bye, Uncle Sam" image to Underwood and Underwood, a stereograph producer and distributor, who bundled it with Forsyth's other images of the round-up and circulated them to customers along with a brief history of bison in Montana. The set of images would have been sold to middle-class owners of stereoscope devices or to schools and offered as an educational spectacle depicting the end of the so-called frontier. The stereograph is an image of capture. The animal is made to symbolise the final form of wildness in territory claimed as America while being transferred between two human worlds, from the domain of "Uncle Sam" to that of the British King of the Dominion of Canada. While hundreds of thousands of bison had already been transformed into material objects of colonial capital – via trade in hides, tongues and bones – this photographed bison and the rest of the herd being rounded up for sale to Canada (and the British King!) were rendered as symbolic capital, circulated as signs of both settler nation-states.[4]

But the image can be analysed in other ways, beyond questions of settler colonial state practices or even critical lenses of alienation and infrastructure. These concepts provide only a partial account of what Forsyth's photograph depicts. Alienation and infrastructure do not create the imaginative space needed for engaging with the questions of multispecies relationality or world-making. These concepts emphasise the tearing Tsing identifies, *but not the lives that are torn.* To consider the relational lifeworlds from which bison were torn by settler alienation and to apprehend the stakes of extermination and conservation via containment, this chapter engages bison world-making and entangled multispecies relationships rather than the translation of lives into assets. I take Forsyth's depiction of colonial processes of extraction and instead address the bison – a being who transforms the place she lives with her

---

4 Shukin 2009.

presence. Refusing the figure-ground relation around which the image is composed, and the tendency in Western art history to foreground the human subject as the only vertical element in the landscape, I direct a multifocal gaze downwards into the dirt – a space where plural multispecies relations proliferate.

By engaging bison and other non-human beings as subjects with histories and agencies, entangled in plural relationships – not only as consumed objects contained by the asset-logics of capital – I offer a disobedient reading of Forsyth's image which activates elements of the stereograph for purposes oppositional to its colonial context of creation, inspired by the work of photo theorist Gabrielle Moser.[5] The stereograph is one moment within the visual and archival record of the rounding-up of bison from the Flathead Valley that could be analysed for what it explicitly contains – men labouring, men observing, their trains and fences, a single bison. But in this chapter, I attend to elements in the scene that are out of focus and not readily available to sight. The result is an experiment in alternative ways of seeing – namely, trying to think with the lifeworld of the bison and the other creatures that coexist in its proximity. My analysis of Forsyth's image and my experiment with other ways of seeing the depicted bison and her world centre's multispecies relations as co-constitutive, active and indeterminate. By engaging in the speculative narration of the depicted bison's world and her relations with the landscape and with non-human beings, my reading activates the photograph in ways that emphasise bison as co-creators of worlds. Looking beyond the demonstration of settler power over bison life – the intended subject of the stereograph – my method instead opens up questions about thinking with and imagining lives that may not be fully visible or knowable.

Indigenous scholarship on multispecies relations and non-human world-making grounds this approach. Non-human protagonists are abundant in Indigenous histories, political and legal orders and philosophies, where land, water and non-human beings are sources of knowledge, origins and relations.[6] For example, in his history of the

5 Moser 2019, 2.

6 For just a few examples, see Kimmerer 2013; King 2003; Little Bear 2000; Simpson 2014; 2011; Todd 2014; Whealdon 2001.

Oceti Sakowin nations of the Mni Sose (Missouri River) bottomlands, Lower Brule Sioux scholar Nick Estes centres the waters of Mni Sose and the fellow human and non-human relatives whose lifeworlds were and are entwined with the river. Citing the account of Oglala prophet Nicholas Black Elk, Estes describes the interconnected beings in the region as kin relations who have mutually suffered waves of colonial invasion that forced Indigenous peoples and their animal kin – including bison, deer, elk and wolves – to flee their homelands.[7] Estes also narrates the history of Pte Ska Win – White Calf Buffalo Woman – who formed the first treaty with bison and other non-humans, a covenant which continues to play a central role in Lakota lifeworlds.[8] These are just two instances from one nation, but they offer a glimpse into the multispecies relationality that has always been at the centre of Indigenous life, scholarship and history. Indeed, as Dakota science scholar Kim TallBear indicates, multispecies relations include "the lands, waters, and other-than-human beings with whom Indigenous peoples are co-constituted".[9] Such relations, TallBear asserts, are central to the very possibility of Indigenous life: "Indigenous peoples come into being *as* Peoples in longstanding and intricate relation with these continents and the other life forms here."[10]

Thinking with non-human beings is also an emergent mode of research in settler-dominated academic disciplines, such as anthropology, critical theory, literary studies and science studies – one that does not always credit the foundational, place-specific and relational contributions of Indigenous scholarship. In emphasising the contingencies, indeterminacies, multiplicities and histories of multispecies world-building, research in this vein articulates how the activities and relations of making a life produce beings and their worlds – often in ways that refuse narratives of human dominance or clean distinctions between nature and culture.[11] For example, in her narrative

7 Estes 2019, 10.
8 Estes 2019, 109.
9 TallBear 2019, 24.
10 TallBear 2019, 24 [emphasis in original].
11 Just a few examples of this work include de la Cadena and Blaser 2018; Haraway 2016; 2008; Hovorka 2017; Kirksey and Helmreich 2010; Sundberg 2014; van Dooren 2019; 2014; van Dooren, Kirksey and Münster 2016.

of mutualist entanglements of matsutake mushrooms with pine forests, Tsing aims to decentre human protagonists. Indicating that her audience is likely not used to stories without human heroes, she asks: "Can I show landscape as the protagonist of an adventure in which humans are only one kind of participant?"[12] Indigenous histories and articulations of relationalities have long demonstrated ways of knowing and telling, in which humans are one among many beings involved in co-creating worlds. Rather than making Indigenous knowledge additive to the more recent environmental humanities literature, this chapter centres Indigenous histories, political theories and science.

I come to the questions of bison world-making and multispecies relations as a white settler scholar who has primarily lived in urban settings. From this position, I do not claim to fully understand how bison are experienced and known as relations to Indigenous peoples on the prairie. My understanding of land and life has been shaped in powerful ways by Euro-Western conceptual frameworks and critiques – limitations which are an effect of white settler privilege and humanities research training. Writing in the Australian context, settler scholar Anja Kanngieser suggests that non-Indigenous peoples working in service of Indigenous peoples' goals ought to begin "by starting with what we don't know".[13] With a similar humility, I engage the knowledge of Indigenous and non-Indigenous conservation biologists in order to think through the roles and relations of bison in prairie ecologies so that I can approach Forsyth's photograph from perspectives beyond the lenses of alienation and infrastructure. Expertise from Indigenous philosophy (particularly Métis scholar Zoe Todd's studies of fish pluralities), Indigenous and settler science and multispecies ethnography provides insight into bison world-making in ways that are located in the specificities of place, relations and histories. With a method of speculative narration and multiple ways of knowing, I present Forsyth's stereograph not only as a depiction of the end of one bison's world, but as an entry point into the plurality of relations bison world-making brings into being.

---

12 Tsing 2015, 155.

13 Kanngieser quoted in Kanngieser and Todd 2020, 392.

Situated and submerged perspectives

With an attunement to plural relations, the complexities of non-human interrelatedness and the multiplicities perceptible from a submerged perspective, I return to Forsyth's image. The six men atop the boxcar likely deemed themselves actors of considerable importance to the scene over which they presided. Beyond the loading of this particular bison, the wider operation of rounding up the wild bison living in the Flathead Valley was a five-year undertaking for which the Dominion of Canada contracted Michel Pablo – the long-time protector and caretaker of the herd, of Pikani Blackfoot and Mexican descent – and fellow residents of the Flathead reservation to chase down more than 700 bison, containing them in a purpose-built system of corrals and chutes and then shipping them across the 49th parallel by rail.[14] One after the next, over a three-year period, each bison was pushed through wooden chutes and into a waiting car, much like the bison in Forsyth's image. To these men in suits and hats, this loading of train cars with wild lives represented the success of a project that early settler conservationists heralded as the "most important act in the interest of conservation of the noblest of our quadrupeds".[15]

Forsyth's composition reiterates the sense of gravitas that the suited men project. Adhering to Renaissance conventions, the stereograph has a defined fore-, middle- and background, with the bison as the men's focal point as well as the point where the image's horizontal, vertical and diagonal lines converge. Forsyth made the image from a high vantage point. He likely perched on a corral fence to protect himself from the bison, while equalising his sightline with the gazes of the men on the boxcar. Activating historical and political ways of looking, the stereograph is the product of European and settler colonial perspectives, knowledges and prerogatives.

There is more going on in the scene than Forsyth's camera intended to frame. Rather than meeting the men's gazes and looking down to the bison, a "submerged perspective" looks up from the muddy foreground

14 For a more detailed history of the origin and round-up of Pablo's herd, see Taschereau Mamers 2020, 129–32.

15 American Bison Society 1911, 36.

and out from the montane background pastures. Submerged perspectives, Macarena Gómez-Barris describes, "perceive local terrains as sources of knowledge, vitality, and livability".[16] Shifting and multiplying vantage points attend to situated relations made invisible by settler colonial ways of seeing: those processes of representation and documentation that simultaneously make Indigenous lives and lands visible to settler state agents while targeting those same lives and lands for assimilation, dispossession and erasure.[17] Looking at the Flathead Valley from a submerged perspective of multiplicity decentres the settler colonial ways of seeing at work in Forsyth's composition and in the calculations of colonial economies to instead create possibilities for a decolonial analysis attentive to worlds made invisible by species hierarchies, alienation and extraction.

The suited men atop the boxcar and those in workwear on the ground – completing a final task of coaxing the bison along – and their infrastructure each impacted life in the Flathead Valley. Yet, bison are also actors of profound importance to the broader scene Forsyth's photograph depicts: one of rolling grasslands and aspen parkland in a glacier-sculpted valley, bordered by mountains covered in montane spruce and subalpine fir forests. As a keystone species, bison have a dramatic influence on the region and have long played an ecological role that no other species can fill. Bison presence and the practical activities herds pursue in making their lives affect the whole ecosystem. Forsyth's photograph depicts not only the removal of a single bison from her lifeworld, but the disruption of an entire ecosystem. The removal of the herd from the Flathead Valley and the extermination of more than 30 million bison in the preceding four decades meant the end of grazing, wallowing and migrating practices that made the land hospitable for other species. The female bison in Forsyth's photo may have weighed more than 500 kilograms, but her life activities made possible the worlds of beetles, toads and birds, as well as supporting those of wolves and humans. Analysing the specificity of these relationships – their contingency, multiplicity and historicity – brings some of the complexity of bison world-making into view. From the

16 Gómez-Barris 2017, 1.
17 Taschereau Mamers, forthcoming.

perspective of bison world-making, settler colonisation and the state-run conservation that followed signalled the end of many worlds.

To provide an analysis guided by the world-making capabilities of bison and their multiple relations and entanglements, I offer a brief illustration of the plural worlds that come into being through bison dung. The largest land mammals in what is currently called North America, bison eat a lot. As generalist browsers who primarily eat grasses and forbs, bison spend more than nine hours per day grazing. Every day, an adult male will eat 10 to 14 kilograms of vegetation to sustain a 900-kilogram body, while adult females need 7 to 10 kilograms of greens to nourish their 500-kilogram frames.[18] Moving up to 25 kilometres a day through open fields, wooded areas, along lakes and rivers and sometimes into the mountains, bison collect plant spores and pollen in their hair and noses along with the vegetation they take into their four-chamber ruminant stomachs. Providing a means of movement for spores and pollen, bison contribute to plant flourishing and biodiversity in the areas they range.[19] The selective browsing of bison – preferring the grasses that can often outcompete other plants – also opens up prairie fields for increased photosynthesis, allowing a wider array of plants to flourish.[20] But a primary contribution to biodiversity and flourishing is the result of all of their grazing: the 11 to 13 litres of dung bison excrete every day.[21] Each excretion – often referred to as a dung pat – becomes a temporary world of microscopic relations, supporting the lives of at least 300 species of insects and worms and more than 1,000 individuals.[22]

One relation whose livelihood is made possible by bison is *Onthophagus knausi*, a very small dung beetle, growing to just 5 millimetres, which flourishes among bison.[23] The small black beetles are the first beings to arrive on a fresh dung pat, attracted to it by their keen sense of smell. A bison's dung pat is a dense source of nutrition

18 Fortin, Fryxell and Pilote 2002.
19 Mueller, Spengler et al. 2020, 8.
20 National Parks Service 2016a.
21 National Parks Service 2016b.
22 National Parks Service 2016b.
23 Barber, Hosler et al. 2019, 425.

for insects, worms, birds, amphibians and other small animals, as well as for the soil itself. An entire microbial community is at work in bison stomachs, helping them digest grasses and forbs, converting plant cellulose to accessible carbohydrate energy.[24] Some of these microbes and bacteria, as well as enzymes and minerals, are excreted along with indigestible plant matter, including seeds. However, these nutrients, enzymes and seeds only become available to other beings through the work of *O. knausi* and other dung beetles. Unlike cattle dung, bison dung remains soft and is an anaerobic environment, but the tunnelling work of dung beetles creates pathways that help open the pat to light and oxygen to create a hospitable environment for other beetles and insects.[25] Along with tunnelling through pats, some beetles form pieces of dung into balls that they bury or roll away from the pat, further dispersing its seeds, microbes and nutrients. The work of the dung beetles brings the nitrogen-rich dung into contact with soil-dwelling microbes, who in turn transform the nitrogen into ammonia that can be absorbed by plants.[26] By activating the process of breaking down the dung, the beetles' work prevents it from becoming a host for parasites. In making nutrients accessible to other insects and the prairie soil, the beetles also keep bison and other animals safe from contracting parasites.

Other insects, including other beetles and flies, as well as an abundance of earthworms, come to dwell in the dung pat in the few days before it is fully broken down or desiccated. The flourishing of invertebrate life attracts insectivores, including frogs, turtles, bats and birds, each of whom further disperse the nutrients and seeds in the dung while supporting other animal communities. For example, bison consultant Wes Olson reported that every anthill at Alberta's Elk Island National Park – the place where descendants of the bison in Forsyth's stereograph live today – is established on a bison pat. Northern flickers flock to the region to feed on the anthills and, while there, create nesting cavities in trees that are later inhabited by flying squirrels when the flickers migrate south.[27] The flourishing of microbial and invertebrate

24 Lott 2002, 48.
25 Olson 2016.
26 National Parks Service 2016b.
27 Olson 2016.

life in bison dung pats is often a lifeline for migrating birds or for black-tailed prairie dogs, who find their first meals in bison dung before other food becomes available on snowy spring landscapes.[28] Finally, after being a source of sustenance for so many, dried dung pats are collected and used to fuel fires by members of the Flathead, Blackfoot and other plains Indigenous nations.

All of this life, reproduction, feeding and nutrient dispersal occurs on a single dung pat. As bison herds moved throughout the prairies, such convergences of interconnected lives repeated on a daily basis, across massive swathes of land. Some of these relations persist in the absence of bison, but their grazing and migration patterns and dung characteristics are unique and not readily replaced. While some dung beetles have adapted to cattle or deer dung, for example, the little *Onthophagus knausi* disappears in the absence of bison.[29]

Pluralities and non-human societies

This brief account of worlds brought into being by bison dung is animated by the work of conservation biologists, but my attention to questions of relations and plurality is guided by the work of Indigenous scholars. In particular, my approach to bison worlds is informed by Zoe Todd's discussion of fish as plural. Describing her research in the Inuvik region of the Northwest Territories, Todd writes:

> In Paulatuuq, I also learned that fish exist and operate in pluralities – fish are simultaneously food; specimens of study for scientific research; sites of memory and stories; non-human persons with agency.[30]

The worlds of lake trout in arctic lakes and of plains bison are vastly different, as are their experiences of landscapes and waterscapes and between fishy and earthy relations. Adapting learning from one

28 Olson 2016.
29 Barber, Hosler et al. 2019, 425.
30 Todd 2018, 61.

situated, local site of observation – what Todd calls a kin study – and applying it to another site risks replicating the case study paradigm popular in much of Western science, where places are made to stand in for one another and situated knowledge is universalised and made to move.[31] Yet it is my sense that Todd's attention to fish pluralities and her call to pay careful attention to both the multiplicities and the specificities of relations offer lessons for understanding bison relations as pluralities. Bison, too, are simultaneously food, objects of human and non-human knowledge, and agential beings who work together as a herd. Their dung also operates in pluralities. It feeds, it shelters, it is a site of convergence for other non-human communities, and it nourishes the soil in ways that create possibilities for future life. The dung pat plurality enacts a reciprocal enlivening of the prairie earth that supports a multiplicity of lifeways – from the microbial to the mammalian.

The notion of dung pat pluralities is also informed by Vanessa Watts' argument that non-human beings are agential and form societies – that society is not restricted to human relationships. Non-human worlds, Watts argues, are more than complex ecosystems. Rather, "non-human beings choose how they reside, interact, and develop relationships with other non-human beings".[32] From her Haudenosaunee and Anishinaabe perspective, Watts explains that "habitats and ecosystems are better understood as societies", where ethical structures and interspecies agreements emerge.[33] The dung pat, then, is not merely an instance of "nutrient cycling" or "ecosystem services", as it might be described by conservation biologists whose research I cited in my description of *Onthophagus knausi* and the many other creatures whose lives converge in bison dung. Rather than project metaphors of human labour practices (and often capitalist metaphors) onto other species, Watts' articulation of non-human societies enacting interspecies agreements acknowledges relationality, experiences and knowledge that exceed the dimensions of life perceptible to humans. While it is true that the activities of *O. knausi* and other dung beetles

31 Kanngieser and Todd 2020, 386–7.

32 Watts 2013, 23.

33 Watts 2013, 23.

provide an important service to the prairie landscape and its inhabitants, describing their activities through human labour metaphors reduces beetle life. Imposing metaphors of human labour – as well as other concepts such as "competition" or "scarcity" – not only delimits non-human lives and lifeways, but also traps human lives within these concepts by treating them as universal or natural rather than constructed. The tunnelling and burrowing of *O. knausi* and others might be the result of mechanistic instinct. But perhaps my human perspective is unable to grasp aspects of the experiences of moving small legs edged with claws and spurs to swim through the warm muck of fresh dung or in the coordination of activities between *O. knausi* and other members of dung pat pluralities. To acknowledge the existences and agencies of the non-human beings with whom humans share the world does not require mutual intelligibility between the worlds of different beings or shared experiences.

Pluralism and the complex array of relations that entangle human and non-human beings are not necessarily questions of harmony or of natural or necessary balance. As I interpret Todd, Watts and other Indigenous theorists, their methods attend to the many ways non-human beings make arrangements as they pursue projects and livelihoods. A vast array of activities makes up the livelihoods and worlds of various species, and these do not necessarily coincide in perfect harmony. Pluralities and webs of relation contain agonism and sometimes antagonism, but also coordination and varying degrees of arrangement and perhaps agreement. Rather than project a fantasy of a harmonious coexistence on bison and the dung pat pluralities they live alongside, the attentiveness to situated relations Todd and Watts advocate engages treaty as a framework for relationality. Gina Starblanket, a Cree/Saultaux political theorist, describes treaty-based frameworks for relating as "diplomatic processes for negotiating relations of non-violent and generative coexistence between living beings in shared geographies".[34] Beyond the transactional – and frequently dishonest – approaches settler states have taken to treaties, Starblanket emphasises that Indigenous elders understand treaties as agreements for using land that includes responsibilities and a

34 Starblanket 2019, 444.

"nonhierarchical co-existence between nations".[35] Crucially, treaty does not transform land into fungible property, nor is it an affirmation of innate, essential harmony or the assumption of underlying consensus. As agreements, treaties are ongoing processes of relation and non-subordination that create conditions for societies living together on shared lands. Both Todd, in the context of human– fish relations in Paulatuuq, and Estes, in the context of relations between bison and other non-human beings and the Oceti Sakowin nations of the Mni Sose bottomlands, identify the reciprocal responsibilities and multispecies coexistence within landscapes and waterscapes as treaty relationships. Affirming these relations as treaties recognises the agency of the many parties involved, even if the kinds of treaties or agreements that may be in place between bison and the other creatures with which herds coexist (including the many species that make up dung pat pluralities) may not bear resemblance to treaties negotiated between human nations.

An expansive view of non-human agency and organisation interweaves with the plurality Todd describes. As Watts explains, non-human societies are active and directly influence how human societies organise themselves. Cree political theorist Kiera Ladner's research demonstrates the influential roles of bison and human–bison relations of Siikisika (Blackfoot) political structures. Buffalo, Ladner reports, were described to her by her Siikisikaawa teachers as their nation's older brother and as an important source for understanding governance structures, they were "acknowledged for teaching Siikisikaawa, directly or indirectly about community".[36] For example, clan systems of social and political organisation were modelled in part on buffalo social structures, which were constantly in flux and responded to seasonal changes. While buffalo gathered in large collectivities of tens of thousands in the summer months, their primary social units were smaller herds with independent, internal social structures.[37] Bison social structures are characterised by non-coercive leadership, shared flexibly across male and female members of the

35 Starblanket 2019, 453.

36 Ladner 2003, 145.

37 Ladner 2003, 137.

herd in response to changing circumstances and conditions. Blackfoot nations, Ladner writes, followed a similar structure of seasonal gatherings and dispersals, collaborative leadership and collective decision-making.[38] Across different examples of bison influence and human–bison relations, Ladner's research demonstrates how bison operate in pluralities: they were crucial sources of food and sustenance, but they were also teachers, objects of observational research across generations of Indigenous scholars, and a society that influenced the social and political organisation of Siikisikaawa peoples and other plains Indigenous nations. Ladner's observations are just one example of bison pluralities and the complex interrelation of plains Indigenous nations and buffalo herds. Métis scholar Adam Gaudry identifies core principles of Métis as originating in political practices of self-ownership, interrelation and consent that structured annual buffalo hunts, arguing that "the buffalo hunt is the Métis constitution".[39] Cree filmmaker and scholar Tasha Hubbard has documented how such relations and the mourning of the loss of buffalo relations animate a wide range of Indigenous cultural productions, including literary works by Mourning Dove, D'Arcy McNickle, and Thomas King, as well as visual art by Dana Claxton and Adrian Stimson.[40]

To engage Forsyth's photograph from a submerged perspective interested in a kin study of non-human societies means attending to plural dimensions of existence and experience. Analysing the stereograph through the theoretical lenses of alienation and white possessiveness might yield compelling critical insights. I have taken this approach to other photographs from the 1907 round-up.[41] But this method often has little to say about the worlds torn and claimed by possessive settler alienation, particularly those extended circles of bison relations such as dung pat pluralities. Indigenous scholars offer critical insights and guidance for attending to relationality in ways that decentre the acquisitive perspectives of settler colonial capital, which I engage with from the perspective of a settler who does not truly know what

38 Ladner 2003, 145–6.
39 Gaudry 2014, 95.
40 Hubbard 2016.
41 Taschereau Mamers 2020.

it means to live in political or spiritual relation with bison. However, learning from Indigenous scholarship is crucial to settler-conducted research like my own, undertaken in service of struggles for decolonisation via disrupting imperial structures of thought and action, disrupting hegemonic modes of interpretation and reimagining worldly possibilities.[42] Todd's engagement with lake trout in Paulatuuq as existing and operating in pluralities and Watts' argument that land, non-human communities and habitats are societies that enact interspecies agreements both demonstrate modes of approaching non-human lives as engaged in agential world-making. The situated approaches modelled by Todd, Watts and other Indigenous scholars ask researchers to take seriously the knowledge that comes from daily lived experiences, emphasising both multiplicity within those experiences and the active yet indeterminate processes of relation that shape them. These experiences are not limited to humans but extend to the complex lives of bison, beetles and other creatures. Such situated approaches are sensitive to pluralities of human–animal relations that extend far beyond consuming animals to attend to non-human beings as relations, as sites of memory and as sources of knowledge and guidance, as Ladner, Gaudry and Hubbard demonstrate. Attending to worlds and world-making in these ways destabilises the singular claims to knowledge and worldliness by wealthy white men, like those overseeing the bison's removal in Forsyth's image.

Conclusion: what does it mean to end a world?

What does it mean to end a world? The extermination of free-ranging bison and the containment of surviving animals within national parks – where the individual in Forsyth's stereograph would have been transported – removed a keystone species from the grasslands ecosystem. Bison extermination was not the accretion of unintended harms inflicted on passive animals.[43] The extermination and removal

42 Smith 2012, 201.

43 For a critique of passive framings of extinction, see Hernández, Rubis et al. 2020.

of bison was an intentional strategy of nineteenth-century westward colonial expansion, through which bison herds were decimated by settler hunters and militias to make way for transcontinental rail and cattle ranching operations. Beyond the expansion of capitalist infrastructure, settler political and military leaders acknowledged the centrality of human–bison relations to plains Indigenous nations and saw the decimation of herds as a primary tactic for undermining Indigenous sovereignty across the western prairies.[44] Not only was the extermination of bison a tactic in the genocide of Indigenous peoples; Hubbard draws on Indigenous epistemologies that apply peoplehood to buffalo and argues that the intensive killing was a genocide against the buffalo nation.[45] The extermination of free-ranging herds radically shifted the world-making of both bison and Indigenous nations on the prairie.

Attending to the ending of worlds – and the making of new worlds in the wake of genocides and environmental catastrophes – requires attunement to relationalities. In his study of corvid lives and deaths, Thom van Dooren examines the modes of entanglement or co-constitution necessary to understand what is at stake in extinction. Extinction, he argues, is not just the tidy excising of a particular species, but "an unraveling of co-formed and -forming ways of life, an unraveling that begins long before the death of the last individual and continues to ripple out long afterward".[46] The unravelling of bison life began long before the 1907 round-up that Forsyth documented. For bison, loss of relations and access to land intensified with the radical increase in slaughter after 1860, but life in the west for animals, lands and peoples had been put under steadily intensifying pressure by expanding colonial settlement from the 1700s. The herd whose round-up Forsyth documented experienced this unravelling of lifeways in different stages, beginning with the herds' formation through a then unprecedented act of conservation by Latatitsa, a Salish man who brought bison calves west over a mountain range, away from intensified slaughter on the plains, and into territory plains bison had not

44 Daschuk 2013, chapter 7; Estes 2019, chapter 3; Smalley 2017, chapter 6.
45 Hubbard 2014, 299–302.
46 van Dooren 2019, 78.

previously inhabited.[47] While the herd thrived for several decades under the stewardship of Michel Pablo and Charles Allard, successive US federal allotment legislation in 1887 and 1904 forced the splintering of reservations into small fee-simple parcels, leaving Pablo with access to only 160 acres of the 1.3 million upon which the herd had flourished. Dispossessed of land, Pablo sold his herd to the Dominion of Canada. At the end of the journey north for the bison in Forsyth's image – and the 600 other animals rounded up and shipped by rail – were corrals in Canada's first national parks: one at the eastern edge of the town of Banff in what was then called the Rocky Mountains Park of Canada and a larger one in east central Alberta, where Buffalo National Park was created on a tract of sandy, arid land deemed by government surveyors as unsuitable for settlement.[48] While spared from direct killing, the last free-ranging herd of plains bison was contained as conservation animals within parks created by settler state agents who understood land as a plentiful natural resource appropriate for exploitation by both government and private enterprise.[49]

Extermination and the removal from the Flathead Valley did not just end the worlds of free-ranging bison. Blackfoot, Flathead, Cree and other Indigenous nations mourned the loss of bison and relationships with herds. In different ways, due to different histories and entanglements, the absence of bison from the Flathead Valley (and the continent) impacted the lives and livelihoods of a vast number of prairie species. *Onthophagus knausi* and the many other invertebrate societies that compose dung pat pluralities had to adapt to other environments, such as cattle or deer droppings, but some disappeared from the area. Birds no longer had access to bison fur to insulate and mask the scent of their nests.[50] In the absence of bison wallows – depressions made when bison roll in dirt – western chorus frogs, northern cricket frogs and plains spadefoot toads were without the ephemeral ponds that formed when the wallows filled with spring rains, and around which these small amphibians

47 Hubbard 2016, 89; Locke 2016, 11–12.
48 Brower 2008, 11–14.
49 Brown 1969.
50 Coppedge 2019; 2009.

chorused and bred.[51] Plant life on the grassland prairies also shifted with the removal of free-ranging bison herds – without the selective grazing that encouraged diversity among grasses and forbs, and without migrations that distributed seeds and pollens across great distances, plant biodiversity decreased and was subject to further pressures with the introduction of settler cattle operations.[52]

These ruptures in the worlds and world-making capacities of human and non-human beings were not the intended subject of Forsyth's stereograph. To seek out such relations requires looking differently at the bison with whom the angles of the image converge, from multiple perspectives and scales. Attending to bison pluralities and the pluralities with which herds are entangled – including and exceeding dung pat pluralities – can be speculative thinking, extending beyond the immediately visible. Guided by the insights of Indigenous scholars such as Todd, Watts, Ladner and Hubbard, such speculative thinking disobeys settler framing of life as commodities readily torn from lifeworlds. Disobedient readings of settler archives to emphasise non-human beings as co-creators of worlds are methods for decolonial animal studies and media studies research that engage lives and lifeworlds, as well as the stakes of their destruction, in ways that destabilise settler colonial ways of knowing and seeing.

References

American Bison Society (1911). *Annual Report 1911*. New York: Wildlife Conservation Society Archives.

Bandhar, Brenna (2018). *The Colonial Lives of Property: Law, Land, and Racial Regimes of Ownership*. Durham, NC: Duke University Press.

Barber, Nicholas A., Sheryl C. Hosler, Peyton Whiston and Holly P. Jones (2019). Initial responses of dung beetle communities to bison reintroduction in restored and remnant tallgrass prairie. *Natural Areas Journal* 39(4): 420–8.

Brower, Jennifer (2008). *Lost Tracks: Buffalo National Park, 1909–1939*. Edmonton: Athabasca University Press.

51 Gerlanc and Kaufman 2003.

52 Rosas, Engle et al. 2008.

Brown, Robert Craig (1969). The doctrine of usefulness: natural resource and national park policy in Canada, 1887–1914. In J. Nelson, ed. *Canadian Parks and Perspectives*, 46–62. Montreal: Harvest House.

Coppedge, Bryan R. (2019). Bison hair reduces predation on artificial bird nests. *Bulletin of the Oklahoma Ornithological Society* 43(3): 13–16.

Coppedge, Bryan R. (2009). Patterns of bison hair use in nests of tallgrass prairie birds. *Prairie Naturalist* 41: 110–15.

Daschuk, James (2013). *Clearing the Plains: Disease, Politics of Starvation, and the Loss of Aboriginal Life*. Regina: University of Regina Press.

Day, Iyko (2016). *Alien Capital: Asian Racialization and the Logic of Settler Colonial Capitalism*. Durham, NC: Duke University Press.

de la Cadena, Marisol and Mario Blaser, eds (2018). *A World of Many Worlds*. Durham, NC: Duke University Press.

Estes, Nick (2019). *Our History is the Future: Standing Rock versus the Dakota Access Pipeline, and the Long Tradition of Indigenous Resistance*. New York: Verso.

Fortin, Daniel, John M. Fryxell and Régis Pilote (2002). The temporal scale of foraging decisions in bison. *Ecology* 83(4): 970–82.

Gaudry, Adam (2014). Kaa-tipeyimishoyaahk – we are those who own ourselves: a political history of Métis self-determination in the North-West, 1830–1870. Doctoral dissertation, University of Victoria, BC.

Gerlanc, Nicole M. and Glennis A. Kaufman (2003). Use of bison wallows by anurans on Konza Prairie. *American Midland Naturalist* 150(1): 158–68.

Gómez-Barris, Macarena (2017). *The Extractive Zone: Social Ecologies and Decolonial Perspectives*. Durham, NC: Duke University Press.

Haraway, Donna (2016). *Staying with the Trouble: Making Kin in the Cthulucene*. Durham, NC: Duke University Press.

Haraway, Donna (2008). *When Species Meet*. Minneapolis: University of Minnesota Press.

Hernández, K.J., June M. Rubis, Noah Theriault, Zoe Todd, Audra Mitchell, Bawaka Country et al. (2020). The Creatures Collective: manifestings. *Environment and Planning E: Nature and Space* 43(8): 838–63.

Hovorka, Alice J. (2017). Animal geographies I: globalizing and decolonizing. *Progress in Human Geography* 41(3): 382–94.

Hubbard, Tasha (2016). The call of the buffalo: exploring kinship with the buffalo in Indigenous creative expression. Doctoral dissertation, University of Calgary, AB.

Hubbard, Tasha (2014). Buffalo genocide in nineteenth-century North America: "kill, skin, and sell". In Andrew Woolford, Jeff Benvenuto and Alexander

Laban Hinton, eds. *Colonial Genocide in Indigenous North America*, 292–305. Durham, NC: Duke University Press.

Kanngieser, Anja and Zoe Todd (2020). From environmental case study to environmental kin study. *History and Theory* 59(3): 385–93.

Kimmerer, Robin (2013). *Braiding Sweetgrass: Indigenous Wisdom, Scientific Knowledge, and the Teachings of Plants*. Minneapolis: Milkweed Editions.

King, Thomas (2003). *The Truth about Stories: A Native Narrative*. Toronto: House of Anansi.

Kirksey, S. Eben and Stefan Helmreich (2010). The emergence of multispecies ethnography. *Cultural Anthropology* 25(4): 545–76.

Ladner, Kiera L. (2003). Governing within an ecological context: creating an alternative understanding of Blackfoot governance. *Studies in Political Economy* 70(Spring): 125–52.

Little Bear, Leroy (2000). Jagged worldviews colliding. In Marie Battiste, ed. *Reclaiming Indigenous Voice and Vision*, 77–86. Vancouver: University of British Columbia Press.

Locke, Harvey (2016). Banff National Park and plains bison conservation. In Harvey Locke, ed. *The Last of the Buffalo: Return to the Wild*, 8–51. Banff: Summerthought.

Lott, Dale F. (2002). *American Bison: A Natural History*. Berkeley: University of California Press.

Moreton-Robinson, Aileen (2015). *The White Possessive: Property, Power, and Indigenous Sovereignty*. Minneapolis: University of Minnesota Press.

Moser, Gabrielle (2019). *Projecting Citizenship: Photography and Belonging in the British Empire*. University Park, PA: Pennsylvania State University Press.

Mueller, Natalie G., Robert N. Spengler III, Ashley Glenn and Kunsang Lama (2020). Bison, anthropogenic fire, and the origins of agriculture in eastern North America. *Anthropocene Review* 8(2): 141–58.

National Parks Service (2016a). Bison eating habits influence the prairie ecosystem. *Bison Bellows*, 24 March. https://www.nps.gov/articles/bison-bellows-3-24-16.htm.

National Parks Service (2016b). A healthy prairie relies on bison poop. *Bison Bellows*, 6 October. https://www.nps.gov/articles/bison-bellows-10-6-16.htm.

Olson, Wes (2016). Wanuskewin: restoring ancestral societies. 5th American Bison Society Meeting and Workshop, Banff, 27 September. Video recording. https://www.facebook.com/watch/?v=745047875649058.

Rosas, Claudia A., David M. Engle, James H. Shaw and Michael W. Palmer (2008). Seed dispersal by *Bison bison* in a tallgrass prairie. *Journal of Vegetation Science* 19: 769–78.

Shukin, Nicole (2009). *Animal Capital: Rendering Life in Biopolitical Times*. Minneapolis: University of Minnesota Press.

Simpson, Leanne Betasamosake (2014). Land as pedagogy: Nishnaabeg intelligence and rebellious transformation. *Decolonization: Indigeneity, Education & Society* 3(3): 1–25.

Simpson, Leanne Betasamosake (2011). *Dancing on Our Turtle's Back: Stories of Nishnaabeg Re-creation, Resurgence, and a New Emergence*. Winnipeg: ARP Books.

Smalley, Andrea L. (2017). *Wild by Nature: North American Animals Confront Colonization*. Baltimore, MD: Johns Hopkins University Press.

Smith, Linda Tuhiwai (2012). *Decolonizing Methodologies: Research and Indigenous Peoples*. London: Zed Books.

Starblanket, Gina (2019). The numbered treaties and the politics of incoherency. *Canadian Journal of Political Science* 52(3): 443–59.

Sundberg, Juanita (2014). Decolonizing posthumanist geographies. *Cultural Geographies* 21(1): 33–47.

TallBear, Kim (2019). Caretaking relations, not American dreaming. *Kalfou* 6(1): 24–41.

Taschereau Mamers, Danielle (forthcoming). *Settler Colonial Ways of Seeing*. New York: Fordham University Press.

Taschereau Mamers, Danielle (2020). "Last of the buffalo": bison extermination, early conservation, and visual records of settler colonization in the North American west. *Settler Colonial Studies* 10(1): 126–47.

Todd, Zoe (2018). Refracting the state through human-fish relations: fishing, Indigenous legal orders and colonialism in North/Western Canada. *Decolonization: Indigeneity, Education & Society* 7(1): 60–75.

Todd, Zoe (2014). Fish pluralities: human-animal relations and sites of engagement in Paulatuuq, Arctic Canada. *Études/Inuit/Studies* 38(1–2): 217–38.

Tsing, Anna Loewenhaupt (2015). *The Mushroom at the End of the World: On the Possibility of Life in Capitalist Ruins*. Princeton, NJ: Princeton University Press.

van Dooren, Thom (2019). *The Wake of Crows: Living and Dying in Shared Worlds*. New York: Columbia University Press.

van Dooren, Thom (2014). *Flight Ways: Life and Loss at the Edge of Extinction*. New York: Columbia University Press.

van Dooren, Thom, Eben Kirksey and Ursula Münster (2016). Multispecies studies: cultivating arts of attentiveness. *Environmental Humanities* 8(1): 1–23.

Watts, Vanessa (2013). Indigenous place-thought and agency amongst humans and non-humans (First Woman and Sky Woman go on a European world tour!). *Decolonization: Indigeneity, Education & Society* 2(1): 20–34.
Whealdon, Bon (2001). *"I Will Be Meat for My Salish": The Montana Writers Project and the Buffalo of the Flathead Indian Reservation*. Robert Bigart, ed. Helena: Montana Historical Society Press.

7

The jaguar gaze: Is it possible to decolonise human–animal relationships through archaeology?

Ana Paula Motta and Martin Porr

Introduction

In this chapter, we argue that despite the advancement of agendas that engage with colonial thought, archaeological research conducted in the context of human–animal relationships is still largely dominated by a colonial gaze. While recent developments have increased the diversity of theoretical frameworks, the study of "non-humans" continues to be guided by deep-rooted assumptions about human nature and categorical distinctions between humans and non-human actors. Within archaeology, understandings of the relationships between humans and non-humans continue to be viewed through economic and symbolic lenses that value animals for their uses to human populations. Therefore, modern interpretations about the past are influenced by Western assumptions of what it means to be human – or not human – and how human populations should relate to the natural world. Furthermore, archaeological interpretations of the past continue to be guided by a Cartesian understanding of space, place and time. For this reason, we are concerned in this chapter with exploring how archaeology can contribute to the decolonisation of animals and to an understanding of the variability of concepts of personhood, animality and life/non-life. As a practice of studying the past in the present, it is the role of archaeology to avoid projecting mirror images of the present into the (deep) past, as this process can easily become a justification of present (power) structures and their historical pathways. We will explore some of the implications of the adoption of a decolonial perspective by examining the multiplicity of meanings associated with the South American jaguar (*Panthera onca*) and how the establishment of natural reserves changed perceptions of the jaguar and human–jaguar relationships.

Animals in archaeology: a brief review

Archaeology is the academic endeavour of understanding past human behaviours through material remains. In the public imagination, archaeology is foremost associated with romantic images of excavations in exotic and remote locations, the uncovering of ancient artefacts, structures and tombs, and the discovery of lost civilisations. However, in contrast, archaeology has developed in the last few decades into a multifaceted discipline that examines the past of humanity beyond a science/humanities division and in all of its complexities. While its conceptual foundations have a long and complicated history, in its present form, archaeology is a relatively recent science that developed during the second half of the nineteenth century together with many closely related processes that shifted the understanding of humanity and its historical and current relationships with environments, animals, plants, etc.[1] During the nineteenth century, archaeology became a crucial element in the establishment of the deep antiquity of the world and humanity.[2] As these processes centred almost exclusively on Europe and North America, archaeology's development was heavily influenced by the contemporary understanding of human diversity within the framework of European imperialism, racism and colonialism. These close practical and conceptual entanglements have long been recognised and studied extensively.[3] The intellectual development of archaeology is conceptually, culturally and

1 Trigger 1989.

2 Gamble 2021; Porr 2020.

geographically closely linked to Western ontological orientations.[4] In other words, "archaeological thought is already firmly inscribed within the academic, scientific, and hence hegemonic knowledge".[5] Others have argued that archaeology is, in fact, a key facilitator for Occidentalism.[6] Western notions of space, place and time are "objectively" used for the reconstruction of the past, through the idea of *longue durée*[7] and the use of universalising terms such as deep time and prehistory.[8] These structures are perpetuated in current archaeological discourses, and this situation is exacerbated by the fact that most of archaeology is still dominated by researchers based in Western Europe and North America. However, some researchers working from/in the Global South have actively countered these tendencies and incorporated other-than-normative conceptualisations into their interpretations. This includes, for example, Luis Guillermo Vasco Uribe's application of Misak's understanding of time as a moving snail.[9] Among Misak or Guambiano Indigenous groups, history and time are conceptualised as a snail performing spiral movements. Traces of these movements are also found in the engraved concentric circles found across Colombia.[10] It has been argued that a linear reconstruction of time that divides (human) history into past (pre-colonial), present (colonial) and future (postcolonial) is intrinsically related to colonialism and presupposes a "conquest of time",[11] in which the present is seen as "ground zero".[12] Given the strong links between archaeology and colonialism, it is impossible to disassociate modern notions of time and their effects on the imagination of past societies from the hegemonising aspects of archaeological practice.

3 Gosden 2012; Liebmann and Rizvi 2008; Lydon and Rizvi 2010; Porr and Matthews 2020a; Trigger 1984.
4 Thomas 2004.
5 Haber 2016, 470.
6 Shepherd 2016a, 13.
7 In the sense of Braudel 1958.
8 Shepherd 2016a, 14.
9 Vasco Uribe 1992; 2002.
10 Vasco Uribe 2002.
11 Shepherd 2016b, 19.
12 Castro-Gómez and Grosfoguel 2007; Mignolo 2011.

Over the last century, approaches towards animals in archaeology have diversified significantly and have reached a considerable degree of methodological sophistication. Harris and Cipolla argue that it was with the advent of processual archaeology in the 1960s that the study of animals evolved as a sub-discipline within archaeology.[13] Subsequently, a dedicated sub-field, zooarchaeology, developed to tackle the myriad questions related to human–animal interactions in the past.[14] When the relevant evidence is available, these approaches can be supplemented by the analysis of figurative representations of animals in the archaeological record, which adds a further dimension to this field and opportunities to learn about the past.[15] Overall, zooarchaeology is conceived as an interdisciplinary endeavour in collaboration with zoology, palaeontology and other related disciplines. With the development of post-processual approaches in archaeology during the 1980s, the focus on the study of animals as "good to eat" shifted towards a symbolic appreciation of other-than-human beings. This symbolic focus on animals was originally inspired by the work of Claude Lévi-Strauss and is encapsulated in his seminal phrase "animals as good to think (with)".[16] Consequently, alternative interpretations of animal remains and representations in the archaeological record emerged. Among them, bones were seen as a window into the study of rituals and ceremonies and in relation to concepts such as totemism and animism.[17]

More recently, a third line of research on the intersections between human and animal lifeways emerged, which could be summarised with the phrase "animals as good to live with". This approach coincides with a wider so-called animal turn and a focus on multispecies approaches in the social sciences, and it includes an engagement with animal ethics, animal communication, new and bi-constructivist approaches to ethology, the codification of animals in the entertainment industry, and animals as companion animals.[18] In this vein, Overton and Hamilakis

13 Harris and Cipolla 2017.
14 Armstrong Oma and Birke 2013.
15 Davidson 2017.
16 Lévi-Strauss 1963, 89.
17 Coulam and Schroedl 2004; Insoll 2012.
18 See e.g. Armstrong Oma and Goldhahn 2020; Haraway 2003; Pilaar Birch 2018a.

have emphasised that despite zooarchaeology's general opportunities "to illuminate the rich and diverse story of engagement of humans with other animals", these potentials have rarely been realised during much of archaeology's research history.[19] The authors suggest the development of zooarchaeology as a social zooarchaeology with a focus on questions about personhood, agency, corporality, the construction of identity and so on, which appear to be more relevant to an examination of the human–animal interface or its critical evaluation. A critical assessment of essentialist perceptions of animals as resources for consumption and symbols has more recently developed into a concern with the embeddedness of animals in human lifeways and the special bonds that emerge from these encounters. These developments have culminated in the publication of the landmark volume *Multispecies Archaeology*, edited by Suzanne E. Pilaar Birch.[20] In the introduction to the volume, it is proposed to move the field towards a multispecies archaeology "that considers animals as agents in animal-human interactions" and "which understands the past through networks and interactions rather than stochastic events".[21] Therefore, this approach aims to critically engage with key aspects of the foundations of Western and modern archaeological thought, human exceptionalism linked to agency and a non-mechanistic/social understanding of animal behaviours and interactions. Within the same volume, Alberti and Fowles furthermore argue that a true multispecies archaeology must not only decentre the human and the creation of meaning, but it must also reject the Western notion of history.[22] The latter can no longer be understood to be connected to the domain of humanity alone but must be dispersed along lines of multiple agencies, materials and their interrelationships. In recent years, numerous studies have been published in this spirit, and it is not possible to review them in greater detail here. However, common themes remain the recognition of animals as social actors, the decentring of human

19 Overton and Hamilakis 2013, 112.
20 Pilaar Birch 2018b.
21 Pilaar Birch 2018a, 3–4.
22 Alberti and Fowles 2018; Ingold 2021; Shepherd et al. 2016.

agency in historical processes and the reconceptualisation of human societies as multispecies assemblages.[23]

While these developments are commendable, we want to argue that these propositions need to be further interrogated within an explicit decolonial framework. Although there has been an increasing interest in incorporating multispecies methodologies and ontologies into archaeology, there has been little problematisation of archaeology's assumptions about how different species perceive the world and how these vary through time and space. In this regard, we want to draw attention to the fact that archaeological research in the Global South and research in other disciplines, such as human geography, have already been dealing with these questions in the last 15 years and have often been ignored by mainstream archaeological research. By embracing a decolonial framework in archaeology, we can further interrogate how past and present societies engaged with other-than-human beings and through a multiplicity of voices,[24] while establishing a greater dialogue between "epistemic worlds".[25] We argue that an engagement with decolonial thought in this context allows greater analytical depth and more extensive connections with current theoretical developments in other relevant fields.

Critique of multispecies approaches in archaeology from a decolonial perspective

> Thinking and being decolonial, originated by detachment, is not a thought that can be "applied" (subsidiary from the distinction between theory and praxis) but rather is the very act of thinking that makes us [decolonial], dialogical and communal. It is not a method, but a way, a path for remaking us in the pursuit of forms of living and (self-)governing, in which we do not live to work/produce/consume, but we work to co-exist.[26]

---

23 Armstrong Oma and Birke 2013; Armstrong Oma and Goldhahn 2020; Hill 2013; Recht 2019.

24 Sundberg 2014, 34.

25 Kuokkanen 2008.

Decolonial approaches in archaeology already have a considerable history. As outlined above, archaeology's entanglement with European imperialism and colonialism has long been recognised. In recent decades, archaeologists have engaged with several elements of the wider postcolonial critique and have explored the consequences for archaeological theory and practice.[27] These developments include the archaeological elucidation of European colonialism itself, the establishment of Indigenous archaeologies and the critical engagement with colonial influences on archaeological analyses and interpretations.[28] Relevant connections can be established in each of these areas with the study of human–animal relationships. For example, in the abovementioned volume, Alberti and Fowles also argue that a multispecies perspective in archaeology and rock art research must engage with the local Indigenous knowledge systems, as they are both constitutive of broader ecological relationships with place.[29] This example points to the fact that there are many links between decolonial approaches and other strands within the social sciences that engage with Indigenous philosophies, posthumanist approaches and other developments that question the dominance of established Western ontologies and epistemologies.[30] However, while we welcome this situation, we would suggest that a closer engagement with decolonial arguments is necessary to push the boundaries further in this respect. We assert that such an engagement allows a deeper consideration of the critiques that have been raised against traditional archaeological approaches through which animals are studied.[31]

---

26 Mignolo 2016, 7; our translation from the Spanish: "El pensar y hacer descolonial, base del desprendimiento, no es tampoco un pensamiento para 'aplicar' (subsidiario de la distinción teoría y praxis), sino que es el acto mismo de pensar haciéndonos, de modo dialogal y comunitario. No es un método, sino una vía, un camino para rehacernos en la búsqueda de formas de vivir y de gobernar(nos) en las que no vivamos para trabajar/producir/consumir, sino que trabajemos para con-vivir".

27 See e.g. Gosden 2012; Hamilakis and Duke 2007; Lydon and Rizvi 2010; McNiven and Russell 2005.

28 Bruchac, Hart and Wobst 2010; Gosden 2004; Liebmann and Rizvi 2008; Schneider and Hayes 2020.

29 Alberti and Fowles 2018.

30 Porr and Matthews 2020b, 4.

The idea of postcolonialism as an intellectual endeavour is a consequence of the political and socioeconomic upheavals after World War II and the dismantling of the formal and institutionalised structures of Western colonialism. Reflecting the differences within European colonialism, reactions, responses and critical engagements also varied. "Postcolonial" approaches often share a challenge against hegemonic epistemologies and knowledge systems, and the representation of colonised "Others" that has been produced in colonial and imperial contexts.[32] An aspect that has been largely overlooked in the context of archaeology is the fact that within postcolonial literature, the notion of humanity itself has been critiqued as Eurocentric and Western. The conclusion of Homi K. Bhabha's foundational book *The Location of Culture* calls for a transformation of "our sense of what it means to live" and what it means to be a human being across different times and spaces.[33] While a critique of the logic and notions of race and racism remains of crucial importance in this context, this aspect needs to be understood in terms of a wider rejection of biological essentialism. This orientation has important consequences for the conceptualisation of human diversity, the nature of social interactions and human relationships with the environment.[34] And, obviously, these considerations must encompass human–animal interactions.

While postcolonialism and decolonialism share many elements, the main difference between the two is connected to the scholars that influenced both schools. The former places emphasis on French poststructuralism and neo-Marxism, whereas the latter is greatly influenced by Latin American theorists. Another substantial difference between the two is that postcolonialism emerged within countries formerly colonised by the British Empire, and the respective outputs were produced predominantly in English, whereas decoloniality embraces many languages and perspectives.[35] An additional point of divergence is related to the positionality of the subjects. Postcolonial

31 See especially Overton and Hamilakis 2013.
32 Liebmann 2008, 5.
33 Bhabha 1994, 367.
34 Anderson 2007; Anderson and Perrin 2018.
35 Lim 2019.

approaches are still very much grounded in the study of the dichotomies between the oppressors and the oppressed and focus on an understanding of the experience of colonisation itself. By contrast, decolonial frameworks are concerned with a more fundamental deconstruction of the modern apparatuses and institutions that facilitate colonialism, which include universities.[36] In sum, the objective of decoloniality is to de-link itself from a Western epistemology intrinsically linked to modernity and capitalism.[37]

In decolonial approaches, it has been recognised that the animal and animal bodies are constructed in opposition to humanity and the human body. The animal is a part of nature and, as such, the colonial subject is always entitled to animals and their bodies as sites of commodification, food production, companionship and so on. The distinction, however, is not absolute. Animality is not restricted to animals but is further extended to non-white people and bodies.[38] Through this logic, racialised people of colour and colonised subjects are conceptualised as hybrid beings along a gradient between full humanity and full animality. Animality becomes a quality that allows and justifies exploitation and use: "settler colonialism *wants* to produce animal bodies as commodities embedded in a global economy of reiterated deathliness".[39] It has been widely recognised that the engagement with and incorporation of Indigenous ontologies provide a better framework within which to understand multispecies entanglements in archaeology and beyond. Such an orientation opens archaeological epistemologies to Indigenous ontologies, which incorporate other-than-human beings, such as animals, plants, the landscape, supernatural beings and elements, among others, into their conceptualisations of the world/s.[40] Thus, engaging with multispecies archaeologies, along with the incorporation of a decolonial discourse, allows us to move further from traditional appreciations of

36 Mignolo and Tlostanova 2006.

37 Mignolo 2009.

38 See Shepherd 2016b, 37; for a further analysis of the (white) colonial gaze on people of colour and their bodies, see Deckha 2012; Lugones 2007, 202.

39 Belcourt 2015, 9 [emphasis in original].

40 Adams 2019; Kawagley 1995.

non-European others, where both non-humans and Indigenous people were conceptualised as being closer to nature. To counter this orientation, Belcourt suggests engaging closely with Indigenous cosmologies and ontologies in which animals are imagined not only as active agents but also as capable of creating kinship relations with humans and other animals.[41] However, Todd warns of the devastating effects that "cherry-picking" sections of Indigenous knowledge without properly contextualising or engaging with local communities has and how it can easily lead to the perpetuation of colonial violence as well as an ongoing promotion of a white narrative of these engagements.[42] Other proposals have also focused on a decolonising approach to animals by moving from nature–culture dichotomies that perpetuate an exploitative view of animals grounded in their economic value.[43] In this sense, animals are perceived as resources for human consumption and survival, where animal meat and by-products are commercialised for subsistence and other activities. The disruption of nature–culture dichotomies in this context can be obtained through an engagement with non-Western ways of being in the world that incorporate "multiple narratives of Indigenous and colonised peoples" in the analysis.[44] In other words, these approaches emphasise other-than-normative knowledge by focusing on local ways of being in the world, and by incorporating co-constituted knowledge in nature–culture,[45] and multiple ontologies[46] in our research agendas. By cutting through these relational and non-essentialist entanglements, colonial epistemologies erase not only animal but also Indigenous bodies.[47] The term "diversity" should not simply refer to human diversity, but rather to the diversity of local entanglements between the agencies of humans and non-humans. These considerations can be understood as part of a wider discourse critiquing the Western notion of nature.

41 Belcourt 2015; see also Harrod 2000.
42 Todd 2016.
43 Hovorka 2017, 388.
44 Szerszynski 2017, 254.
45 Sundberg 2014, 41.
46 Howitt and Suchet-Pearson 2006.
47 Watts 2013.

While we believe that multiple ontologies and local entanglements have not been adequately addressed in the context of archaeological interpretation, it also needs to be stressed that the relationships that are constructed between animals, humans and nature continue to be temporalised in problematic ways.[48] It has long been recognised that modern Western thought is based on a linear conception of time.[49] Accordingly, the differences among humans and between humans and non-humans are viewed not only in a hierarchical but also in a temporal fashion. White people are constructed as younger and more advanced than coloured people and both are younger than animals. While these characteristics are sometimes described in a systematic and clear-cut fashion, in the spirit of the Great Chain of Being (a hierarchical structure that describes all matter and life-forms), the reality is much more contradictory and messy.[50] Animality and humanity intersect in each creature and are differently established and evaluated within changing contexts and circumstances.[51] This logic allows for the giving or denying of rights, agency and capabilities. It can allow or deny any human being or animal a life in the present.[52]

Consequently, we propose that, in its analysis and interpretation, archaeological research needs to integrate more specifically a decolonial critique of the essentialist constitution of non-human animals and human beings and their temporalisation in its analysis and interpretation. We believe that such a movement allows connections to a range of recent approaches and frameworks in relevant fields outside of archaeology that have already developed a decolonial agenda and respective methodologies of human–non-human interactions. Recognition of these elements will allow a more specific integration of Indigenous philosophies in research designs and interpretations.

Within human geography, some recent papers have integrated a specific decolonising approach that considers the active contribution of human, animal and more-than-human agencies. For example,

48 Mignolo 2011.
49 Porr 2020; Thomas 2004.
50 Smail and Shryock 2013.
51 Corbey and Lanjouw 2013.
52 Hovorka 2017, 388.

Sundberg exposes the struggles of geographical literature that engages with posthumanism as still being deeply charged with colonial/Eurocentric ideas. She argues that posthumanism is intimately linked to Eurocentric scholarship, in which universalising notions of being human are perpetuated and other ontologies are neglected.[53] Many authors have engaged with decolonising practices and have established different pathways that could be applied to their research agendas. Overall, many have argued that decolonising is a means of exposing systemic violence perpetuated by Eurocentric epistemologies[54] or is a way of disassociating oneself from Western epistemologies.[55] Others have used the term decolonial to open a dialogue between different worlds,[56] as a way of *walking* or performance,[57] or as a way of disrupting hegemonic and colonial power.[58] Walking in this context refers to the performativity of knowledge production, in which the world is known by experiencing, walking or dwelling in it, thus re-creating connections between people, other beings and landscapes.[59] The notion of walking highlights the different ways in which coloniality is enacted and further reproduced during the research process. Sundberg argues that walking with also involves changing our perception of solidarity while fostering ethic collaborations between Indigenous and non-Indigenous scholars and knowledge-holders.[60]

In other words, decoloniality should not be seen as a separate framework but rather as a movement within, a way forward.[61] In this sense, the idea of walking with developed by human geography is a starting point for decolonising archaeological practice. Walking *with* in this context highlights an experiential ontological knowledge of the world, in which relationships with people, non-human beings and

53 Sundberg 2014.
54 Mignolo 2011; Sundberg 2014, 34.
55 Mignolo 2009.
56 Kuokkanen 2008.
57 Sundberg 2014.
58 Todd and Robert 2018.
59 Turnbull 2007.
60 Sundberg 2014; see e.g. Bawaka Country et al. 2018; Suchet Pearson et al. 2013.
61 Gnecco 1999; Haber 2016.

places are discovered and constructed. Publications in this spirit take seriously the decolonising agenda as a movement *within*, and this understanding can serve as inspiration for "a movement toward the abandonment of the hegemonic standpoint of archaeological knowledge".[62] These insights profoundly affect the ways in which research and fieldwork are conducted with a greater level of involvement, immersivity and humility. Researchers need to open themselves more profoundly to the local dependency of knowledge production and to the symmetrical and non-hierarchical engagement with people, animals and other actors. As we have highlighted, modernity cannot be conceived without coloniality; notions like modernity, coloniality and capitalism are intrinsically related and cannot be separated.[63] However, by embracing a decolonial perspective, we are able to steer away from the coloniality of power and knowledge.[64] Other recent literature in environmental history and human geography has also adopted a specifically multispecies orientation to decentre humanity in past and present narratives.[65] In these cases, the conceptualisation of humans, animals and their interactions is related to questions of multispecies justice in the negotiations of solutions to present and future environmental challenges. In relation to archaeological research and imagination, these questions draw attention to the dangers of inscribing an essentialist and universal understanding of humanity into the deep past and of a colonialist reading of human origins, which narrows future pathways out of the current climate crisis.[66] Along these lines, decisions about environmental conservation are also made from an anthropocentric point of view, in which other-than-human beings and Indigenous people are "othered" and deemed incapable of preserving nature.[67] This last point will be further expanded below in relation to the evolving perceptions of the jaguar in Mexico and South America.

62 Haber 2016, 470.
63 Mignolo 2009.
64 Quijano 2009.
65 Celermajer et al. 2020; Tschakert 2020.
66 Porr and Matthews 2020b, 21–3.
67 Motta 2023.

While it is not possible to address all of these aspects in the case study presented in this chapter, we want to demonstrate how some key aspects can be integrated into archaeological methods and interpretations.

On being jaguar in South America

Human–jaguar relationships have a long history in South America and other parts of the world. "Being jaguar" has strong associations to certain "desirable" qualities that are often connected to rulers, warriors and priests, and it is also used as a phrase to describe a mode of being. Here, we discuss multiple archaeological contexts in which jaguars emerge, including the discovery of early jaguar-shaped statuettes, the representation of the jaguar's iconography across different cultures and historical periods, the meaning of jaguars at the time of colonisation of America by Europeans, and contemporary perceptions of jaguars in two villages in Mexico. We disentangle the links between different *Panthera* felines and how these have influenced modern perceptions and archaeological interpretations of jaguars. In doing so, we hope to highlight how Eurocentric notions of big cats influenced archaeological reconstructions of jaguars and how modern notions of this feline negatively impacted conservation efforts in some areas. Finally, we propose that jaguar is a way of being, an action, which cannot be universalised and disassociated from a "way of being in the world".

Jaguars (*Panthera onca*; Figure 7.1) – also called *yaguareté*, *uturuncu*, *balam* and *ocelotl* – are part of the feline genus *Panthera*, coined by Lorenz Oken in 1816, after he classified spotted felines in a single group. Among the other felines that compose this category are the African lion (*P. leo*), Asian tiger (*P. tigris*) and leopard (*P. pardus*). Big cats have played numerous roles in Western culture and imagination for many centuries. Over time, our understanding has moved from reflections of real human encounters with them (in North Africa, the Middle East and Southeast Europe) to mere symbols in art, heraldic imagery and so on. Big cats are generally employed to represent physical power, danger, social dominance and strength. As such, there is a certain degree of ambivalence involved. The big cat's

Figure 7.1 Photograph of a jaguar at El Pantanal, Mato Grosso do Sul, Brazil. Human–jaguar encounters in this area are frequent, mostly due to the presence of tourists that want to visit one of the largest diversity hotspots in the world. Photo provided by Walmyr Buzatto.

power is a source of both fascination and fear across the humanity/animality boundary.[68] Perhaps the most classic example in this respect is the ambivalent imagination of the lion in Greek mythology, particularly the depiction of Heracles clothed in the skin of the Nemean lion. The conceptualisation of human–feline interactions within archaeology and palaeoanthropology has traditionally been coloured by whether the feline is seen as an antagonist to humanity (or not). The genus *Panthera* (*P. pardus*) and early hominins (*Australopithecus robustus* and *Homo ergaster*) crossed paths at Swartkrans (Members 1 and 2) in South Africa. Bone remains suggest that these early hominins

68 Quammen 2003.

fell prey to leopards who inhabited the area.[69] Human relationships with large carnivores are a common theme in human evolutionary studies, and they are usually framed in terms of competition for similar resources or in terms of predator–prey relations. These aspects slightly changed with the discovery of the Early Upper Palaeolithic painted cave of Chauvet and its surprising amount of big-cat depictions (*P. spelea* and *P. pardus*), which was preceded by lesser known, but similarly structured, mobiliary art from Southwest Germany. These finds have been the subject of a limited number of explorations that attempt to situate the human–feline relationships expressed through these bodies of imagery in context and to understand them as reflections of past lifeworlds and ontologies.[70] Overall, it is certainly the case that general Western understandings of big cats have been structured in a simplified fashion as overly negative and homogenised across all big cats such as lions, tigers and leopards.[71] As a result, this situation has negatively affected contemporary perceptions of jaguars as well.[72] In this sense, jaguars in South America have often been interpreted from a Eurocentric point of view in which ethological knowledge obtained from Old World *Panthera* felines was indiscriminately applied to the study of jaguars. As a result, jaguars were portrayed as vicious animals that attacked humans systematically.[73]

It has been estimated that jaguars arrived in South America between 510 ka and 280 ka BP and are the largest predator on the continent.[74] In South American Indigenous cultures, jaguars are the most well-known and venerated feline[75] and have been at the centre of artistic representations, myths, legends and cosmologies across many groups. Remains of jaguars and humans were found in the same stratigraphic layers at Schulze Cave in Texas, United States, and dated to as early as 11,000 BP.[76] However, the character of human–jaguar interactions from

69 Lee-Thorpe, Thackeray and van der Merwe 2000.
70 Hussain and Floss 2015a; 2015b; Porr 2010; 2015.
71 But see Cueto et al. 2016.
72 Hoogesteijn et al. 2016, 446–9.
73 Hoogesteijn et al. 2016, 449.
74 Rabinowitz 2014.
75 Alvarsson 2012, 107.
76 Dalquest 1969.

these remains is still unclear, as the jaguar bones do not seem to have been intentionally placed in this layer, nor do they exhibit any anthropic marks.[77] Despite this lack of direct archaeological and zooarchaeological evidence, jaguars are part of artistic repertoires in this period across the entire American continent. The earliest depictions of jaguars are currently found in Central America and Mesoamerica, across different media, such as ceramics, plates, ornaments, metallurgy, figurines and rock art. For example, in Suriname, jaguar iconography found on ceramics at the Kaurikreek site have been dated to 4,200–3,700 BP.[78] At Pedra Pintada, Brazil, rock engravings depicting jaguars are proposed to have been made between 3,900 and 3,000 BP.[79] Other early depictions of jaguars include mobiliary art made by the Olmec dated to 3,200 BP[80] and funerary objects with designs depicting were-jaguars (beings that can adopt the form of a jaguar) found in the Early Formative Village of San Jose de Mogote, Oaxaca, dated to 3,000 BP.[81] More recently, jaguar images were found in different material remains and ornaments made by La Tolita, Jama-Coaque, Bahia and Guangala/Guayas groups with a proposed chronology of 2,500–1,500 BP.[82] In sum, as suggested by archaeological remains, jaguars were deemed as important animals and omnipresent across different types of material culture. Some anthropologists have even suggested that jaguars were viewed as gods.[83] Others have considered jaguars as the element that separates nature from the supernatural[84] and therefore, linked to the underworld (see for example the Lanzón found at Chavín de Huántar ca. 1200–700 BCE),[85] as evidenced by many representations of anthropomorphic motifs of shamans transforming into jaguars.[86] This transformation was facilitated

77 See Dagget and Henning 1974 for a review.

78 Rostain 2008, 284.

79 Roosevelt 1996; but see Motta and Romero Villanueva 2020 for a review of other findings and chronological contextualisation of Central and South American cultures.

80 Coe 1972, 10.

81 Blanton et al. 1981; Whalen 1983.

82 Masucci 2008.

83 Reichel-Dolmatoff 1978; Saunders 1998.

84 Hoogesteijn et al. 2016, 446.

85 Cruz 2002, 230.

by the consumption of entheogenic plants[87] and the suggestion has been supported by the discovery of drug paraphernalia such as pipes and plaques across Central and South America[88] and by the fact that it was still practised after colonial contact.[89] In some regions, jaguars have also been associated with the Solar cult, which is the spiritual basis of social organisation of some Andean groups.[90] Although jaguar–human associations vary across time and space, overall, jaguars have been linked to warfare, high social status, witchcraft, priests, shamans and chiefs.[91] Jaguar images also evoke fierceness, bravery and strength,[92] and supernatural protection.[93] Jaguar body parts have been incorporated into human bodies (in the form of tattoos, headdresses, hair decorations, masks, etc.), while there are many depictions of humans wearing jaguar skins, claws and fangs.[94] Dillehay and Kaulicke argue that some of the jaguar's body parts (head, snout, canines and claws) were of special significance, which would explain why certain groups, like Chavín de Huántar, Aguada and Ciénaga-Condorhuasi, depicted jaguars showing their teeth (Figure 7.2).[95]

---

86 Cruz 2006, 6; Gómez Augier and Caria 2009; Gordillo 2009.
87 Métraux 1948; Reichel-Dolmatoff 1978.
88 Cruz 2006, 7; Gordillo 2020; Pochettino, Cortella and Ruis 1999.
89 Furst 1968, 154.
90 Pérez-Gollán 1992.
91 Furst 1968; Reichel-Dolmatoff 1978; Saunders 1992.
92 Goldman 1979, 225.
93 Karsten 1968, 123.
94 Cruz 2002, 227.
95 Dillehay and Kaulicke 1984; González 1974.

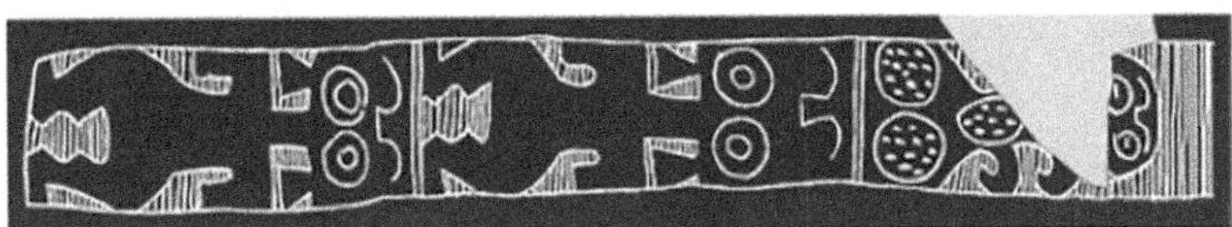

Figure 7.2 Aguada iconographic designs found at La Rinconada site, Catamarca, Argentina. Top: engraved designs found on a ceramic bowl depicting the changing states of a shaman after ingesting hallucinogens. Bottom: engraved motifs found on a ceramic container showing a jaguar lying on its back and a compositional motif with mixed human and jaguar features. The figure has been depicted with a tail, canines, jaguar rosettes and claws. Modified from an image provided by Inés Gordillo.

Saunders points out that the importance of jaguars in archaeology has been regarded as self-evident.[96] He proposed in turn to think of the jaguar's significance as the result of a long history of encounters, where animal symbols are part of Indigenous constructions of nature.[97] In this sense, the animals' place in nature is the product of human classification[98] and, therefore, not a natural kind.[99] Furthermore, Saunders argues that the portrayal of jaguars in images and archaeological remains created a "straight jacket" view, in which jaguar interpretations were deeply influenced by Eurocentric perceptions of felines from the Old World.[100] The comparisons drawn between jaguars and other *Panthera* felines, which were heavily influenced by colonial attitudes towards these animals, along with the indiscriminate use of sixteenth-century ethnographic theory to interpret Pre-Classic and Classic groups,[101] perpetuated the idea that feline images did not change through time.

The use of ethological approaches drawn from other feline species to assess the role of jaguars in archaeology is also made difficult by the many names used across Mexico and Central and South America to refer to them. There was a great amount of variability across the region. For example, archaeological research conducted among Aztec and Mayan societies shows the great diversity linked to their etymological origin. In Aztec Nahuatl, jaguars are called *ocelotl*, which was regularly confused with the English word ocelot[102] or tiger.[103] Among Mayans, jaguars are called *balam* or *bolom*.[104] It is interesting to note that for both Aztec and Mayan societies, *ocelotl* and *balam* were regarded as powerful predators loaded with meanings around warfare and social status.[105] Reconstructions of Aztec writing systems revealed

---

96 Saunders 1994.
97 Saunders 1994, 104.
98 Douglas 1990.
99 Saunders 1994, 104.
100 Saunders 1994, 105.
101 Saunders 1994, 106.
102 Davies 1973, 143.
103 Vaillant 1944, 127.
104 Álvarez 1984, 328.
105 Saunders 1994, 108.

that Aztecs used the words *ocelopetlatl* and *oceloyote* to describe brave and courageous individuals and warriors.[106] A similar case can be made for how jaguars have been conceived in Mayan societies, where *balam* is etymologically associated to the word *boolay*, which means savage and fierce.[107] This group has coined the phrase *Balam-Tah*, which that means "be like jaguar" or "to hunt like the jaguar".[108]

Jaguars are not only found in the archaeological record and imagery; they are also an integral part of contemporary societies' oral memory. At San Nicolás del Monte, Mexico, a group of Mexican researchers conducted interviews to understand contemporary attitudes towards jaguars and disentangle modern conflicts between humans and jaguars.[109] As a result, they report that conflict between these two populations increased in the last few decades due to deforestation, which has severe effects on prey availability, with jaguars attacking domesticated animals as a result.[110] At Sierra de Manantlán, Mexico, Álvarez and co-authors argue, social knowledge of jaguars has been lost since the declaration of the area as a natural reserve, which affected jaguar–human relationships.[111] In a survey conducted by the authors among the town inhabitants, it was found that older people have a better understanding of jaguars' hunting practices than younger people, who do not express much knowledge about jaguars and their behaviour. This change in human–animal relationships is partly the result of colonisation and industrialisation, where young people migrate to bigger cities in search of higher education, work opportunities and other endeavours. As a result, human relationships with the environment are forever affected, with Indigenous communities experiencing drastic changes to their lifestyles and knowledge about their surrounding worlds.[112]

Deforestation and the illegal hunting of jaguars have deeply changed the relationship between humans and these big cats across their entire

106 Simeon 1988, 352.
107 Saunders 1994, 110.
108 Álvarez 1984, 329.
109 Ávila-Nájera et al. 2011.
110 Ávila-Nájera et al. 2011, 1022.
111 Álvarez, Gerritsenm and Gómez Llamas 2015.
112 Toledo 2000; Toledo and Barrera-Bassols 2008.

living range. The loss of ecosystems that drives jaguars to hunt domesticated animals and become a threat to humans creates conflicts between these two populations, heightened by the loss of knowledge about jaguars as traditional lifeways are abandoned. To overcome this situation, there needs to be a transformation from a conflict-based relationship to a complementary one.[113] This change needs to lead to a new balance between humans and jaguars and the re-establishment of their dynamic and practical entanglements. Only in this way can the whole breadth of the jaguar's existence be appreciated and re-appreciated.

According to some North, Central and South American populations, jaguars are not "only" animals, but are a way of being in the world, a world in which jaguars, as well as other beings, can see and represent.[114] To paraphrase Ingold,[115] animals do not just exist; they *are* "not nouns but verbs". This conceptualisation of animals as action, as a form of "animaling", or movement *within,* has also been noted among Mayan and Aztec societies, in which the terms *balam* and *ocelotl* are used to describe the state of being fierce, savage, brave, in association to being jaguar. Kohn's work among the Runa, in Ecuador, is relevant for highlighting contemporary perceptions of jaguars and how these affect people's perception of the environment.[116] The author raises the question of the jaguar gaze. While conducting fieldwork with the Runa, he was informed to sleep facing up, so that the jaguar would see him as a person and not "dead meat".[117] This description of jaguars as being able to recognise humans as persons and not just as food is grounded in the knowledge that jaguars, and other beings, also see us. Humans are not the only species able to see and represent others; other-than-human beings also have the capacity to do so. Kohn argues that it is in these encounters that transformation occurs, that the "other" becomes something new, and in this process, we change as well.[118] Overall, the concept of animaling, of animals seen as verbs

113 Álvarez et al. 2015, 52.
114 Kohn 2013, 2.
115 Ingold 2011, 175.
116 Kohn 2013.
117 Kohn 2013, 1–2.
118 Kohn 2013, 2.

instead of nouns, in this context highlights the fact that Indigenous groups have long considered some non-human animals as persons, in particular the jaguar, as humans and jaguars see and represent each other. This way of understanding jaguars is essential for decolonising archaeological appreciations of these animals.

In our discussion of jaguars we have considered how changing perceptions of these animals have influenced their archaeological interpretation as well as their conservation status and the contemporary knowledge held by Indigenous populations. The perception of the jaguar among the Runa as well as other groups is grounded in a deep understanding of the surrounding environment, in which animals and humans are co-constituted and deeply entangled in a series of co-becomings inherently linked to human and animal identities. As we have discussed, jaguars have been understood in archaeological contexts as "frozen" in time. They have either been conflated with universalised interpretations that are based on the colonial imagination of Old-World big cats, or our understanding of them has been based on ethnographic sources that were gathered at the time of European colonisation and were indiscriminately applied to understand the past. In these reconstructions, contemporary perceptions of jaguars are disregarded, misrepresented or portrayed in a romanticised way. As the Mayans and Aztecs, and other countless groups, have reported, jaguars are not mere animals; they are embedded in all aspects of human lifeways and, as such, are strong symbols. Decolonising jaguars entails conceptualising them as a way of being, as action, as *jaguaring*. Through the acceptance of the historic relationships between humans and jaguars, a decolonising practice within archaeology can be realised.

(Some) concluding remarks

> [...] we are colonised by certain ways of thinking about relationality. We can only imagine the ways in which selves and thoughts might form associations through our assumptions about the forms of associations that structure human language. And then, in ways that often go unnoticed, we project these assumptions onto nonhumans. Without realising it we attribute to

> nonhumans properties that are our own, and then, to compound this, we narcissistically ask them to provide us with corrective reflections about ourselves.[119]

The study of animals in the social sciences has developed from an early understanding of animals as resources for human consumption (animals good to eat), to a consideration of the symbolic values of animals (animals good to think with) and to a nuanced understanding of animals that takes into consideration the relational intersection of humans and animals in everyday life. These changes are reflected in archaeological research projects and practices and related questions. Compared to other related disciplines, the adoption of relational approaches that consider other-than-normative ways of being in the world and Indigenous and subaltern knowledges was clearly delayed in archaeology. Only recently have new approaches been emerging, with researchers beginning to be more open to the exploration of multiple epistemologies and ontologies. The advancement of a social zooarchaeological method[120] that explores alternative analyses of faunal remains with a focus on animal agency or the development of multispecies approaches can be seen as the beginning of a series of research approaches in archaeology that will tackle these questions in new and critically informed ways.

The postcolonial critique has focused on the colonial entanglements of archaeology and its emergence as a discipline from which to study the *past*. In its early origins, archaeology was a medium through which to study distant cultures and set the stage for a nationalistic agenda, whereby European nations could recover the distant past and their ancestors.[121] Further on, postcolonial studies focused on ideas of humanity and selfhood, deeply rooted in a European conception of what it means to be human and, therefore, animal.[122] This critique also raised questions about the dominance of culture over nature and was used as a justification of human control

119 Kohn 2013, 21.
120 Overton and Hamilakis 2013.
121 Trigger 1989.
122 Bhabha 1994, 367.

over the environment and other beings. Animals are consequently denied agency and self-determination. A decolonial critique of animal studies must focus instead on a rejection of nature–culture dichotomies that perpetuate exploitative relationships with animals[123] and must be conceived as a movement towards subversive, Indigenous and local knowledges of animals.[124] Decolonisation is here not to be seen as a separate theoretical field, but rather gained through performance. Following Sundberg, it can be seen as a movement *within* and a way of walking with.[125]

An earlier version of this chapter was delivered by Ana Paula Motta at the Australasian Animal Studies Association conference hosted in Ōtautahi/Christchurch, 1–4 July 2019, Aotearoa/New Zealand. We thank audience members for their insightful comments and suggestions. We would like to thank Rick De Vos for inviting us to participate in this edited volume and for his encouragement during the earlier stages of writing this chapter, and the two anonymous reviewers for their thoughtful comments and input in improving our manuscript. We are grateful to Emily Hoffman and Walmyr Buzatto for facilitating and providing, respectively, the jaguar's photograph illustrated in Figure 7.1. We are also thankful to Bruno Vindrola for his comments on an earlier version of this chapter. The research conducted by Ana Motta was funded by the Forrest Research Foundation and the University of Western Australia.

References

Adams, M. (2019). Indigenising the Anthropocene? Specifying and situating multi-species encounters. *International Journal of Sociology and Social Policy* 41(3/4): 282–97.

---

123 Hovorka 2017.
124 Sundberg 2014.
125 Sundberg 2014, 40.

Alberti, B. and S. Fowles (2018). Ecologies of rock art and art in northern New Mexico. In S. Pilaar Birch, ed. *Multispecies Archaeology*, 133–53. New York: Routledge.

Álvarez, C. (1984). *Diccionario etnolingüístico del idioma maya yucateco colonial. Volumen I: Mundo Físico.* (Ethnolinguistic dictionary of the colonial Mayan Yucateco language). Mexico City: Universidad Nacional Autónoma de México.

Álvarez, N., P.R.W. Gerritsen and J.C. Gómez Llamas (2015). *Percepciones campesinas del Jaguar en diez localidades de la Reserva de la Biosfera Sierra de Manantlán en el Occidente de México: implicaciones para su conservación* (Farmers' perceptions on jaguars in ten localities at the Sierra de Manantlán Biosphere Reserve in Western Mexico: implications for their conservation). *Sociedad y Ambiente* 1(7): 35–54.

Alvarsson, J-Å. (2012). *El individuo y el ambiente – Cosmología, etnobiología y etnomedicina* (The individual and the environment: cosmology, ethnobiology, and ethnomedicine). *Etnografía 'weenhayek* vol 6. Bolivia: Uppsala University and FI'WEN.

Anderson, K. (2007). *Race and the Crisis of Humanism*. New York: Routledge.

Anderson, K. and C. Perrin (2018). "Removed from nature": the modern idea of human exceptionality. *Environmental Humanities* 10(2): 447–72.

Armstrong Oma, K. and L. Birke (2013). Archaeology and human-animal studies. *Society and Animals* 21(2): 113–19.

Armstrong Oma, K. and J. Goldhahn (2020). Introduction: human-animal relationships from a long-term perspective. *Current Swedish Archaeology* 28: 11–22.

Ávila-Nájera, D.M., O.C. Rosas-Rosas, L.A. Tarango-Arámbula, J.F. Martínez-Montoya and E. Santoyo-Brito (2011). *Conocimiento, uso y valor cultural de seis presas del jaguar (Panthera onca) y su relación con éste, en San Nicolás de los Montes, San Luis Potosí, México* (Knowledge, use, and cultural value of six jaguar (*Panthera onca*) preys and their relation with it in San Nicolás de los Montes, San Luis de Potosí, Mexico). *Revista Mexicana de Biodiversidad* 82: 1020–8.

Bawaka Country, S. Suchet-Pearson, S. Wright, K. Lloyd, M. Tofa, J. Sweeney et al. (2018). Gon Gurtha: enacting response-abilities as situated co-becoming. *Environmental and Planning D: Society and Space* 37(4): 682–702.

Belcourt, B-R. (2015). Animal bodies, colonial subjects: (re)locating animality in decolonial thought. *Societies* 5: 1–11. https://doi.org/10.3390/soc5010001.

Bhabha, H.K. (1994). *The Location of Culture*. London: Routledge.

Blanton, R.E., S.A. Kowalewski, G. Feinman and J. Appel (1981). *Ancient Mesoamerica: A Comparison of Change in Three Regions*. Cambridge: Cambridge University Press.

Braudel, F. (1958). Histoire et Sciences sociales: La Longue durée. *Annales* (14)4: 710–8.

Bruchac, M.M., S.M. Hart and H.M. Wobst, eds (2010). *Indigenous Archaeologies: A Reader in Decolonisation*. Walnut Creek, CA: Left Coast Press.

Castro-Gómez, S. and R. Grosfoguel (2007). *El giro decolonial: reflexiones para una diversidad epistémica más allá del capitalismo global* (The decolonial turn: reflections for an epistemic diversity beyond the global capitalism). Bogotá, Colombia: Iesco-Pensar-Siglo del Hombre Editores.

Celermajer, D., D. Schlosberg, L. Rickards, M. Stewart-Harawira, M. Thaler, P. Tschakert et al. (2021). Multispecies justice: theories, challenges, and a research agenda for environmental politics. *Environmental Politics*: (30)1–2, 119–140. https://doi.org/10.1080/09644016.2020.1827608.

Coe, M.D. (1972). Olmec jaguars and Olmec kings. In E.P. Benson, ed. *The Cult of the Feline: A Conference in Pre-Columbian Iconography*, 1–18. Washington, DC: Dumbarton Oaks.

Corbey, R. and A. Lanjouw, eds (2013). *The Politics of Species: Reshaping our Relationships with Other Animals*. Cambridge: Cambridge University Press.

Coulam, N.J. and A.R. Schroedl (2004). Late Archaeic totemism in the greater American Southwest. *American Antiquity* 69(1): 41–62.

Cruz, P. (2006). A garden for the gods: entheogenic plants use and archaeology in the Yungas of Northwest Argentina (Calilegua, Jujuy). Working paper. http://bit.ly/3Uv7MRX.

Cruz, P. (2002). *Entre pumas y jaguares. Algunas reflexiones acerca de la iconografía del valle de Ambato (Catamarca–Argentina)* (Between mountain lions and jaguars: some reflexions on the iconography from the Ambato Valley (Catamarca–Argentina)). *Revista Andina* 34: 217–35.

Cueto, M., E. Camarós, P. Castaños, R. Ontañón and P. Arias (2016). Under the skin of a lion: unique evidence of Upper Paleolithic exploitation and use of cave lion (*Panthera spelaea*) from the Lower Gallery of La Garma (Spain). *PLoS ONE* 11(10): e0163591. https://doi.org/10.1371/journal.pone.0163591.

Dagget, P.M. and D.R. Henning (1974). The jaguar in North America. *American Antiquity* 39(3): 465–9.

Dalquest, W. (1969). The mammal fauna of Schulze Cave, Edwards County, Texas. *Bulletin, Florida State Museum Biological Science* 13(4): 205–76.

Davidson, I. (2017). Images of animals in rock art: not just "good to think". In B. David and I. McNiven, eds. *The Oxford Handbook of the Archaeology and Anthropology of Rock Art*, 435–67. Oxford: Oxford University Press.

Davies, N. (1973). *The Aztecs*. London: Macmillan.
Deckha, M. (2012). Toward a postcolonial, posthumanist feminist theory: centralizing race and culture in feminist work on nonhuman animals. *Hypatia* 27(3): 527–45.
Dillehay, T.D. and P. Kaulicke (1984). *El comportamiento del jaguar y la organización socio-espacial humana* (A methodological approach: jaguar behaviour and human socio-spatial organisation), *Relaciones de la Sociedad Argentina de Antropologia* 16: 27–36.
Douglas, M. (1990). The pangolin revisited: a new approach to animal symbolism. In R.G. Willis, ed. *Signifying Animals: Human Meaning in the Natural World*, 25–36. London: Unwin Hyman.
Furst, P. (1968). The Olmec were-jaguar motif in the light of ethnographic reality. In E.P. Benson, ed. *Dumbarton Oaks Conference on the Olmec*, 143–75. Washington DC: Dumbarton Oaks.
Gamble, C. (2021). *Making Deep History: Zeal, Perseverance, and the Time Revolution of 1859*. Oxford: Oxford University Press.
Gnecco, C. (1999). Caminos de la Arqueología: de la violencia epistémica a la relacionalidad (Archaeological roads: from epistemic violence to relationality). *Boletim do Museu Paraense Emílio Goeldi Ciências Humanas* 4(1): 15–26.
Goldman, I. (1979). *The Cubeo*. Urbana: University of Illinois Press.
Gómez Augier, J.P. and M. Caria (2009). La simbología prehispánica e histórica del Noroeste Argentino y su relación con los cambios paleoambientales (Prehispanic and historic symbology in northwestern Argentina and its relationship with palaeoenvironmental changes). *Anales del Museo de América* 17: 96–105.
González, A.R. (1974). *Arte, estructura y arqueología* (Art, structure and archaeology). Buenos Aires: Ediciones Nueva Visión.
Gordillo, I. (2020). *De quimeras y transformaciones: Arqueología del arte y figuras polisémicas en los Andes del sur* (Chimeras and transformations: archaeology of art and polysemic figures in the Southern Andes). In *Congreso internacional sobre iconografía precolombina, Barcelona 2019, Actas*. Lincoln: University of Nebraska.
Gordillo, I. (2009).). Dominios y recursos de la imagen: iconografía cerámica del valle de Ambato (Domains and resources of an image: ceramic iconography from the Ambato Valley). *Estudios Atacameños* 37: 99–121.
Gosden, C. (2012). Post-colonial archaeology. In I. Hodder, ed. *Archaeological Theory Today*. 2nd edn, 251–66. Cambridge: Polity.
Gosden, C. (2004). *Archaeology and Colonialism: Cultural Contact from 5000 BC to the Present*. Cambridge: Cambridge University Press.

Haber, A. (2016). Decolonising archaeological thought in South America. *Annual Review of Anthropology* 45: 469–85.

Hamilakis, Y. and P. Duke (2007). *Archaeology and Capitalism: From Ethics to Politics*. Walnut Creek, CA: Left Coast Press.

Haraway, D. (2003). *The Companion Species Manifesto: Dogs, People and Significant Otherness*. Chicago: Prickly Paradigm Press.

Harris, O.J.T. and C.N. Cipolla (2017). *Archaeological Theory in the New Millennium: Introducing Current Perspectives*. London: Routledge.

Harrod, H.L. (2000). *The Animals Came Dancing: Native American Sacred Ecology and Animal Kinship*. Tucson: University of Arizona Press.

Hill, E. (2013). Archaeology and animal persons: toward a prehistory of human-animal relations. *Environment and Society: Advances in Research* 4: 117–36.

Hoogesteijn, R., A.L. Hoogesteijn, F. Tortaro, E. Payán, W. Jedrzewski, S. Marchini et al. (2016). Consideraciones sobre la peligrosidad del jaguar para los humanos: ¿quién es letal para quién? (Considerations on the dangers of jaguars to humans: who is lethal to whom?). In C. Castaño-Uribe, C.A. Lasso, R. Hoogesteijn, A. Diaz-Pulido and E. Payán, eds. *II. Conflictos entre felinos y humanos en América Latina*, 445–66. *Serie Editorial Fauna Silvestre Neotropical*. Bogotá: Instituto de Investigación de Recursos Biológicos Alexander von Humbolt.

Hovorka, A.J. (2017). Animal geographies I: globalising and decolonising. *Progress in Human Geography* 41(3): 382–94.

Howitt, R. and S. Suchet-Pearson (2006). Rethinking the building blocks: ontological pluralism and the idea of "management". *Geografiska Annaler: Series B, Human Geography* 88(3): 323–35.

Hussain, S.T. and H. Floss (2015a). Sharing the world with mammoths, cave lions and other beings: linking animal-human interactions and the Aurignacian "belief world". *Quartär* 62: 85–120.

Hussain, S.T. and H. Floss (2015b). Regional ontologies in the Early Upper Palaeolithic: the place of mammoth and cave lion in the 'belief world" (*Glaubenswelt*) of the Swabian Aurignacian. In P. Bueno-Ramirez and P.G. Bahn, eds. *Prehistoric Art as Prehistoric Culture*, 45–58. Oxford: Archaeopress Archaeology.

Ingold, T. (2021). Posthuman prehistory. *Nature and Culture* 16(1): 83–103.

Ingold, T. (2011). Naming as storytelling: speaking of animals among the Koyukon of Alaska. In *Being Alive: Essays on Movement, Knowledge and Description*, 166–75. London: Routledge.

Insoll, T. (2012). *The Oxford Handbook of the Archaeology of Ritual and Religion*. Oxford: Oxford University Press.

Karsten, R. (1968). *The Civilisation of the South American Indians*. London: Dawsons of Pall Mall.
Kawagley, A.O. (1995). *A Yupiaq Worldview: A Pathway to Ecology and Spirit*. Prospect Heights: Waveland Press.
Kohn, E. (2013). *How Forests Think: Toward an Anthropology beyond the Human*. California: University of California Press.
Kuokkanen, R. (2008). *Reshaping the University: Responsibility, Indigenous Epistemes, and the Logic of the Gift*. Vancouver: UBC Press.
Lee-Thorpe, J., J.F. Thackeray and N. van der Merwe (2000). The hunters and the hunted revisited. *Journal of Human Evolution* 39(6): 565–76.
Lévi-Strauss, C. (1963). *Totemism*. Boston: Beacon Press.
Liebmann, M. (2008). Introduction: the intersections of archaeology and postcolonial studies. In M. Liebmann and U.Z. Rizvi, eds. *Archaeology and the Postcolonial Critique*, 1–20. Lanham, MD: AltaMira Press.
Liebmann, M. and U.Z. Rizvi, eds (2008). *Archaeology and the Postcolonial Critique*. Lanham, MD: AltaMira Press.
Lim, C.M.S. (2019). Postcolonial and decolonial: "same but different". In *Contextual Biblical Hermeneutics as Multicentric Dialogue: Towards a Singaporean Reading of Daniel*, 193–4. Leiden: Koninklijke Brill.
Lugones, M. (2007). Heterosexualism and the colonial/modern gender system. *Hypatia: Writing against Heterosexism* 22(1): 186–209.
Lydon, J. and U.Z. Rizvi, eds (2010). *Handbook of Postcolonial Archaeology*. Walnut Creek, CA: Left Coast Press.
Masucci, M.A. (2008). Early regional polities of coastal Ecuador. In H. Silverman and W. Isbell, eds. *Handbook of South American Archaeology*, 489–504. New York: Springer.
McNiven, I.J. and L. Russell (2005). *Appropriated Pasts: Indigenous Peoples and the Colonial Culture of Archaeology*. Lanham, MD: AltaMira Press.
Métraux, A. (1948). Tribes of eastern Bolivia and Madeira headwaters. In J.H. Steward, ed. *Handbook of South American Indians*, vol. 3, 381–454. Washington: Smithsonian Institution.
Mignolo, W.D. (2016). Preface. In N. Shepherd, C. Gnecco and A. Haber, eds. *Arqueología y decolonialidad* (Archaeology and decoloniality), 7–8. Buenos Aires: Del Signo.
Mignolo, W.D. (2011). *The Darker Side of Western Modernity: Global Futures, Decolonial Options*. Durham, NC: Duke University Press.
Mignolo, W.D. (2009). Introduction: coloniality of power and de-colonial thinking. In W.D. Mignolo and A. Escobar, eds. *Globalisation and the Decolonial Option*, 303–68. New York: Routledge.

Mignolo, W.D. and M. Tlostanova (2006). Theorising from the borders: shifting to geo- and body-politics of knowledge. *European Journal of Social Theory* 9(2): 205–21.

Motta, A.P. (2023). On living heritage and painted images: performance and the transformation of "paintings" in rock art. In M. Porr and N. Weidtmann, eds. *One World Anthropology and Beyond: A Multidisciplinary Engagement with the Work of Tim Ingold*, chapter 16. London: Routledge.

Motta, A.P. and G. Romero Villanueva (2020). South American art. In C. Smith, ed. *Encyclopedia of Global Archaeology*. https://doi.org/10.1007/978-3-319-51726-1_2914-1.

Overton, N.J. and Y. Hamilakis (2013). A manifesto for a social zooarchaeology: swans and other beings in the Mesolithic. *Archaeological Dialogues* 20(2): 111–36.

Pérez-Gollán, J. (1992). La cultura de La Aguada vista desde el valle de Ambato (Aguada culture as seen from the Ambato Valley). *Publicaciones del CIFFyH, Universidad Nacional de Córdoba* 46: 157–73.

Pilaar Birch, S. (2018a). Introduction. In S. Pilaar Birch, ed. *Multispecies Archaeology*, 1–7. New York: Routledge.

Pilaar Birch, S., ed. (2018b). *Multispecies Archaeology*. New York: Routledge.

Pochettino, M.L., A.R. Cortella and M. Ruis (1999). Hallucinogenic snuff from northwestern Argentina: microscopical identification of *Anadenanthera colubrina* var. *cebil* (Fabaceae) in powdered archaeological material. *Economic Botany* 53(2): 127–32.

Porr, M. (2020). The temporality of humanity and the colonial landscape of the deep human past. In M. Porr and J.M. Matthews, eds. *Interrogating Human Origins: Decolonisation and the Deep Human Past*, 184–207. London: Routledge.

Porr, M. (2015). Beyond animality and humanity: landscape, metaphor and identity in the Early Upper Palaeolithic of Central Europe. In F. Coward, R. Hosfield, M. Pope and F. Wenban-Smith, eds. *Settlement, Sociality and Cognition in Human Evolution: Landscapes in Mind*, 54–74. Cambridge: Cambridge University Press.

Porr, M. (2010). Palaeolithic art as cultural memory: a case study of the Aurignacian art of Southwest Germany. *Cambridge Archaeological Journal* 20(1): 87–108.

Porr, M. and J.M. Matthews, eds. (2020a). *Interrogating Human Origins: Decolonisation and the Deep Human Past*. London: Routledge.

Porr, M. and J.M. Matthews (2020b). Interrogating and decolonising the deep human past. In M. Porr and J.M. Matthews, eds. *Interrogating Human Origins: Decolonisation and the Deep Human Past*, 3–31. London: Routledge.

Quammen, D. (2003). *Monster of God: The Man-Eating Predator in the Jungles of History and the Mind*. New York: W.W. Norton & Company.
Quijano, A. (2009). Coloniality and modernity/rationality. In W.D. Mignolo and A. Escobar, eds. *Globalisation and the Decolonial Option*, 303–68. New York: Routledge.
Rabinowitz, A. (2014). *An Indomitable Beast: The Remarkable Journey of the Jaguar*. Washington, DC: Island Press.
Recht, L. (2019). Animals as social actors: cases of equid resistance in the Ancient Near East. *Cambridge Archaeological Journal* 29 (4): 593–606.
Reichel-Dolmatoff, G. (1978). *El Chamán y el Jaguar: Estudio de las Drogas Narcóticas entre los Indios de Colombia* (The Shaman and the Jaguar: Study of Entoptic Drugs among Indigenous People from Colombia). México DF: Siglo Veintiuno Editores.
Roosevelt, A.C. (1996). Paleoindian cave dwellers in the Amazon: the peopling of the Americas. *Science* 272: 373–84.
Rostain, S. (2008). The archaeology of the Guianas: an overview. In H. Silverman and W. Isbell, eds. *Handbook of South American Archaeology*, 279–302. New York: Springer.
Saunders, N.J. (1998). *Icons of Power: Feline Symbolism in the Americas*. New York: Routledge.
Saunders, N.J. (1994). Predators of culture: jaguar symbolism and Mesoamerican elites. *World Archaeology* 26(1): 104–17.
Saunders, N.J. (1992). The jaguars of culture: symbolising humanity in Pre-Columbian and Amerindian societies. Doctoral dissertation, Department of Archaeology, University of Southampton.
Schneider, T.D. and K. Hayes (2020). Epistemic colonialism: is it possible to decolonise archaeology? *American Indian Quarterly* 44(2):127–48.
Shepherd, N. (2016a). Introducción: ¿Por qué arqueología? ¿Por qué decolonial? (Introduction: Why archaeology? Why decolonial?). In N. Shepherd, C. Gnecco and A. Haber, eds. *Arqueología y Decolonialidad (Archaeology and Decoloniality)*, 13–18. Buenos Aires: Del Signo.
Shepherd, N. (2016b). Arqueología, colonialidad, modernidad (Archaeology, coloniality, modernity). In N. Shepherd, C. Gnecco and A. Haber, eds. *Arqueología y decolonialidad (Archaeology and Decoloniality)*, 19–70. Buenos Aires: Del Signo.
Shepherd, N., C. Gnecco and A. Haber, eds (2016). *Arqueología y Decolonialidad* (Archaeology and Decoloniality). Buenos Aires: Del Signo.
Simeon, R. (1988). *Diccionario de la lengua Nahuatl o Mexicana* (Dictionary of Nahuatl or Mexican language). Mexico City: Siglo Veintiuno.

Smail, D. L. and A. Shryock (2013). History and the "Pre". *American Historical Review* 118(3): 709–57.

Suchet-Pearson, S., S. Wright, K. Lloyd and L. Burarrwanga (2013). Caring as Country: towards an ontology of co-becoming in natural resource management. *Asia Pacific Viewpoint* 54(2): 185–97.

Sundberg, J. (2014). Decolonising posthumanist geographies. *Cultural Geographies* 21(1): 33–47.

Szerszynski, B. (2017). Gods of the Anthropocene: geo-spiritual formations in the Earth's new epoch. *Theory, Culture and Society* 34(2–3): 253–75.

Thomas, J. (2004). *Archaeology and Modernity*. London: Routledge.

Todd, Z. (2016). An Indigenous feminist's take on the ontological turn: "ontology" is just another word for colonialism. *Journal of Historical Sociology* 29(1): 4–22.

Todd, K.L. and V. Robert. (2018). Reviving the spirit by making the case for decolonial curricula. In N.N. Wane and K.L. Todd, eds. *Decolonial Pedagogy: Examining Sites of Resistance, Resurgence, and Renewal*, 57–72. Switzerland: Palgrave Macmillan.

Toledo, V. (2000). *La Paz en Chiapas: Ecología, Luchas Indígenas y Modernidad Alternativa* (La Paz in Chiapas: Ecology, Indigenous Struggles, and Alternative Modernity). Mexico City: Ediciones Quinto Sol and UNAM.

Toledo, V. and N. Barrera-Bassols (2008). *La Memoria Biocultural: La Importancia Ecológica de las Sabidurías Tradicionales* (The Bio-cultural Memory: The Ecological Importance of Traditional Knowledges). Barcelona: Icaria Editorial.

Trigger, B. (1989). *A History of Archaeological Thought*. Cambridge: Cambridge University Press.

Trigger, B. (1984). Alternative archaeologies: nationalist, colonialist, imperialist. *Man* 19: 355–70.

Tschakert, P. (2020). More-than-human solidarity and multispecies justice in the climate crisis. *Environmental Politics* 1–20. https://doi.org/10.1080/09644016.2020.1853448.

Turnbull, D. (2007). Maps, narratives and trails: performativity, hodology and distributed knowledges in complex adaptive systems – an approach to emergent mapping. *Geographical Research* 45: 140–9.

Vaillant, G. (1944). *The Aztecs of Mexico*. New York: Doubleday.

Vasco Uribe L.G. (2002). *Entre Selva y Páramo: Viviendo y Pensando la Lucha India* (Between Rainforest and Paramo: Living and Thinking the Indigenous Fight). Bogotá, Colombia: Instituto Colombiano de Antropología Histórica.

Vasco Uribe L.G. (1992). Arqueología e identidad: el caso Guambiano (Archaeology and identity: the Guambiano case). In G. Politis, ed.

Archaeology in Latin America Today, 176–91. Bogotá, Colombia. Biblioteca Banco Popular.
Watts, V. (2013). Indigenous place-thought & agency amongst humans and non-humans (First Woman and Sky Woman go on a European world tour!). *Decolonization: Indigeneity, Education and Society* 2(1): 20–34.
Whalen, M.E. (1983). Reconstructing early formative village organisation in Oaxaca, Mexico. *American Antiquity* 48(1): 17–43.

8

The birdwomen speak: "Storied transformation" and non-human narrative perspectives

Kirsty Dunn

> At primary school I saw a play about Hatupatu and the birdwoman.
> The birdwoman had wings for arms, claws in place of fingers,
> lips formed into a beak.
> She wore a cloak of colourful feathers.
> Her hair was on fire.
>
> Nobody mentioned her name.
>
> – Stacey Teague ("Kurangaituku")

> Kurungaituku picked up the big, heavy bag, bundled it into her pīkau. Leaning over Hatupatu, she wiped her talons on the fine, soft flax of his kaitaka and she sighed to herself.
> His voice was gone.
>
> – Ngahuia Te Awekotuku ("Kurungaituku"[1])

Although one of the first stories involving the famous Māori shapeshifting demigod Māui that I remember hearing as a child is the story of the contest between the trickster and the colossal ika (fish) that would later be renamed the "North Island" of New Zealand,[2] it is another Māui tale which has become a favourite in our household: that which depicts the

1 Te Awekotuku 2003, 86.

journey Māui makes into the underworld.[3] In the version we tell (courtesy of Glenda Kauta, Mārara Te Tai and Janet Piddock's bilingual, picture-book retelling[4]), Māui becomes curious as to why his mother, Taranga, makes a habit of leaving at first light while others remain sleeping. One evening, Māui deceives Taranga by covering the small holes in the whare (house) with his sleeping mat to prevent the dawn light from entering. Taranga thus misses her usual cue and does not wake until birdsong rouses her, much later in the morning. Realising she has been tricked, Taranga quickly flees the whare with Māui following in hidden pursuit. Māui watches Taranga descend into an opening in the ground and he resolves to follow her; but first, he returns to the whare and dons his mother's cloak, which she has left behind in her hurried departure.[5] Māui then recites a karakia (incantation) and turns himself into a kūkupa (wood pigeon),[6] flies down into the opening in the earth and arrives in Rarohenga (the underworld), where he learns that Taranga regularly visits with his father, Mākea; Māui then returns to human form, whereupon Taranga introduces father and son. Thus, not only does this narrative explain the circumstances surrounding the meeting between Māui and his father, it also incorporates the source of the colourful plumage of the kūkupa: for the hues of the feathers of the bird are said to originate from the colours of the cloak of Taranga.

Reflecting on this narrative and on my son's affinity for it, it is of no surprise to me that he is drawn to a story about an inquisitive adventurer who can shapeshift into a bird, a brave trickster who can move between worlds, and a son who successfully tricks his mother

---

2 One name for this island, Te Ika a Māui (The Fish of Māui), references the events whereby Māui fished up the gigantic ika that his brothers then took to with their hoe (oars), thus creating the island's undulating landscape.

3 I note that translations provided in brackets are approximations only; many of the concepts referred to here (such as "pūrākau", "whakapapa", "atua", "kaitiakitanga" and "taonga") defy easy translation into English.

4 Kauta and Piddock 1985.

5 In other versions of this narrative, it is not a cloak but a maro (a short garment worn around the waist) that Māui utilises: "[Māui] changed into the form of a kererū (wood pigeon), taking the colours and the sheen of the feathers of his mother's maro. The belt became the snowy throat, and the fastenings the black feathers" (Reed and Calman 2008, 121–4).

6 The other common name for this bird is kererū.

(the last of these may well be what appeals to him the most). For me, like the tale of Māui and the great ika, it is also a story about the journeys we often take in order to learn more about ourselves – our origins, our motivations and our aspirations – and a narrative which acknowledges that these transformative expeditions not only require entering into unknown or unfamiliar territories, they might also involve circumventing authority and breaking with tradition.

This pūrākau (narrative) is also one of many in Te Ao Māori (the Māori world) which feature the shapeshifting abilities of tūpuna (ancestors) and transformations from human to non-human and which provide numerous opportunities to consider human–non-human kinships, representations, associations and comparisons.[7] In one narrative, for example, warrior Titapu changes into a kōtuku (white heron) upon his death after an ambush and seeks revenge while in bird form;[8] in another, Māui turns Irawaru (brother of his companion, Hinauri) into a kurī (dog) after a feud;[9] and in some accounts, Ngāti Porou tupuna Paikea (Kahutia Te Rangi) is able to transform himself into a whale and operate "fluidly between his human form and his ocean form".[10] In some versions of the story in which Māui attempts to gain immortality, he turns into a tīrairaka (fantail) before attempting to enter the womb of Hine-nui-te-pō;[11] there is also a version of the story of Te Ika a Māui which explains that upon realising his brothers had gone fishing without him, Māui changed into a tīrairaka, followed the waka out to sea and slowly shed his feathers to reveal himself.[12] In addition, Cleve Barlow describes the return of "illustrious ancestors" who had the ability to "direct and influence the affairs of the family they had left behind"; in some instances, these tūpuna "were able to transform themselves into birds, fish or insects".[13]

---

7 "Pūrākau" here refers to narratives passed down through generations. For more, see Lee 2009.

8 Pohatu 2001.

9 Pohatu 2001.

10 Ihimaera 2019, 191.

11 Kupenga, Rata and Nepe 1993. Hine-nui-te-pō is the atua (deity) who cares for those who have passed into the spirit world.

12 Reed and Calman 2008.

13 Barlow 2015, 41.

Sometimes transformations also explain the origins of certain species. Pīoi (pīhoihoi, the ground lark) and Kūkuruwhatu (tūturiwhatu, the dotterel), for example, were once not birds but men who fell in love with the same woman, Wharo; they were transformed into birds after attempting to deceive her mother, Hineitemorari.[14] These transformations and metamorphoses are not limited to human and animal forms. The atua (deity) Rongomai takes the form of a sleeping whale prior to his altercation with the atua Maru;[15] a family of whales becomes a range of hills around the Welcome Bay area;[16] migratory manu (bird) Taiāmai evades capture by transforming into stone;[17] famous explorer Tamateapōkaiwhenua turns wahine (woman) Turihuka into stone (and shortly after transforms Kōpūwai into a lizard for abandoning her)[18]; the "ogre" Matukutakotako transforms into a bittern in order to escape Rata, a celebrated mokopuna (descendant) of Tāwhaki[19]; and Pania – woman of the sea – famously becomes a rock in her beloved ocean.[20]

There are also narratives which describe people with abilities or appearances akin to those of our animal whanaunga (relations). For example, some tūpuna are credited with the ability to fly, such as Tarāpunga[21] and Tamarau; the latter's appearance was "usually that of a pākura (pūkeko) and occasionally that of a meteor".[22] There are other pūrākau which describe human–animal hybrid people, including the well-known "birdwoman", Kurangaituku (also known as Kurungaituku), and her conflict with Hatupatu, which took place in the Rotorua rohe (a retelling of which features in this chapter)[23]

---

14 Reed and Calman 2008.
15 Reed and Calman 2008.
16 Haami 2006.
17 Brown 2013.
18 Reed and Calman 2008.
19 Reed and Calman 2008, 183.
20 Reed and Calman 2008. The son of Pania, Moremore, is also said to have turned into a taniwha in the form of a shark which resides at the reef near Hukarere and at the harbour near the Ahuriri river mouth. See Reed and Calman 2008, 454.
21 Riley 2006.
22 Reed and Calman 2008, 448.
23 Reed and Calman 2008, 249.

as well as Kōpuwai and Moeahu, the "dog-headed men".[24] Animal hybrids are found in whakairo (carved works), too: combinations of bird, serpent or fish with human features have been the subject of analysis, with various suggestions as to what these hybrid figures might represent.[25]

The transformation Māui makes from human form to bird form and back again in the pūrākau is one of many examples of the prominence of animal whanaunga within Māori narratives. In a similar vein to the origin story regarding Māui and the great ika, the pūrākau describing Māui and his journey to the underworld exemplifies the ways in which human and non-human whakapapa (genealogies)[26] and experience are so often intertwined; animal whanaunga are frequently implicated in these narratives and in many works by Māori writers, as observers, as adversaries, as kai (food), as tohu (signs), as guardians and in this particular instance (if only momentarily) in the form of the protagonist themselves.

While containing historical, geographical, genealogical and ecological knowledge as well as moral and ethical guidelines, these narratives involving transformation, metamorphosis, hybridity and "more-than-human" behaviours and attributes also provide opportunities to reflect upon human–non-human kinships and connections described within whakapapa. Works that incorporate similar representations – including those that retell or reference pūrākau, which feature these transformations, qualities and characteristics – are thus apposite avenues for considering this kinship, as well as the genealogies of the stories themselves, the information they contain, and the perspectives they represent.

The narrative regarding Māui and his visit to Rarohenga also exemplifies the layers of knowledge and narrative within pūrākau and illustrates the interplay of relationships within these stories: between environments, family members, and human and non-human – and,

24 Brown 2013, 161.
25 See e.g. Brown 2013.
26 Whakapapa encompasses much more than genealogy; whakapapa not only describes relationships between all things but provides guidelines for living in relation. Whakapapa is also a process of layer-making.

consequently, between different narrative points of view. It is the representation of these relationships and, in particular, the ways in which alternative narrative perspectives can illuminate and examine these connections that is my key concern in this chapter. While taking the form of a bird gives Māui the ability to view the interaction between his parents from an alternative and advantageous perspective, these narratives which feature non-human points of view provide opportunities to consider alternative experiences and subjectivities: to decentre the human experience and the more dominant voices within that sphere in order to imagine other lives, stories and points of view; to undertake, as Daniel Heath Justice writes, a kind of "storied transformation" from "self, to other, and back again".[27] "It's amazing what you discover", notes Tina Makereti, "when you look in a different direction, speak with a different voice".[28]

While it is the transformation Māui makes from man to manu and his observing the world through the eyes of the kūkupa that helped to inspire various lines of literary inquiry, it is portrayals of birdwomen and mother birds and narrative perspectives within two short stories by Māori authors which have come to form the basis of the analysis here. Karl Wixon's "Te Karaka o te Tītī" (1997), which portrays a whānau (family) mahi tītī (muttonbirding) excursion from the perspectives of both human and bird, and "Kurungaituku", a retelling of the story of Hatupatu and the birdwoman by Ngahuia Te Awekotuku, each engage with these themes in various ways. In doing so, they prompt reflections upon the power of narrative perspective and initiate the consideration of voices and experiences – including those of our non-human relatives – which both compare and contrast with our own. These texts also provide means by which issues regarding the creation, dissemination, appropriation and suppression of certain narratives may be explored, as well as the effect and impact that particular narratives have upon our relationships with each other, our non-human relations and the environments we inhabit.

Karl Wixon's "Te Karaka o te Tītī" (The Cry of the Muttonbird) and his unsettling representation of both human and non-human

---

27 Justice 2018, x.
28 Makereti 2018, n.p.

perspectives provide an apt entry point into this analysis. Published in the second short fiction anthology released by Huia in 1997,[29] Wixon's subversive narrative juxtaposes two perspectives: the first belongs to Karl, who engages in muttonbird harvesting with his family and in doing so helps to ensure that connections to lands and to ancestral practices and knowledges are maintained; the second belongs to a female tītī (muttonbird), which likewise depicts her relationships with the ocean and land, as well as her place within her whānau as both mother and mokopuna. Wixon's text moves between the shared views and connections between human and non-human, the stark contrasts in their perspectives of the same series of events and the power dynamic at work between the two protagonists – man and bird – who share the same environment.

The twinned narratives which constitute the story represent both our relationships and similarities shared with other species, as well as the ways in which humans exercise control over their non-human counterparts and their habitats. A sense of the responsibilities which accompany that power, including concepts such as kaitiakitanga (guardianship and caretaking), is also implicit within Wixon's narrative. The dual perspectives in the story also go some way towards decentring the human subject in order to consider the experiences of non-human whanaunga and the ways in which human behaviour impacts upon their lives.

Karl's narrative begins as he looks out beyond the light of his kerosene lamp towards a walking track. In the deep shadow, the "unhindered mind of a child sees ghostly figures appear and disappear", and he considers how his ancestors "probably walked this same track";[30] he notes that sometimes he feels their presence, "their triumphs" and "their pains".[31] He then hears a "ghostly cry": the "karaka o te tītī" (cry of the muttonbird) as it reaches a "crescendo", "eeeee,eee,eee,ooah, ooah ooah oooahh, eeee eeeee uu uu", and soon after observes a "kaiak" (parent bird), which crosses his path "scuttling erratically on feet more suitable for

29 Established in 1991, Huia is an independant, Māori-owned and -operated publisher.

30 Wixon 1997, 137.

31 Wixon 1997, 137.

the domain of Takaroa" as it hurries towards the beach.[32] The bird pauses, and Karl narrates: "It hesitates momentarily and looks at me, as if it has seen me before. Disturbed by the light it takes off again".[33]

This series of events is then told from the perspective of the mother tītī. She too considers her ancestors, as she steals away from "the warm embrace of Papatūānuku" (atua of land – also sometimes referred to as earth mother), and she is also situated within a family environment, as she leaves her "babies" to sleep.[34] Then, after flicking her feet to cover the entrance to their home with leaf litter, she becomes immediately aware of and in tune with the "currents and forces" which surround her. She hears "the distant thumping of the surf" as well as the cry of her "babies" in much the same way that Karl is aware of the "ghostly" forces which surround him and of the sound of the tītī crying out above him.[35] Connections between ancestors, human, non-human and environment are thus established early and reaffirmed by the corresponding narratives. The omnipresence of the past is also accentuated here via the mention of the deeds of tūpuna, the repetition of "ghostly" in regards to Karl's experience (both visual in terms of the figures which "appear and disappear" and aural in terms of the cry of the tītī chicks) and in the notion that manu and man may have met before. The recognition of and reference to the past are thus depicted from the outset of Wixon's text and mirrored in the bird's narration which appears later; this emphasises the theme of maintaining those connections, histories and relationships which reverberates throughout the story.

After leaving her chicks in their burrow, pushing through the undergrowth and stumbling upon open ground, the mother

---

32 Wixon 1997, 137. Takaroa is the name for the atua of the ocean and sea-dwelling species in the Kai Tahu mita (dialect).

33 Wixon 1997, 137.

34 Wixon 1997, 139. This connection with whānau also appears later in the narrative: after arriving at the clifftop, the tītī spreads her wings and senses the currents and narrates: "with a flick I am gliding gracefully alongside my whānauka [...] We sing together, while keeping a watching eye on the murky depths beneath us" (Wixon 1997, 140). Again, the similarities between the tītī and Karl are made apparent: both belong to families and both are keenly aware of the environment that surrounds and sustains them.

35 Wixon 1997, 139.

tītī narrates: "I am dazzled by a bright light, a tall creature looming over me, looking at me as if it has seen me before. Frightened I race on".[36] This passage is particularly powerful in both its similarity to Karl's narration and in the important difference that it illuminates. While the response is almost identical, in that both bird and man sense a recognition in the eyes of the other, the actual outcome of this mirrored response is that neither of them really does recognise the other, nor do they share the memory of a previous encounter. It is here that Wixon subtly represents the connections and similarities between human and non-human in terms of shared environments, histories and family relationships, as well as the ways in which our understandings of and communication between each other remain elusive.

This interplay between sameness and difference, connection and separation, is present throughout the story. For example, within Karl's narration, various bird species are referred to as though they are people who go about their daily lives and "speak" to each other as their human relations do, as well as to the human in their midst. "Laughing, chattering kakariki" (a type of parrot), for example, bid Karl "good day" as they go about their "patrol across the tree-tops", while the tūī "ducks, dives, swerves and glides" through the canopy: "Look-out, outa my way, comin' through, move aside, up we go, look-out, comin' through."[37] A pītakataka (fantail) also "flits around" and informs him of "the latest gossip, its black and white tail flickering with excitement as endless chatter spouts forward".[38] The bird shares "all the latest news" before flying elsewhere "chattering as it goes".[39] The "guttural cry of the weka" is also mentioned and its "gargled call", "eee we, eee we, eee, we…", is translated: "come over here, I've found some tītī, eyes ripe for the picking".[40] Karl is "startled" by the reply from a weka nearby, which he translates as: "I am coming, I'm bringing my whānau, save some for us."[41] Karl addresses a kākāriwai (robin) as "friend"; "I know what you

36 Wixon 1997, 139–142.
37 Wixon 1997, 138.
38 Wixon 1997, 138.
39 Wixon 1997, 138.
40 Wixon 1997, 138.
41 Wixon 1997, 138.

want," he says, and proceeds to share a piece of his fruit cake with the bird.[42] Here, the connection between Karl and the manu around him is made clear; he observes their behaviours closely, listens to their calls and compares their thoughts and actions to those belonging to humans, including himself.

This connection is also evident in Karl's assumption of the perspective of the weka; it is here that more details regarding the tītī harvest emerge: "Be careful, there is a creature here, pulling tītī out of the earth and breaking their necks. Don't be tricked, she lays many irresistible shiny objects on the ground around her."[43] Given that the word "creature" is usually employed by humans with reference to animal species, Karl's use of it in regards to humans in this context provides yet another representation of connections between species and our shared origins: the word applies to human and non-human beings. The appearance of "creature" here also foreshadows the perspective of the tītī in the second narration, whereby the bird also refers to Karl as a "creature" who looms over her when she first encounters him, as previously mentioned.[44]

Connections between human and non-human, however, are clearly punctuated by the realities of the customary harvesting of tītī. Given the chatty conversations and connections between bird and man that have been established and which surround the description of the "creature" who is "pulling tītī out of the earth and breaking their necks", the sudden intrusion of death into the narrative sharply fetters this relationship.[45] Wixon's narrative thus demonstrates the key whakapapa which underpin human and non-human relationships in Te Ao Māori: while non-humans are considered as kin, they are also utilised as sources of sustenance. In this way, he shows that human and non-human connections and similarities operate in tandem with the ways in which humans can and do exercise this supreme power over their non-human relations.[46]

42 Wixon 1997, 139.
43 Wixon 1997, 138.
44 Wixon 1997, 139.
45 Wixon 1997, 138.

This "punctuation" occurs once more in Karl's narrative, immediately before the perspective of the tītī is introduced. Karl's mother tells him that it's "Smoko time" and asks him to "chase the wekas away"; "they're at our birds again", she explains.[47] Karl then throws a stick as hard as he can, killing a weka in the process: "Weka stew for dinner," he says to himself. Given the previous description of the weka, which portrays the industrious birds in a similar vein to the human family gathering tītī, Karl's actions here once more provide an abrupt reminder of the complexity of human–animal relationships and the push and pull inherent within them – the simultaneous existence of both similarity and difference, and a kinship that nevertheless entails unequal power relations which result in human dominance and the slaughter and consumption of other species. And, while the narrative as a whole reads as a potent reminder of both the realities of the relationship between human and non-human and the power held by humans within that relationship, it might also be possible to read Wixon's representation here (particularly in light of the emotive perspective of the mother tītī) in a different way, in light of Craig Womack's assertion that "[a]nimals, not just us humans, have kin, and we would do well to imagine them if we want to take into account all – not some – of our relations."[48] Wixon's narrative might also be a potent way of this "imagining" other kin and thus prompts a closer interrogation of both our attitudes and our actions in regards to animal relations.

Wixon's narrative also represents the responsibilities encompassed within the concept of kaitiakitanga as constraints upon that power. Just before the narration switches to the point of view of the tītī, Karl counts up the tītī that have been harvested thus far, "tahi, rua, toru, whā, rima", as he ties the birds together "five in each end";[49] "I count up thirty-seven," he narrates, before asking: "Mum, how many tītī are

46 This is also reflected in the description of the fearful tītī chick who is "cowering in the far reaches of its burrow" as Karl's mum uses an adze to break fresh turf in order to capture it (Wixon 1997, 137).

47 Wixon 1997, 139.

48 Womack 2013, 24.

49 Wixon 1997, 139.

there?" The perspective then shifts to that of the tītī, who, after recounting the earlier meeting between herself and "the tall creature", explains that the food stocks which sustain her and her relatives are diminishing: "We sing together", she narrates, "while keeping a watching eye on the murky depths beneath us. According to some of my older whānauka [relations], the moana [ocean] was once filled with kai. Our tūpuna used to only venture as far as Rakiura in their search. Today the search is long, we have lost sight of Poutama and I worry about my babies."[50]

This representation of intergenerational knowledge (the food available to the ancestors of the tītī) reflects the story's opening sentences, in which Karl considers the journeys and deeds of his ancestors in the same environment. Thus, when Karl's counting up of birds (individually and then in groups) is juxtaposed with the decreasing amount of food available for the tītī and her relatives, the notion of imbalance, and the possibility of being unable to continue intergenerational practices or maintain ancestral connections with particular places (land and sea), is made apparent.

The role of humans within this imbalance is then emphasised by the bird's description of the fate of her kin as some of them dive towards a "squirming mass of squid" near the ocean's surface: "Something doesn't feel right" to her, but her attempts to stop them come too late, as the other birds "dive to fill their gullets only to be embraced by an invisible wall of death".[51] "I had been warned about these floating taniwha that line the horizon at night, their thousands of eyes glowing brilliantly at night," she thinks, and she recalls how other members of her whānau had witnessed these taniwha "on their great heke [migration] around Te Moana Nui a Kiwa [The Pacific Ocean]".[52] These human-made "walls of death" meant for ika (which are most probably responsible for the diminishing kai stocks previously referred to) are thus responsible for the killing of tītī. It is these representations which reflect the consequences of and contrasts between large-scale means of exerting power over other species and customary practices; the

50 Wixon 1997, 140.
51 Wixon 1997, 140.
52 Wixon 1997, 140.

narrative also suggests the effect that the former may have over the latter. At the same time, the effects of commercial fishing and customary harvesting upon an individual (the mother tītī, who describes her relatives and her young) are also highlighted, which not only mirrors the contrasts between the macro and micro level harvesting of species but poignantly prompts a reflection on the individual, subjective experiences of our animal kin.

Kaitiakitanga, then, acting in a way that preserves connections to ancestors, to the environment and to other species, appears to be a key theme within Wixon's text, and one that is made particularly potent when presented through the eyes of non-human relations. Foregrounded on an acknowledgement of genealogical connections and the similarities between human and non-human, the text also represents the realities of the ways in which humans utilise power and dominance over non-human kin – in regards both to other species and to the environment. A call to remember these realities and responsibilities is at its most effective in a question Karl poses which appears twice in the narrative, once as a bridge between his own narrative and the perspective of the tītī and once more as the story's closing line: "Mum, how many tītī are there?"[53] The question hangs in the air at these two important locations in the narrative, appearing as somewhat of a challenge to consider not just "how many" birds, fish and so on have been harvested, but how many of them remain. It appears that the answer to this question will be determined by the extent to which these human connections to non-human kin are maintained. Wixon's representation of the mother bird's perspective, and others which imagine likewise, may well be considered as an additional and effective means by which the continuation of these relationships may be achieved and the responsibilities which accompany them may be remembered and enacted.

The representation of alternative perspectives also features in the short story "Kurungaituku" by Ngahuia Te Awekotuku: a retelling of the famous tale of the "half human and half bird" creature's "capture" of a young man named Hatupatu and his subsequent escape and victory.[54] This retelling also demonstrates the ways in which reimagining

53 Wixon 1997, 139, 141.

existing narratives provides provocative means to examine storytelling authority. Rather than being told with an emphasis on the wily Hatupatu and his getting the better of the "bird ogress", this version places the perspective of Kurungaituku at the centre;[55] here, it is Kurungaituku who is the victor and it is she who robs Hatupatu of his voice. In a similar vein to "Te Karaka o te Tītī", this evocative retelling and its focus on the birdwoman's experience emphasise the operation of narratives for, about and at the expense of others; it also serves as a reminder of kinship responsibilities which caution against assumed superiority and greed.

"Kurungaituku" sits alongside eight other stories which centre the views and experiences of wāhine (women) in *Ruahine: Mythic Women* (2003), and which, as Bach, Luh and Schult note, enrich women with "elements of physical power and mental strength".[56] Together, these retellings challenge not only the dominance of male protagonists within certain narratives but those responsible for this apparent dominance. As Ani Mikaere explains in her book *Colonising Myths, Māori Realities*, the "re-telling of Māori cosmogony by Māori males to Pākehā ethnographers led to shift in emphasis away from the powerful female influence in the stories and towards male characters."[57] "Kurungaituku" and the other stories within *Ruahine: Mythic Women* have thus been collectively described as means by which the "mythological moulds within which Māori women have been cast" can be dismantled and by which new representations and interpretations are offered.[58] In addition, both the representations of the wāhine within the collection and the author's act of producing them provide space within which the experiences and narratives of Māori women and

54 Te Awekotuku 2003, 73–86.

55 Reed and Caman 2008, 252. In this version, Hatupatu is killed by his brothers Hānui and Hāroa for raiding the whata (food stores), and he is buried under a pile of feathers. Upon inquiring about their son's whereabouts, Hatupatu's parents call on the aid of Tamumu (a spirit) to find him; he does so, and Hatupatu is brought back to life and subsequently encounters Kurungaituku as he hunts for manu to satisfy his hunger.

56 Bach, Luh and Schult 2003, 35.

57 Mikaere 2011, 220.

58 Murphy 2017, 6.

expressions of mana wāhine in contemporary Aotearoa (New Zealand) can be brought into focus.[59]

In the introduction to "Kurungaituku", Te Awekotuku explains that the well-known story is already subject to change and perspective according to its teller and notes for example that in some versions of the narrative Hatupatu is abducted by the birdwoman, while in others he is invited into her lair.[60] Despite these alternative versions, the story usually concludes in much the same way: with Hatupatu killing the cave-dwelling animal companions of Kurungaituku and stealing treasured items before escaping and hiding from her in a hollow rock beneath a hill; he then leads the birdwoman to her death in the boiling hot pools. "Kurungaituku perished in the scalding water", writes Te Awekotuku, "[…] but I could never accept it. Why didn't she fly away if she had wings like a bird? And why was she punished when Hatupatu was the thief and murderer?"[61] These questions create the foundation for this alternative narrative: one which emphasises the birdwoman's strength, patience and dedication to her relations in opposition to the greed and deceit shown by Hatupatu – a greed that is aided by his alluring words and song but ultimately leads to his downfall.

In addition to this introduction, numerous references to voice, story and song are located throughout this reimagining and illustrate constant power shifts between the key players in the narrative. We learn, for example, that it is the voice of Hatupatu which attracts Kurungaituku to him in the first place. As she walks through the forest contemplating the need for a "human friend" to help take care of her

59 Bach, Luh and Schult 2011, 33. While Aotearoa is often considered the Māori name for New Zealand, it is important to note that in narratives pertaining to this name, it related to the first sighting of Te Ika a Māui (the North Island) by Kuramarotini (the female companion of the voyager Kupe). Debate continues over whether or not this name should therefore extend to encompass the country's other islands.

60 In the version provided by Reed and Calman, Hatupatu is captured by the birdwoman and dragged to her cave, "where he was thrown into a corner to be kept as a mōkai" (pet) 2008, 251. Stacey Teague's poem "Kurangaituku" also highlights the existence of different versions of the narrative; of Hatupatu she writes: "[S]ome say she abducted him, others say he was invited" (2020).

61 Te Awekotuku 2003, 75.

home and companions, she hears a "strange, unusual voice that soared high into the trees" and even causes the birds to halt their own song in order to listen.[62] Then, as she silently flies down to land in front of Hatupatu, we are told that the young man "swallowed all his words" at the sight of the birdwoman.[63] This interplay between song and silence continues throughout the story and foreshadows the narrative's violent climax.

It is also during this initial meeting that the stark contrast between the characters – and a more sympathetic version of the birdwoman – becomes clear. Kurungaituku, for example, is "kind and curious and eager to talk" to Hatupatu, and she invites him to meet her pets and stay with her a while. Hatupatu, however, covets the "fabulous, richly feathered cloak" Kurungaituku wears: "I would like a cloak like that," he thinks, and he agrees to accompany her.[64] Miromiro, close companion of Kurungaituku, becomes aware of the newcomer's intentions as she watches him "touching the birdwoman's special taonga" (items of value), one of which is a cloak consisting of a "woven mantle of bright, fresh blood: a silky soft, sorrowful memory of Kurungaituku's favourite feathered cousins, killed by humans for their beauty" that the birdwoman has reclaimed.[65] Miromiro sees Hatupatu fondle the cloak "lovingly with a faraway look in his eye and a humming, greedy song upon his breath".[66]

As winter draws nearer, Hatupatu persuades Kurungaituku to venture further into the forest to obtain karaka berries for the group. Utilising his oratorical skill, he describes the succulence and deliciousness of the berries and convinces her to go. He also promises to take care of their companions, again with the use of his voice and song: "He reassured her that all he had to do was sing to them and quietly, easily, they'd settle down, not missing her at all."[67] Then, once Kurungaituku has left the cave, it is song once more that Hatupatu

62 Te Awekotuku 2003, 76.
63 Te Awekotuku 2003, 77.
64 Te Awekotuku 2003, 77.
65 Te Awekotuku 2003, 77. Miromiro and Kōmiromiro are names for the white-breasted North Island tomtit.
66 Te Awekotuku 2003, 78.
67 Te Awekotuku 2003, 78.

utilises as he sings "slowly, gently, and softly", though his voice is used in order to disguise his intentions and to move undetected so as to succeed in killing the ngārara (insects), kurī (dogs), kiore (rats), mokomoko (lizards) and other companions of Kurungaituku. With "soundless tread" and with his song "low and lingering", he injures and kills them all except Miromiro. He "crushed" wings to a "pale ashy powder", "snapped thin bones" and "shredded cool, soft flesh".[68] He then fills a kete (basket) with the treasures he has coveted, puts on the cloak and leaves; again, "his voice soared".[69] Thus, the oratorical prowess and "magical" singing voice of Hatupatu are directly related to his ability to exert power over others: to deceive, to inflict pain and to silence.

After Miromiro informs Kurungaituku of what has happened, the birdwoman contains her anger and grief and sets off in search of Hatupatu. She locates him, and in the meeting and chase that follows, the interplay between voice and silence becomes increasingly evident. While Hatupatu moves swiftly through the forest "pacing himself with song", the birdwoman stops him in his tracks – arriving before him "wordlessly" and "without a sound".[70] Then, once Hatupatu has successfully led Kurungaituku to the boiling hot pools, the earth gives way beneath her, causing the birdwoman to fall into the pools and fill the air with her screams as the pool boils and hisses:

> She howled, she screamed; the horror of little crushed wings, and thin snapped bones, and frail shredded flesh swelling in her voice, the horror. [...] She howled, she screamed. And then, suddenly she stopped. Suddenly. Silent, silent as defeat. Silent as death.[71]

The cries and subsequent silence of the birdwoman in this passage powerfully reflect the climax of the usual version of events: that which ends in the demise of Kurungaituku and which denies the birdwoman her side of the story. At the same time, however, the incorporation of the birdwoman's grief for her slaughtered companions within her

68 Te Awekotuku 2003, 79.
69 Te Awekotuku 2003, 79.
70 Te Awekotuku 2003, 80.
71 Te Awekotuku 2003, 83.

screams of pain in this retelling is a significant departure – her voice encompasses not only her pain but that of her kin. In addition, the sudden silence which follows the screams of Kurungaituku represents a significant shift in power. For while Hatupatu utilises his voice to deceive, here, the birdwoman employs silence to do the same; it is her silence that leads Hatupatu to erroneously believe that he has defeated Kurungaituku and that he has succeeded in leading her to her death.

As Kurungaituku patiently waits and heals her wounds with her animal companions, the strength, greed and supposed success of Hatupatu are once more made evident through voice, story and song. Upon his return to his family, "new songs were sung and new stories told", and these "Hatupatu rolled over his tongue, chanted lustily with his ever-glorious magical voice".[72] He also boasts about the bounty he stole from Kurungaituku and left back in the forest, and with "lifting words and shining melody" he weaves a "spell of expectation" that disperses throughout the village.[73] However, when he encounters what he believes to be the ghost of Kurungaituku, his attempts to sing so that she will "remember his beauty, his specialness, his voice" are cut short as the birdwoman violently puts an end to his singing and storytelling:

> Claws reached down into his mouth and tore out his tongue. Crushed his back teeth to a pale, ashy powder; snapped the front ones, so thin and white; shredded the cool, soft flesh of his gums, hacked deep into his throat muscles.
>
> Silenced his voice. Forever.
>
> Kurungaituku picked up the big, heavy bag, bundled it into her pīkau. Leaning over Hatupatu, she wiped her talons on the fine, soft flax of his kaitaka and she sighed to herself. His voice was gone. His beauty ruined. Kai toa.
>
> All that would be left of him, from that moment on, was the story. The legend. That, she grimaced to herself as she left his crumpled breathing body in the fern, should be more than enough.

72 Te Awekotuku 2003, 83.
73 Te Awekotuku 2003, 84.

And so it was.[74]

Here, this visceral description reflects the prior violent actions of Hatupatu, in his crushing and snapping of bones and shredding of flesh of the birdwoman's companions, and the same use of these terms to describe the pain contained within the screams of Kurungaituku as she falls into the hot pools. This powerful repetition in this retelling and its appearance at these distinct moments in the narrative further emphasise the potency of alternative perspectives and reimaginings of existing narratives. The use of the same descriptions to represent acts of violence, the grief caused by that violence and the revenge undertaken for that violence, demonstrates the power of narrative perspective in operation.

Finally, while Kurungaituku puts an end to the songs and storytelling of Hatupatu, she does not kill him, nor does this version of events cancel out the existing versions of the story. As she leaves Hatupatu, silent but still breathing, in the fern, the narrative concludes: "All that would be left of him, from that moment on, was the story. The legend. [...] And so it was".[75] This potent reimagining and the many versions and retellings of the story in existence (as well as those yet to come) are thus able to sit alongside one another, without any suggestion that contemporary versions assume authority or superiority. "Kurungaituku" therefore stops short of becoming that which it critiques; rather, it provides a persuasive representation of the interplay between silence and dominant voices, offers an opportunity to consider alternative perspectives and is an invitation to contemplate the ways in which narrative sovereignty operates within the realm of pūrākau. It also reflects the ongoing process of storytelling, the changes that occur within that process and the fact that neither narrative nor its audience and the world in which they live remain fixed or static. In addition, the voices of animal relations sing out loudly in this narrative: they are not characters on the margins; rather, their experiences and subjectivities are integral to the story.

74 Te Awekotuku 2003, 85–6.
75 Te Awekotuku 2003, 86.

I will admit that my selections and interpretations of these two texts are very much influenced by my own experiences as a woman and as a mother; have much to do with my long-held fascination with the famous story of Kurungaituku and the ways in which she is often depicted as a terrifying, grotesque and callous foe; and reflect my interest in and affinity for imaginings pertaining to the experiences and narratives of our non-human kin. I find the representations of perspectives belonging to non-human and hybrid characters within these texts particularly profound, as they offer opportunities to consider the potential implications of privileging certain narratives over others. The constant oscillations between sameness and otherness embedded in the portrayals of these birds and bird-like protagonists provide means to reflect on both the narratives we tell about ourselves and those told about us by others; they also offer creative avenues to imagine how human qualities and behaviours might be perceived by – and might significantly impact upon – non-human relations. "Like whakapapa with its many layerings and time phases", writes Jon Battista, "the concept of 'story' owes its existence to its own multifaceted and historied nature. A story has the potential intrinsically to have many tellers even when, or even especially through, the privileging of a particular point of view".[76] Both of these texts exemplify this multifaceted nature of story via the various ways in which they engage with and represent unique and alternative narrative perspectives of our non-human kin.

The amalgamations of human and non-human characteristics in Wixon's text and Te Awekotuku's retelling, and the alternative viewpoints of the same series of events that each of them utilises in different ways, reflect the multiplicity of identity: the various characteristics, experiences and narratives – and the layers of whakapapa – that constitute the writer, the subjects they portray and the readers who interpret them. For me, in highlighting this multiplicity, these two narratives also powerfully represent the ways in which we are included within – and therefore are responsible to – multiple communities simultaneously. Together, these portrayals of alternative perspectives thus provide us with means to recognise,

76 Battista 2004, 213.

acknowledge and, importantly, reflect upon the current status of human–non-human kinships and relationships in the communities within which we reside. Not only that, but in reminding us of our relationships with other species, and in light of the whakapapa woven through them, these narratives require us to remember our obligations to them too.

References

Bach, Lisa, Katharina Luh and Ulrike Schult (2011). "The samenesses and the differences": representations of Māori femininities and sexualities in Ngahuia Te Awekotuku's short story collections *Tahuri* (1989) and *Ruahine: Mythic Women* (2003). *Women's Studies Journal* 25(2): 26–42.

Barlow, Cleve (2015). *Tikanga Whakaaro: Key Concepts in Maori Culture*. Oxford: Oxford University Press.

Battista, J.L. (2004). Me he korokoro kōmako "With the throat of a bellbird": a Māori aesthetic in Māori writing in English. PhD thesis, University of Auckland.

Brown, Deirdre (2013). Indigenous art animals. In Annie Potts, Philip Armstrong and Deirdre Brown, eds. *A New Zealand Book of Beasts: Animals in Our Culture, History and Everyday Life*, 159–75. Auckland University Press.

Haami, Bradford (2006). Te Whānau Puha – whales – whales and Māori society. *Te Ara – The Encyclopedia of New Zealand*. http://www.TeAra.govt.nz/en/te-whanau-puha-whales/page-3.

Ihimaera, Witi (2019). A story from the sea. In Witi Ihimaera and Whiti Hereaka, eds. *Pūrākau: Māori Myths Retold by Māori Writers*, 188–94. Auckland: Penguin Random House New Zealand.

Justice, Daniel Heath (2018). *Why Indigenous Literatures Matter*. Waterloo, Ontario: Wilfred Laurier University Press.

Kauta, Glenda and Janet Piddock (1985). *Maui in the Underworld – Maui ki te Ao-i-raro*. Marara Te Tai, trans. Auckland: Reed Methuen.

Kupenga, Vapi, Rina Rata and Tuki Nepe (1993). Whāia te iti kahurangi: Māori women reclaiming autonomy. In Witi Ihimaera, Haare Williams, Irihapeti Ramsden and D.S. Long, eds. *Te Ao Mārama: He Whakaatanga o te Ao – The Reality*, 4–9. Auckland: Reed.

Lee, Jennifer (2009). Decolonising Māori narratives: pūrākau as a method. *MAI Review* 2(3).

Makereti, Tina (2018). Māori writing: speaking with two mouths. *Journal of New Zealand Studies* NS26. https://doi.org/10.26686/jnzs.v0iNS26.4842.

Mikaere, Ani (2011). *Colonising Myths, Māori Realities: He Rukuruku Whakaaro*. Wellington: Huia and Te Wānanga o Raukawa.
Murphy, Leola (2017). Intersectional feminisms: reflections on theory and activism in Sara Ahmed's *Living a Feminist Life*. *Women's Studies Journal* 31(2): 4–17.
Pohatu, Warren (2001). *Maori Animal Myths = Mokai Rangatira*. Auckland: Reed Children's.
Reed, A.W. and Ross Calman (2008). *Raupō Book of Māori Mythology.* North Shore, NZ: Raupo/Penguin Group.
Reilly, Michael (2018). E Tiu, Wāhia: an introductory note. In Michael Reilly (Michael Patrick Joseph), Gianna Leoni, Lyn Carter, Suzanne Duncan, Lachy Paterson et al., eds. *Te Kōparapara: An Introduction to the Māori World*, 1–6. Auckland: Auckland University Press.
Riley, Murdoch (2006). *Manu Māori: Bird Legends and Customs.* Kapiti Coast, North Island, NZ: Viking Sevenseas NZ Ltd.
Teague, Stacey (2020). Kurangaituku. Audio file in Paula Green, Poetry Shelf connections: celebrating *Landfall* 238 with a review and audio gathering. NZ Poetry Shelf. 23 April. https://nzpoetryshelf.com/tag/stacey-tengue/.
Te Awekotuku, Ngahuia (2003). Kurungaituku. In *Ruahine: Mythic Women*, 73–86. Wellington: Huia.
Wehi, Priscilla (2009). Indigenous ancestral sayings contribute to modern conservation partnerships: examples using *Phormium tenax*. *Ecological Applications* 19(1): 267–75.
Whaanga, Hemi, Priscilla Wehi, Murray Cox, Tom Roa and Ian Kusabs (2018). Māori oral traditions record and convey indigenous knowledge of marine and freshwater resources. *New Zealand Journal of Marine and Freshwater Research* 52(4): 487–96. http://doi.org/10.1080/00288330.2018.1488749.
Wixon, Karl (1997). Te Karaka o te Tītī. In *Huia Short Stories 2*, 137–41. Wellington: Huia.
Womack, C.S. (2013). There is no respectful way to kill an animal. *Studies in American Indian Literatures* 25(4): 11–27.

About the contributors

Rick De Vos conducts research in animal studies and in anthropogenic extinction, in particular its cultural and historical significance and the ways in which it is articulated and practised. He is an adjunct research fellow in the Centre for Culture and Technology at Curtin University in Western Australia, and before that coordinated the Research and Graduate Studies Programs at the Centre for Aboriginal Studies at Curtin. He is a member of the Extinction Studies Working Group and has published essays on extinction in various academic journals and essay collections, including *Knowing Animals* (Brill, 2007), *Animal Death* (Sydney University Press, 2013), *Extinction Studies: Stories of Time, Death and Generations* (Columbia University Press, 2017), *The Edinburgh Companion to Animal Studies* (Edinburgh University Press, 2018) and *Life Writing in the Anthropocene* (Routledge, 2021). With Matthew Chrulew he edited a special issue of *Cultural Studies Review* in 2019 entitled "Extinction Studies: Stories of Unravelling and Reworlding".

Kirsty Dunn (Te Aupōuri, Te Rarawa, Ngāpuhi) is a lecturer at the University of Canterbury, Aotearoa (New Zealand). She completed her PhD in English, entitled "'Into the dark, we are moths': reading animal whanaunga in Māori writing in English", in 2021. Her doctoral thesis is a Kaupapa Māori analysis of various literary representations of animals and human–animal relationships in Te Ao Māori; she has also completed research projects regarding representations of meat culture in contemporary fiction, and Māori perspectives on veganism and plant-based kai. Kirsty's creative works have been published in Aotearoa and overseas.

Katarina Gray-Sharp is of Ngāti Rangi, Ngāti Raukawa, Ngāti Kauwhata and Ngāti Rangiwēwehi (among others). She is a māmā, pouaru (widow), ringawera (worker) and kaikaranga (first voice). She is an early career academic, the author of a chapter on being Māori in the academy and co-editor of a volume on Te Tiriti o Waitangi. After a decade in teaching and learning, Katarina completed a doctoral thesis on her responsibility in the face of mass extinction. She shares a home with a teen daughter, a tail-less tabby and a huntaway cross.

Kelsey Dayle John (Diné) is an assistant professor with a joint appointment in gender and women's studies and American Indian studies at the University of Arizona. Her work is centred on animal relationalities, particularly horse–human relationships as ways of knowing, healing and decolonising education. Alongside her work in Indigenous animal studies, Kelsey's research interests also include Indigenous feminisms, decolonising methodologies and foundations of education. In her spare time, she hangs out with her horses and dogs.

Rowena Lennox lives on unceded Gweagal Country and is the author of two books: *Dingo Bold: The Life and Death of K'gari Dingoes* (Sydney University Press, 2021), about emotional relationships between people and dingoes on K'gari/Fraser Island; and a biography of an East Timorese church leader, *Fighting Spirit of East Timor: The Life of Martinho da Costa Lopes* (Pluto Press/Zed Books, 2000), which won a NSW Premier's History Award. Her poems, essays and stories have been widely published, and she holds a doctorate of creative arts from the University of Technology Sydney, where she is an honorary in the Australian Centre for Public History. Her current research interests are colonialism, dingoes, decolonisation, and family and maritime history.

Susan McHugh is professor of English at the University of New England and researches and teaches courses in writing, literary theory, animal studies and plant studies. She is the author of *Love in a Time* *of Slaughters: Human-Animal Stories Against Extinction and Genocide* (Penn State University Press, 2019), *Animal Stories: Narrating Across Species Lines* (University of Minnesota Press, 2011) and *Dog* (University of Chicago Press, 2004) and a co-editor of *The Palgrave Handbook of Animals and Literature* (Palgrave Macmillan, 2020), *Indigenous Creatures, Native Knowledges, and the Arts: Animal Studies in Modern Worlds* (Palgrave Macmillan, 2017) and *The Routledge Handbook of Human-Animal Studies* (Routledge, 2014).

Ana Paula Motta has recently completed a PhD in archaeology at the University of Western Australia, where she looked at social identity and human–animal relations in rock art in the Kimberley, Australia. She obtained an MSc in palaeoanthropology and Palaeolithic archaeology at University College London and a BSc in anthropology and archaeology from the University of Buenos Aires. She was awarded a Forrest Research Foundation scholarship to conduct her doctoral studies, an Institute of Archaeology master's prize, and was included in the Faculty of Social and Historical Sciences Dean's List. Her research interests include ontology and epistemology, decolonising archaeology, Indigenous knowledge, social identity and hunter-gatherer archaeology and anthropology..

Martin Porr is associate professor of archaeology and a member of the Centre for Rock Art Research + Management at the University of Western Australia. He has published widely on Palaeolithic art and archaeology and on general theoretical aspects of archaeological and rock art research. He is co-editor of the volume *The Hominid Individual in Context: Archaeological Investigations of Lower and Middle Palaeolithic Landscapes, Locales and Artefacts* (with C.S. Gamble; Routledge, 2005), the volume *Southern Asia, Australia and the Search for Human Origins* (with R. Dennell; Cambridge University Press, 2014) and the volume *Interrogating Human Origins: Decolonisation and the Deep Human Past* (with Jacqueline M. Matthews; Routledge, 2020).

Danielle Taschereau Mamers is the managing director of the Critical Digital Humanities Initiative at the University of Toronto. Danielle holds a PhD in media studies and has held postdoctoral fellowships at McMaster University, the University of Pennsylvania and the University of Toronto. Bringing together decolonial media theory with archival, ethnographic and visual studies methods, she conducts disobedient readings of settler archives and conservation policy in order to centre Indigenous knowledge and engage bison as world-making subjects.

Index